PHILOSOPHY

BETWEEN

FAITH

AND

THEOLOGY

PHILOSOPHY

B E T W E E N

FAITH

A N D

THEOLOGY

ADDRESSES TO CATHOLIC INTELLECTUALS

ADRIAAN THEODOOR PEPERZAK

University of Notre Dame Press

Notre Dame, Indiana

Manufactured in the United States of America

Library of Congress Cataloging-in-Publication Data

Peperzak, Adriaan Theodoor, 1929–
Philosophy between faith and theology : addresses to Catholic intellectuals /
Adriaan Theodoor Peperzak.
p.   cm.
Includes bibliographical references and index.
ISBN 0-268-03886-4 (cloth : alk. paper)
ISBN 0-268-03887-2 (pbk. : alk. paper)
1. Catholic Church and philosophy.
2. Catholic philosophers—Religious life.   I. Title.
BX1795.P47P46   2005
261.5'1—dc22

2005021957

To the memory of
Corrie Arens-Peperzak (1917–2004)

CONTENTS

Preface   ix

PART ONE
CHRISTIAN FAITH AND SCHOLARSHIP

CHAPTER ONE
Roots of Thought   3

CHAPTER TWO
Christianity and Academic Life   16

CHAPTER THREE
On the Relationships between Life, Scholarship,
and Faith in a Catholic University   29

CHAPTER FOUR
The Future of Christian Philosophy   43

CHAPTER FIVE
Does Theology Have a Role to Play in the University?
A Philosophical Perspective   56

PART TWO
FROM PHILOSOPHY TO PRAYER AND VICE VERSA

CHAPTER SIX
Philosophy—Religion—Theology   73

CHAPTER SEVEN
Retrieving Onto-Theo-Logy   85

CHAPTER EIGHT
Wonderment and Faith   103

CHAPTER NINE
About Salvation   119

CHAPTER TEN
God across Being and the Good   129

CHAPTER ELEVEN
Freedom and Grace: Some Reflections on Gratitude   140

CHAPTER TWELVE
Affective Theology/Theological Affectivity   155

CHAPTER THIRTEEN
The Address of the Letter   168

CHAPTER FOURTEEN
Provocation: Can God Speak within the Limits of Philosophy?
Should Philosophers Speak to God?   180

Notes   195

Index   209

Philosophers think. But before they think, they have learned to live. How does their thinking emerge from their lives?

A life cannot be lived without any trust. Does trust play a role in philosophy? Does it guide the way thinking proceeds?

Philosophers who enjoy the good fortune to be Christian are bound by a double allegiance: they belong to one catholic Church, while also participating in the universal Republic of thought. While they try to offer arguments that all their fellow humans can understand, their deepest convictions originate in a message that cannot be demonstrated by scientific or speculative means. The blinding light of faith overshadows their thinking and amplifies the space in which it unfolds.

How do and how should Catholics who practice philosophy perform and explain the personal union of their philosophy with their faith? How can we understand the difference between philosophy and theology within the existential unity of their operations?

Must Catholic philosophers choose between crypto-theology and autonomous but faithless thought? Does their faith disqualify them from the rigors of authentic philosophy? If so, how can their thinking still be passionate, or even alive?

These are some of the questions that prompted the writing of this book. While searching for the answers, it offers arguments for a new, no longer modern, practice and understanding of philosophy. After the bankruptcy of an enlightened "faith in reason" (Hegel) and its grandiose, but never finished, monuments, we must reconsider the limits of philosophy's independence and analyze its essential connections with life and faith.

This book concentrates on the relations between Catholic faith, life, and thought. Such a concentration remains too abstract, however, if it does not involve us also in an analysis of other phenomena that codetermine the course of thinking. Thus, the cultural situatedness of thought, its affective and ontological determinations, its link to the past and the future, and the conversational character of its practice will be part of the explorations attempted here.

The perspective from which these explorations are presented is not the faithless viewpoint of a solitary thinker, but rather the perspective of a faithful community that is concerned about all creation and stretches from the beginning to resurrection thanks to the Eternal who heeds the universe. Thus, the philosophy of a Catholic becomes part of a farther-reaching contemplation that should be as rigorously scholarly as sensitive to the most desirable truths of an inspired life.

Within the Catholic universe, philosophers can be challenged to show how their search for insight is intertwined with the light that their faith sheds on world and history. Faith indeed opens possibilities that reason on its own cannot discover, even if, *post factum*, the latter might notice certain mirrorings of God's presence in all things. However, within the space of contemplation that unfolds when a faithful person is also a philosopher, the boundary between philosophy and theology cannot be drawn with the presumed clarity of modern treatises on the relations between these disciplines.

————

Although the chapters that compose this book originated in separate papers that were given on invitation at loosely connected occasions, each one of them unfolds a unifying core. The title "Philosophy between Faith and Theology" is an attempt to indicate their common denominator, but their coherence owes more to the constellation of topics and theses that underlies all of them. Desire and affection, responding and correspondence, movement and purification, study and conversation, dedication and education, God and world, history and tradition are some key elements of this constellation. In *Elements of Ethics* I offer a more systematic analysis of the phenomena to which these notions refer, but here they come to the fore as needed by the particular topics and the more religious context of the various chapters.

To facilitate the reading of this book, I will indicate here how each of its chapters illustrates the possibility of a philosophy that can be recognized as emerging from a Catholic position without ceasing to be philosophy.

The first, introductory chapter sketches the horizon of such a philosophy and some contours of its research program. It examines how Christian philosophers, after the end of modernity, can combine their participation in their own religious tradition with participation in the surrounding culture and the operations of universal thought.

The next four chapters show how the interdependence of philosophy, theology, and the sciences should codetermine the organization of a Catholic university that believes in its own catholicity. Chapter 2 focuses on the question of how a Catholic scholar, without dishonesty or secrecy, can integrate the various loyalties that are at stake, while chapter 3 argues that the idea of a Catholic university demands and conditions a specific cooperation of life and scholarship with faith. Chapter 4 tries to answer the famous question of whether a "Christian philosophy" is possible at all. Instead of developing their philosophical investigations as parts of a separate system, Catholics need to integrate them in their overall search for a mature *gnōsis* of faith. Chapter 5 concludes this part by showing how theology should play an integrative role in Catholic universities.

In the course of the first five chapters, the word "philosophy" has received another meaning than the usual one. If its integrative function is taken seriously, a critique of its modern definition, according to which reason's autonomy is sacrosanct, is inevitable. The transformation proposed in this book brings "philosophy" closer to the *philosophia* that was practiced from the pre-Socratic thinkers to Proclus (a period of more than a thousand years) and from Philo to Cusanus (a period of fourteen hundred years). Perhaps contemporary pluralism has to develop into a more confident, but also more humble practice of contemplation, which no longer denies but enjoys being inspired by rich traditions from the past.

After the chapters on personal and institutional conditions of a Catholic philosophy, chapters 6 through 14 present samples of such thought. Each chapter is an experiment in overcoming modernity, while refusing to follow other postmodern paths.

Chapters 6 and 7 make a transition from philosophy in its usual sense to a form of thought that is closer to theology. Both chapters consider some epistemological problems that emerge from the confrontation of philosophy with religion and faith. Chapter 6 uses a very broad definition of religion and faith in order to show that *all* philosophy is guided by a prephilosophical "faith." It refers back to chapter 1 and forward to chapter 9. In a discussion with Martin Heidegger and Emmanuel Levinas, chapter 7 argues that the European project of philosophy as onto-theo-logy is not exhausted, but, in some sense, has hardly begun. The onto-theo-logical tradition has neither been able to do justice to the Other, nor to show how persons are. Consequently, neither humans nor God have been approached in an appropriate way. One of the most important conditions for a promising transformation of ontology (and consequently for a renewal of theology) lies in a phenomenology of speaking and responding that shows how radically these differ from anything that can be captured in textuality. Only such a phenomenology can (at least somewhat) clarify our talking about God's Word, Incarnation, and the sacramental presence of the Spirit.

Chapters 8 through 14 are prompted by various topics that are central in philosophy, but they unfold in a wider space of investigation, being unafraid of overstepping the threshold between "universally human" thought and Catholic theology.

Chapter 8 contrasts the attitude of Greek and modern philosophers with the attitude of Christian thinkers by examining the difference between the amazement that gave birth to the philosophies of Plato and Aristotle, on the one hand, and the amazement caused by Jesus's appearance, as interpreted by the synoptic Gospels, on the other. Both forms of wonder tend to induce a certain kind of search, but the understanding sought by Plato and Aristotle differs profoundly from the *gnōsis* about which Paul and John write. Whereas Greek wondering results in *theōria,* the amazement that affected Jesus's audience develops into admiration and adoration.

Chapter 9 likewise has an epistemological aspect. While asking what philosophers can say about the Christian faith in salvation, it reflects on the most radical longing that motivates human lives. Such a reflection can hardly avoid taking a position with regard to the theological debate on the "natural" or "supernatural" character of human desire and its desideratum.

Desire also plays a central role in the next three chapters, but each of them approaches it from a different perspective. Chapter 10 reacts to a contemporary debate about the priority of being or the Good. Connecting with the discussion of onto-theo-logy presented in chapter 7, it retrieves the Neoplatonic tradition of "the Good beyond being." The search leads through a renewed analogy of being to the Incomparable, whose generosity hides and reveals itself in a human history of passion and compassion. Starting from a new critique of modernity's obsession with freedom and rights, chapter 11 reaches the same conclusion as the preceding one, but it focuses on the past and the future of God's presence in all things and pays more attention to the affective and symbolic aspects of the human response to that presence in gratitude and hope.

Chapter 12 analyzes the philosophical and theological importance of affectivity by drawing a parallel between affecting and speaking. It emphasizes the transcendental importance of speaking, as distinct from all spoken or written texts and contents. The positive and the negative aspects of our speaking about God must be analyzed, but neither positive nor negative theology, nor the combination of both, can tell us much, if our speaking is not driven by an originary movement that reaches beyond any text or theory toward the most desirable but unsayable. Desire and correspondence appear again to be the keys to an appropriate definition of theology.

The last two chapters contain indications for a phenomenology of speaking and responding and its relevance for philosophy and theology. They extend their analyses to other modes of addressing, such as dedication, giving, living for, and devotion; and they draw conclusions with regard to the relations between speaking *about* (observation, examination, scientific, philosophical, and theological language) and speaking *to* (conversation, listening, commanding, dedication, prayer). When reflection triumphs, it disregards all speakers and listeners; only addressing allows a good respondent to glimpse the truth of other speakers. As far as God's Word addresses us, we are enabled to speak about God, but such a speech cannot surpass the level of marginal notes that somewhat clarify the meaning of our prayers.

———

Many people have contributed to the production of this book. I thank all of them, known and unknown, from my educators to the readers. Here I want to express my gratitude particularly to the following friends:

Catriona Hanley, Laurel Madison, and Ryan Madison, who, for years, graciously assisted me in translating, editing, and revising;

Xiaoling Sun, who helped me, with perfect dedication, in the last stage of editing;

Margaret Hyre, who, with insight and precision, took care of the final text;

the philosophers whose invitations were at the origin of the various chapters—especially Professor Marcomaria Olivetti, who invited me to participate in the colloquia where I presented the first versions of chapters 8, 10, 11, 13, and 14;

the two reviewers, Kevin Corrigan and Jeffrey Bloechl, who gave me good advice and encouraged me to publish this book;

the administration and the philosophy department of Loyola University Chicago, which generously granted me time for writing;

Dr. James Wiser and Dr. James Brennan, who, some years ago, supported my efforts to organize discussions about the relations between Christianity and culture.

More than anyone else, it is my wife, Angela, to whom I am profoundly grateful for her unrelenting patience and unselfish encouragement that made my time-consuming writing possible.

Adriaan T. Peperzak
Chicago—Wilmette
3 July 2004

Christian Faith and Scholarship

ONE

Roots of Thought

Philosophy has always been a problem for itself, but never before have philosophers been as obsessed with questions about its nature, its proper task, its conditions, its possible end, its meaning, and so on, as they are today. Is philosophy a science or a metascience? If the latter, is it nevertheless scientific? Or is it rather hermeneutics, a skill, a practice, an engagement, a virtue, or a way of life? Is philosophy even capable of answering all these questions about its own mode of being and operating or must it look elsewhere for illumination?

A brief look at the ongoing business of philosophy shows that it is practiced in various ways: besides professionals who earn their salary from nine to five, others think night and day; some have limited themselves to historical reflection on the past, while others are redoing all the basic work, which in their judgment has never been sufficiently accomplished; certain philosophers emulate the sciences, while others show more affinity with literature; those who delight in analysis contrast with more synthetic thinkers.

Different schools teach different kinds of metaphilosophy, but on the whole the scene remains dominated by the concept of "enlightenment," according to which philosophy proves its theses on the basis of experiential and logical evidence. Even if this idea is heavily criticized by a variety of "post-modern" theories, most of these criticisms remain faithful to the ideal of an autonomous, theoretical, thematic, and disengaged reflection. Very few thinkers practice philosophy as a question of life or death, although the number of those who insist on the original meaning of *philosophia* as a way of life is growing.[1]

A Way of Life

If philosophy is not merely a skill but a mode of life, several theses of modern metaphilosophy must either be abandoned or transformed into subordinate elements of a self-aware life in which thinking plays an important, though not necessarily supreme, role. As an integral element of an existential search for wisdom, theoretical reflection is radically motivated by the basic orientation and thrust of the life in which it is at home. Thinking is then codetermined by the philosopher's basic desires and the manner in which he has made himself at home in the world. The existential elements of a life—a particular "stance" and a characteristic orientation—cannot be separated from the social and cultural network in which a thinker is involved. Therefore metaphilosophy also includes an analysis of the society and the culture from which one's thoughts emerge. It thus encompasses a study of the cultural and personal pattern in which this or that thinking is rooted. However, such a metaphilosophy stops being philosophical when it *reduces* the interpretation of someone's thinking to sociological, historical, or psychoanalytical conditions. A philosophical analysis of rooted and embedded thought cannot surrender itself to the sciences unless these become philosophical by radically reflecting on their own basic presuppositions. Although it must carefully listen to all scientific discoveries, only philosophy can lead the examination of the ultimate relations between its own activity and the life from which it emerges. Metaphilosophy itself is part of a radical philosophy of human life; as a re-turn upon the implicit logic and motivation of a philosophical life, it belongs to a thorough anthropology (which, in turn, is codetermined by a certain level of implicit or explicit metaphilosophy). Even so, as a self-reflective philosophy of human life, thinking is embedded in that very same life under investigation, which, being more and deeper than philosophy, expresses itself in it. Life and philosophy are thus entangled in a mutual embrace.[2]

Philosophy as a Tradition

If philosophy is a way of life, it cannot be practiced outside of a philosophical community with mores and opinions of its own, i.e., outside of a specific tradition and history. The business of philosophy is socially and culturally formed, structured, patterned, (co)determined. Having learned a specific language, we participate in particular discussions of preselected issues; authorities of a specific school or style have initiated us by directing our readings and attempts at argumentation; we venerate a small group of classics and look up to leading stars, while obeying the rules of progress set by the acknowledged powers in the field. What does autonomous thinking mean in this context? Little more than an invitation to check by our own means whether the experiences and arguments on which the established authorities base their theories are valid and to discover new questions and arguments that further the state of the art. Of course, the results of our checking will likewise be evaluated by established judges who can refuse or recommend publication. Once in a while we participate in the rituals of conferences and symposia to promote our own variations on accepted patterns, in the hope that, one day, we too will be recognized as authorities, perhaps even—if our marketing works—as stars.

A deeper sociological, political, and historical study of philosophical stars and constellations would show how much inequality, veneration, tradition, authority, and power is invested in their operations, despite the modern belief that reason is autonomous and experience democratic. However, in this chapter I will focus on one aspect only: the genealogical self-presentation of modern and postmodern philosophy.

Genealogies

Neither individuals nor communities can live an intellectual life without situating themselves in space and time. *A fortiori* they cannot even begin to think without having an idea of how they relate both to contemporary and past philosophers. Spatio-temporal contextualization is necessary to provide us with a general framework, an orientation, a memory, a milieu, a family, and an ongoing conversation about specific issues. Especially in a time of confusion and general doubt, we need to belong somewhere in order to know how and to whom we are related as heirs, colleagues, leaders, and supporters.

Even if such a framework remains implicit, reflection makes us aware of the specific way in which we belong to a particular community and history. Much could be said about the spatial aspect of our situation, especially about the tensions between nationalism and the (at least verbally recognized) necessity of cosmopolitanism, but here I will focus instead on a few temporal aspects of our philosophical situation.

In situating ourselves in history, we cannot avoid telling a highly selective and simplified story about the founding events and figures of our past and the connections that relate our epoch to previous epochs of our tribe. Most often we mix this story with symbolic anticipations and mythical self-interpretations, thus constructing a half-historical, half-mythical narrative about our origin and mission, the ways in which "we" have accomplished our task, the future toward which we have always wanted to go, and the predicament in which we presently find ourselves. In other words, we offer a genealogy. Well-known examples of such genealogies are Hegel's *Phenomenology of Spirit,* Nietzsche's *Genealogy of Morals,* and Freud's Mosaic phantasies; but many other genealogies from Hesiod to Teilhard de Chardin can be added.

We should not underestimate the hermeneutic power of a genealogy; it inclines us to certain prejudices and preferences, especially when it remains half-conscious or merely implicit. The way we situate our thought shapes our perspective on the world in which we live and the tasks we must fulfill. The Enlightenment saw itself as the renewal of a progress begun by the ancients that was interrupted by the Middle Ages. Hegel's version of progress encompassed not only the philosophical history from Parmenides and Heraclitus up to his own synthesis, but also the whole of world-history from its primitive beginnings to modern politics and religion. In the last century, this enlightened optimism has been broken and reversed. Several famous authors have deemed the cultural decadence of the Occident more striking than its progress in science and technology. Heidegger, for instance, retrieved the recurrent nostalgia for Greece by seeking inspiration in pre-Platonic experiences of Being in order to overcome the technological faith of "enlightened" modernity, while others presented the philosophical history from Parmenides to Aquinas as a glorious ascent followed by an infamous descent into the depths of postmedieval perplexity. Some postmodern authors, however, see all metaphysics as condemnable atavisms whose naïveté lies behind "us," so that "we" can make a new beginning, assuming we have not become too skeptical to engage in philosophy at all.

The danger of being seduced by a particular genealogy before we even begin a discussion of the issues at hand, can only be met by an ongoing reassessment of the historical pattern through which we set the scene for our past and present. It is, for example, difficult not to consider our generation as more knowledgeable and more mature than previous ones; often we are guided by a Hegelian idea of progress, except perhaps when we ponder the various disasters of the last one hundred and fifty years. But even then we might think highly of our advances in thinking and feeling about human rights, war, exploitation, injustice, and ecology.

The philosophical legitimation of a particular genealogy is perhaps a task too difficult for us. How can we prove that history must be schematized in this way? Who possesses the knowledge required to *prove* the simplifying myths about our past and present and what grounds our expectations for the future?

Instead of dwelling on a general hermeneutics of genealogies, let me try to contrast a popular story about the actual situation of philosophy with another contextualization that might be more promising or more urgent. Although the modern story often remains implicit, it is attested to abundantly in many famous texts of the last four centuries. Several variations have been attempted, but few alternatives have been seriously considered. Though the following presentation neglects many nuances, I believe that it is an acceptable though simplified portrait of the standard genealogy on which philosophical modernity relies.

A Modern Interpretation of the Past

As the modern story has it, in the beginning of our civilization, myth and magic ruled human life, but the emergence of philosophy in Greece was the dawn of a first, albeit still clumsy enlightenment. Empirical observation and rational argument replaced invocation of the gods. For a few centuries the new mentality was maintained, scientific discoveries were made, systematic interpretations of the natural and social cosmos were developed. When Christianity conquered Europe, however, myths and magical practices regained their power. The heritage of the Greeks became an amalgam of Oriental and Mediterranean beliefs, trading its scientific orientation for mysticism and religiously motivated forms of oppression. The Dark Ages continued until, after more than a millennium of obscurantism, the second emancipation of human intelligence began, with the glorious rise of modern science in the sixteenth century. The philosophers were seduced into imitation, and together, science and philosophy have finally found their way. By the modern account, the last four centuries have amply demonstrated how much humanity on its own is able to discover and create. Autonomous thought on the basis of experiential and experimental evidence has made us possessors of the world and healers of its biological, social, and cultural diseases. Oppression has been overcome by freedom of thought and experience—democratic goods shared by most educated adults. Extraordinary experiences, exceptional wisdom, good taste, and other relics of elitism are no longer relevant. The paradigm of thinking is calculation, because everybody can learn how to cope with quantities. Qualitative truths, if they cannot be translated into statistics, must be set aside as subjective.

Obviously, this picture is simplistic. Certain psychologists, for example, do not compete with natural scientists, and most theologians do not use scientistic models to explain God's Trinity. Some philosophers, such as Pascal and Husserl, have resisted the pressure to follow the modern paradigm, even though they themselves were specialists in mathematics; but few thinkers have been able to combine authentic philosophy with a refusal of Enlightenment's self-interpretation.

Does such a genealogy, even if it is a caricature, belong to the past? Yes and no. No, insofar as most universities and research centers are still dominated by modern ideas and ideals—a situation that might remain the case for a while because the formation of young philosophers in the most renowned schools still follows the modern tradition. Yes, insofar as modern Enlightenment no longer responds to the most genuine desire of young and old intellectuals who demand that philosophy have a vital rapport with the human search for wisdom and meaningful practice. In order to justify their desire and express their disappointment with modern Enlightenment, some of these intellectuals refer to the premodern practice of philosophy as part of an ongoing exercise in spirituality,[3] while others focus on contemporary sources of renovation through existential experiments, literature, or non-Western cultures.

The response to modern Enlightenment that I will be suggesting is not the standard one offered by many currents of thought gathered under the title "postmodernity" (an expression as eloquent as the term "Middle Ages"). I use this title here only "strategically," because the various styles of "postmodern thought" are perhaps too different to be classified as species of a single genus. What, for example, do Kierkegaard, Nietzsche, Heidegger, Wittgenstein, Derrida, and Levinas have in common? Most "postmoderns," however, do share a greater affinity with the modern idea of philosophy than with the premodern search for rational wisdom as part of a beautiful, holy, honest, or successful life.

If, by trying to overcome modernity while keeping as much as possible of its achievements, we reach a position of our own, this position will both determine and be determined by the genealogy through which we situate our reflections within the troubling turmoil of our time. The following sketch of a genealogy other than the modern one is meant as an invitation to critical rejoinders. Mutual understanding concerning the question of where we have come from and where we are going seems to me an indispensable condition for any genuine discussion of the fundamental problems of our profession.

The Genealogy of a Christian Philosopher

As a Christian who is also a philosopher, I would think that our history neither begins with the myths of Homer and Hesiod, nor with the philosophies of Parmenides or Socrates, but much earlier: with Abraham, whose exodus from idolatry expressed his faith in the one savior of humankind. Christians are children of Abraham; the religious history of Israel, including its subsequent exiles, wanderings, and exoduses constitute the first, enduring part of our past. As followers of Christ, we are the heirs of Moses, the Prophets, and ancient Jewish wisdom. Graced by the Spirit, we participate in the Word's Incarnation, Passion, and Resurrection. Existence "in Christ" develops into a kind of spirituality for which trust, gratitude, and hope are both basic and central.

Early Christians have used the word "*philosophia*" to characterize a serious and self-conscious Christian life. With the growing influence of the contemplative ideal, "*philosophia*" took on a more theoretical tone, but for centuries it maintained its ties with the spirituality of a holy life.[4]

The inculturation of Christian faith was inevitably an encounter with Hellenistic and Roman kinds of *philosophia*. The Neopythagorean, Middle-Platonic and Neoplatonic, Stoic, and Epicurean movements offered their adherents ways of life in which meditation on the classics was a required practice.[5] For a Christian it was neither necessary nor even common to be an intellectual, but well-educated Christians could not avoid thinking about the meaning of their own faith in terms of the existing culture. They inevitably took a stand with regard to the beliefs and arguments upheld by leading philosophers and schools. Their interest, which initially might have been apologetic, developed into a more positive endeavor when they explained the Christian form of life in a culturally acceptable theology. Over and above their Judaic heritage, Christians could not but borrow Greek and Roman elements from the surrounding culture — and here began the long struggle for a language and thought of their own by sifting through, rejecting, integrating, and transforming the heritage of the ancients within the context of Christian "philosophia."

The task was not merely theoretical. Even if *theōria,* as contemplation, was a much more serious and existential affair than modern theories, Christian faith was a different commitment than the one required by the various philosophical schools. To what extent could the categories, theses, and theories of pagan schools be accepted as elements of Christian *philosophia?* Or, to formulate the question in a more general manner: how, on which conditions, and thanks to what transformation, is it possible to "convert" a non-Christian philosophy into an integral part of a Christian theology?

A definitive answer to this question has not been given in Western history, but some thinkers and periods were more successful than others in their struggle to discover one. Between the extremes of Tertullian's separation between Jerusalem and Athens and the absorption of Christianity in Hegel's gnosticism, many have tried to rethink the theoretical and practical elements of the inherited culture within the climate of their faith. Not only had they to unfold a fundamentally different belief while using the available linguistic, representational, and conceptual patterns; they had also to maintain the union of their new theories with the spirituality and practice into which the faith of their community developed. Origen, Gregory of Nyssa, Augustine, Maximus the Confessor, Dionysius, Anselm, Bonaventure, Thomas, Scotus, Eckhart, Cusanus were some of the leaders in the radical transformation of pagan *philosophia* into a contemplative spirituality that flourished for more than a thousand years in Western Europe. When philosophy became autonomous and scientific, however, it bade farewell to wisdom, and when theology distanced itself from prayer and charity, a chilling separation between mysticism and science became a fact. One *summa* or system after the other could emerge without profoundly changing the readers' experience or challenging their religious and moral attitudes. Reason either became so formal that she could prostitute herself to any conviction or she conquered and killed the Spirit of Jesus Christ by demanding entire and absolute allegiance to her manners of certitude and progress.

Modern faith in Reason[6] revealed a temptation implicit in the Greek conception of philosophy, though in Greece it was still restrained by existential demands. We now know that, contrary to its modern interpretation, ancient philosophy was not a merely theoretical affair, but the dominant role of reflection in the form of life it propagated, could easily develop into a supreme, autarkic, and divine *gnōsis* with fading interest in the emotional and practical needs of a human life. Modern philosophy was the attempt to find out whether Reason indeed could justify itself as absolute ruler of the universe. It developed an enlightened spirituality and a religion of its own—not based on admiration, gratitude, and compassion, but rather on the celebration of human intelligence, possession, engineering, and mastery.

Emancipated from its servitude,[7] philosophy would finally enjoy its autonomy, but the price it was forced to pay was high. Admirable advances in formal, analytical, and technical skills have been made during the time of philosophy's emancipation, but it has lost much of its vitality by severing its connections with the wealth of nonscientific experience, including contemplation, poetry, good taste, the search for wisdom, and deep-rooted faith in God. What always happens when a great but finite idea or principle is idolized, happened also in philosophy. By making itself autarkic, it lost its roots. No wonder that it is withering. Rationality without receptivity yields disappointment; life itself has found other ways not to be bored or desperate.

Christian Theology and Philosophy

My story is not meant to suggest that we should ignore or despise modern enlightenment in order to abandon ourselves to premodern ways of doing philosophy. Not only would such a move be ungrateful and impossible; it would falsely suggest that the problem at stake had been solved in some other period of Western history. Enlightened scholars' ignorance of what they call the "Dark Ages" is no reason to depreciate their work in the service of reason— even if this service was idolatrous. More importantly, however, Christian philosophers must critically examine the (explicit and implicit) theoretical conscience of their own Christian community in order to see how, in this half-modern, half-postmodern time, they should approach the perduring

question of an existential union between faith, spirituality, and philosophical theory.

Even apart from its spiritual and theological importance, this question is
philosophical, because philosophy cannot restrict its curiosity by ignoring the
basic principles of its subjects' own lives. Rooted in faith *and* passionately devoted to philosophy, a scholar cannot avoid asking and answering the double
question of their mutual embrace: How does faith accept, urge, use, transform, and enjoy philosophy; and how can philosophical reflection clarify its
own being rooted in, nourished, and oriented by that faith? A philosophy
without roots dies from irrelevance and disinterest. If Christian faith is not
the source of a human life, this life must be inspired by another faith; for reason cannot by itself provide thinkers with a stance, an absolute beginning, an
unshakable foundation, or an existential home. Many other faiths exist, for
example scientism, atheism, skepticism, agnosticism, materialism, relativism,
and fideism; but none of them can be proved. As fundamental trust, faith has
its own certainty, but the worth of this certainty becomes manifest only in its
fruits. It is therefore necessary for philosophers to unfold, as much as possible, the characteristic stance and inspiration on which they rely in discussing common issues with philosophers of other faiths.

If simultaneously being a Christian *and* involved in philosophy is a philosophical problem for Christian philosophers, it is *also* a theological problem,
of course. Any Christian concerned about the destiny of philosophy joins the
theological quest for a renewed alliance between theology and philosophy.
Since neither philosophy nor theology can be genuine unless they are inti-
mately connected with the emotional, intellectual, and ethical elements of an
authentic spirituality, the latter must also be integrated with the thought of
a postmodern Christianity. Renewal is here not repetition, but hard work
on a new task in a kind of continuity with fifteen hundred years of Christian
thought, even if this great tradition is still despised by most modern and postmodern intellectuals.

There is at least one reason why a simple repetition of premodern
philosophy and theology is impossible, although their classics are the rich-
est, albeit insufficiently explored, sources of inspiration. Not only has modern history profoundly changed the world, but even in their own time the
Christian classics have not given a final answer to the ultimate questions.
We must therefore approach them as critically as we do non-Christian authors. Concerning such a self-critical retrieval, I think especially of two issues that are certainly characteristic and basic to a Christian life: prayer and

charity. But to what extent are these issues philosophical and not exclusively theological?

A Task for Philosophy and Theology

The word "prayer" may comprise the entire enactment of faith in God. In this broad sense, it embraces not only several ways of external and internal speaking to God, but also the unfolding of faith in feelings of admiration and praise, enjoyment of all things as given, gratitude for this wonderful earth, sadness and compassion in the face of so much injustice and torture, acceptance of suffering in memory of God's passion, endurance of aging as time given and mortality, hope of deliverance, and love in response to over-whelming grace. In prayer we express the trust of all trusts, which separates us from all proclamations of God's death or absence. We certainly must not deny the authenticity of individual and collective experiences in which God appears as painfully hidden and far away, but even these experiences testify in a Christian context to the incomprehensible greatness of God's presence. Loyalty to faith resists fashionable discourses that misinterpret the nights and deserts of the mystics as the absence or death of God. It is a good ques-tion, however, to ask in what sort of presence we believe when confessing "I believe in God." How does God's hiddenness present itself? The long tradi-tion of Christian theology offers a wealth of thought on this question. Is God a person? A no-thing? The supreme being? Being itself? The Good be-yond being? Can God be contextualized? Is God caught in a horizon? Does God enter into personal relationships with human individuals? Does God constitute communities? And so on. Instead of discussing such questions immediately, let me here only state a thesis and a task.

The Western tradition of thought has not developed a satisfactory un-derstanding of personality and interpersonal activities (including speaking, communication, giving, loving, suffering); therefore neither has it been able to understand the meaning of being in general and what it could mean to "be" beyond personality or even "beyond being." A consequence of this fail-ure is that philosophy has been incapable of showing the compatibility of the addressing attitude and the reflexive attitude and their unity in one and the same human subject who prays to God and thinks about God. Attempts to combine prayer with reflection are found, e.g., in Augustine's *Soliloquia* and *Confessions* and in Anselm's *Proslogion*, but the alternation of prayers and arguments found in such works does not fully explain how it is possible to philosophize in "the spirit of prayer."[8] Here lies a task that must be accomplished if we want to understand how philosophy can be Christian and how faith can be philosophical. If it is true that modern scholarship has taken the shape of a secular religion, our task involves the attempt to convert its devotion to the god of reason into an element of the search for a more authentic wisdom, one that is granted only to a praying attitude. How to maintain the most rigorous skills of logic and phenomenology without separating them from the most genuine and complete experience of faith—that is the issue at stake.

The direction of scholarship must be oriented and channeled in another way than that of modern theory. It will then come closer to the ways of purification and illumination thematized in medieval theology. But even so, an appropriate answer will not be possible as long as God and the earth (or humanity) are conceived as rivals. If God's incarnation (including creation as its initial moment) is identical with the divinization of humanity, the solidarity of God with human history is established forever. Whether human lives and thoughts will ever be able to unfold this truth appropriately, is another question; but a sustained approximation must be attempted.

Such an approximation presupposes that we do justice to God's being simultaneously personal *and* beyond personality. We must therefore rethink the meaning of all the metaphors "father," "mother," "lord," "judge," "savior," "friend," and "lover." But first, we must (re)discover how persons are and how they deal with one another. And here lies the connection between speaking about God and our understanding of human interpersonality. The meaning of God cannot be dissociated from the question of human love and solidarity.

As obviously Christian as trust in the omnipresence of God is the basic commandment according to which God's love of all humans, human love of God, and love for all human persons (including ourselves) are identical. Because the Western tradition of philosophy has been ruled by impersonal paradigms, it has been incapable of adequately understanding the phenomenon of love. This has hampered not only a theology of the basic and central commandment, but also an understanding of its intimate connections with the Incarnation and the triune life of God. Despite the admirable attempt of St. Augustine in his *De doctrina christiana*,[9] St. Thomas's analysis of *caritas* as *forma virtutum*,[10] and the attempts of more recent theologians, the unity of the divine and human loves has remained a scarcely understood, though well-experienced and often preached mystery. It will always remain a mystery, but Christians who philosophize cannot avoid focusing on the unity of God and humanity in love, which is the orient of their lives and of all thought that serves their own and all others' salvation. Though the chapters of this book will not accomplish the task articulated above, their incursions into the dimension where Christian faith meets with "*philosophia*" are presented in the hope that all who sympathize with their orientation may advance toward the ideal of an intellectual community bound together by the liberating diversity of hopeful charity.

Christianity and Academic Life

To introduce the perspective from which the following chapters have been written, I would like to begin with a few autobiographical remarks.

When I was studying at the public gymnasium of Hilversum in the Netherlands, I delighted in being introduced to Greek and Roman literature, art, and philosophy. Born and educated in a devout Catholic family, I was fascinated by the beauty of that past world whose traces were still found everywhere in the literature, the architecture, and the sculpture of the surrounding Dutch, French, English, German, and Italian cultures. While reading Plato's dialogues, I naïvely combined his thoughts about the soul and a spiritual way of life with the lessons of the Catholic catechism, without stumbling on the deep differences between the Athenian culture of the fourth century before Christ and the Christian tradition from which I had received my spiritual food. Plato's description of *erōs* as the radical motivation that pushes us upward from one level to the next towards the pure ocean of beauty itself struck me as a wonderful description of the desire for God, which, at that time, had caught me. While I was studying philosophy and theology in Franciscan friaries, excellent teachers and texts revealed to me many differences between Greek antiquity, medieval Christianity, and modern culture. My heroes became Saint Augustine, on whom I wrote my first paper, and Saint Bonaventure, who is the most Franciscan of all great thinkers. Like them, I hoped to learn how to contribute to a new synthesis of philosophy and contemporary culture with theology, faith, and spirituality.

While studying at the Institute for Philosophy at the University of Leuven in Belgium, I continued to discover the spiritual world of old and new philosophers. Kant, Hegel, Heidegger, Husserl, and French phenomenology were interpreted and admired by my professors, several of whom were priests; but, although the Institute had been founded as a school in Neo-Thomism, most of them refused to speak about the links between philosophy, faith, theology, and spirituality. They accepted the modern postulate that separates autonomous reason, as displayed in philosophy and the sciences, from a theology that appeals not only to historical sciences and philosophical thought, but also, and principally, to the authority of Scripture and the Church. Although the climate of Leuven was Catholic, the theoretical assumptions on which most professors in philosophy based their teaching were hardly different from those that ruled the University of Paris, where I obtained my doctorate. There the only professor who thematized the links between philosophy and theology was Paul Ricoeur, whom I got to know and greatly admire while he was the director of my dissertation.

I have always been convinced—even more so now than before—that it is a great mistake of many intellectuals not to reflect on the connections that tie their scholarly pursuits to the primary dynamism of their lives and the basic convictions by which these are guided. In this chapter I will try to justify this conviction by giving some arguments for a renewed integration of scholarly work with Christian faith as it unfolds in spirituality and theology.

Academic Life

As academics, we are familiar with one or more scholarly disciplines; we have developed appropriate skills and through the years we have acquired enough experience to guide others in the field. Once in a while, we reflect upon the methods we practice in our research and teaching and we exchange our ideas with others in conferences and colloquia. We know what is going on in our specialty and follow the relevant developments.

How does this knowledge relate to the rest of our lives? Our jobs are only a part of these lives, even if they frequently absorb so much time and energy that we must wait for special days to enjoy extra-scholarly activities and pleasures. However, teaching and research, science and skills alone cannot fulfill a life; they are not equivalent to happiness or salvation. One could live a good life, even a wise life, without being at home in scholarship; but it is impossible to become happy without discovering what a human life is good for. The meaning of each, your and my, human life—or at least a certain, sufficient meaning of life—must be realized if living is to be worthwhile. We like our jobs, but how are they situated in the lives we want to be meaningful?

When is a human life meaningful and what is the role scholarship should play in our search for meaning? These are questions that no academic can avoid. To be up-to-date about the methods of science, without being knowledgeable and experienced about the ways that lead to success in life, would constitute a strange lack of balance, but in fact highly learned people can be ignorant with regard to the wisdom that is necessary for a fulfilled life. Apparently, such wisdom cannot be acquired through research and erudition alone. If scholars are people who do not stop thinking until they understand what they are doing, experiencing, planning, and hoping for, they cannot avoid reflecting on the connections that unite their scholarship with the broader and deeper life from which it emerges.

Christian Spirituality

Each human life is led by a mentality or "spirit" that gives it some sort of orientation. The unfolding of this mentality into a characteristic style of feeling, acting, imagining, practicing, and thinking can be called spirituality. The spirituality of a model Jesuit, for instance, can be described, but so can the characteristic style of behavior and speech of an enlightened agnosticist or a Nietzschean postmodernist. The roots of spirituality lie in a depth that we may call "religious," if we take this adjective in a broad and vague sense of the word. "Religion" indicates then the depth of a fundamental trust or distrust or suspicion or certitude or enthusiasm or melancholy with regard to the most fundamental events and problems of human life: What is it good for? Why do I exist? Why is there a human world at all? What is the meaning of all this, of the cosmos, of existence as such?

All religions are attempts to answer such questions, thus placing their members within a universal framework of ultimate meaning. Christianity is faith in God, the almighty Creator, whose Word, Jesus, through his life and work, suffering, death, and resurrection, reveals God's humility, endurance, and transforming grace. Creation, incarnation, passion, and re: punctuate the history of God and humanity in the spirit of Jesus, the Christ. Christians belong to a history that is more fundamental than any history of science and scholarship. The Christian community began with Abel and Abraham, and the time of Christianity is the time of humanity. Sharing with all humans a basic dimension of spirituality and religion, we see all of them as brothers and sisters in search of ultimate meaning. With all other Christians we share the desire to be true to the mystery of God's involvement in human history and of our involvement in God's own trinitarian life. As Catholics, we love our traditions without silencing the conversation with other Christians. Each having a style of our own within the worldwide Church, we maintain a solidarity with all creatures in the love of one God who wants all people to become holy. A communication without barriers opens up from this faith. Let us not narrow it through any variety of spiritual provincialism, political nationalism, dogmatic exclusivism, or moralistic self-righteousness!

———————

The question of how our academic pursuits emerge from our lives in order to realize part of their meaning can be approached as a question about the interaction between the inspiration that directs our lives and the "spirit" that characterizes our participation in contemporary scholarship. Assuming that all of my readers are somehow involved, or at least interested, in the characteristic spirituality of Christianity, I would first like to sketch a succinct outline of Christian spirituality—while being conscious that my perspective can be replaced by several others—and then ask how the style and spirit of the contemporary university can relate to it.

Christian faith is neither a theory nor a worldview; it is not a species of "theism" or a set of beliefs, but it is a most fundamental and total trust in God. This trust is a movement; through it we respond to God's addressing us while revealing that He loves us. God is good, God is concerned, God loves all beings that owe their existence to this love. This is perhaps the most incredible aspect of faith, and indeed the most exciting one. This love is also the most difficult to understand not only because we hardly even know what and how perfect love among humans is, but also because God is not an individual or a person in the finite and "normal" sense of these words. While being the absolute origin that requires nothing to exist, God's infinity reveals itself in our experiences of joyous and painful lives.

The trust that moves Christians toward God is first of all acceptance and gratitude; second, it encompasses the normal response that love elicits: love in return, albeit in a clumsy and inconstant way. Our failure to love God passionately enough might make us doubt whether we can really count on God's unconditional compassion, but, while struggling for a tested and purified faith, we discover not only that hope is as basic as faith and love, but that faith, hope, and love themselves are gifts of grace, rather than conquests through which we show how good *we* are. Total dependence on grace *and* total transcendence toward God define a Christian life, even if it is hampered by fragility and sin. The Spirit of God's grace is "greater than our heart"; it precedes our very existence and carries our development "on eagles' wings."

I could not utter any of these words if they had not been handed down to us by the Christian tradition, as keys for the interpretation of our history. The secret of this history, the mystery to be fully revealed at the end of times, is traditionally named Creation-Incarnation-Passion-Resurrection. Perhaps "Incarnation" alone would suffice to summarize the core of Christianity, if we do not forget that God's humanity realizes itself in all human beings who are driven by the Spirit of grace. Neither must we forget that God's participation in the history of an unholy humanity implies rejection and betrayal, suffering, torture, and murder. And what else is resurrection than the full triumph of incarnation? If God is humble enough to endure a human existence, the assumption and transfiguration of this existence into God's own life has taken place long before it is manifested in the divinization of all flesh.

Jesus Christ, the central sacrament in which the Spirit unites God with the human universe, is the living presence from which a Christian life receives its inspiration. Being "in Christ," following the principal way-guide, we are living the life of God's Spirit in our historical mixture of dusk and dawn, endurance and delight.

Is all this not too beautiful, too ethereal and too unreal to have any impact on our daily life? Something for Christmas and Easter or for religious poetry on exceptionally sad or sunny days? To answer this question, we could start from the Cross. For this, at least, stands at the heart of all realistic history. Without passage through the Passion, all other words of faith, including creation, incarnation, resurrection, and ascension are hollow. They would suggest that an ascent to heaven is possible without descent into the suffering of corruption, injustice, hatred, murder, and abandonment. For now, however, I must break off this kind of sermon in order to approach the question from another side by asking the following questions: How does the spirit of Christian faith penetrate our academic activities? How can these be integral elements of a concrete Christian spirituality?

Two Spirits

Spirit, inspiration, spirituality do not float above the real world of real lives; they penetrate and stylize all our deeds, words, gestures, thoughts, and emotions. Even our ways of eating and walking somehow express the kind of spirit that inspires us. But are we inspired by one single, all-encompassing spirit? Being "children of Abraham" and followers of Jesus, we are also children of our country and time. The culture in which we have grown up has shaped our minds and bodies, the language of our communication, the customs of our ethos, and the assumptions of our affluent and democratic mentality. Does the spirit of this culture, at the beginning of the twenty-first century, fit into the spirituality of the Christian tradition? Are we able to combine loyalty to the Gospel with the mentality of contemporary America?

The culture of our time is not a monolithic block. It offers space for a great variety of convictions, opinions, practices, ideas, and ideologies; yet it does have a general character in which, for example, pluralism, relativism, enlightenment, and boundless curiosity are at home. Individuals must find out how to integrate elements of the surrounding culture and transform them into their own personal characters. The family, the school, chance encounters, study, jobs, marriage, children, the Church, and many other factors intervene in this process. If faith has been accepted as the basic framework of life, it will have strongly influenced the formation of the faithful person's character, but tensions between the life of faith and being at home in the prevailing culture can easily cause a certain disharmony. Christian spirituality is neither a worldview nor a culture; it is open to all cultures, but it demands their adjustment and purification.

To what extent can our academic culture be an expression of Christian inspiration? Must it not be purified, bent, transformed, or converted to be compatible with the Holy Spirit? If, like Paul, we want to be Greek with the Greeks and Hebrew with the Hebrews, does this mean that we, intellectuals, should simply do what everybody else in academia does?

My first observation is that faith cannot be real unless it becomes concrete in the patterns of a particular culture, which culture thereby receives a deeper source of inspiration and purification, so that its patterns are also transformed. However, faith can never be identified with any specific culture because it creates a human community of all times and places by maintaining a certain distance toward all particular cultures. Faith remains free to criticize, correct, or convert all cultures, but it cannot do without them.

Second, I will approach the difference between the spirit of today's academe and the spirit of the Christian tradition by contrasting the self-awareness typical of secular scholarship with the self-awareness of Christians who know their own history. The difference between these two spirits can be captured by studying how each of them situates itself in time through a genealogy of its own position.[1]

To fully justify this approach, I should examine several presuppositions, but I can give here only a few indications for such a justification. For Western intellectuals, it is hardly possible to interpret the meaning of their own work without seeing it as a contribution to Western history as a whole. For Christians, it is even "more" impossible to forget the ongoing story in which Adam, Abraham, Moses, David, Mary, Jesus, the Apostles, and the history of the Church play leading parts. We can therefore approach the relations between culture and faith by looking at the way in which Western Christians, according to their self-consciousness, have become what they are. To assess in what sense such a genealogical consciousness differs from a scientific reconstruction of the past would demand a treatise on memory, remembrance, retrieval, history, and genealogy. Instead, I will simply state boldly that the way in which we imagine ourselves as belonging to a specific family with its own history and traditions, greatly determines the confidence that lies at the base of a purposeful life.

Genealogies

Among the many possibilities of belonging to one or more specific traditions there are several standard types. I will oppose here a Christian genealogy to another, "enlightened" one. The latter seems to be presupposed in much of the scholarly literature, while Christian genealogies are often treated with contempt. The contrast I will draw is schematic and unrefined, maybe even in some respects a caricature, but its purpose here is only to invite reflection on a double allegiance.

The genealogy of the secular university—a genealogy that is often presented as objective history—divides the Western civilization into three or four main periods. According to this account, ancient Greece was the cradle of enlightenment through science and philosophy; it opposed *logos* to *mythos* and conquered magic by discovering an autonomous kind of rationality. The invasion of Christianity into the refined world of Hellenistic and Roman culture is here interpreted as a countermovement that introduced or reintroduced belief in supernatural, mystical, and magical forces, religious authorities, and dogmatic certainties. With the death of antiquity began the "dark" age—a period of more than a thousand years that many pseudoscholars deemed so retrogressive and uninteresting that they did not even have a name for it. As the "middle ages" between antiquity and modernity, this epoch from the Hellenistic age to the sixteenth century could be ignored because its beliefs and speculations made no contribution to the development of modern science, of which the modern university is heir and guardian. The spirit of the modern university is the spirit of modern autonomy and rationality, calculus and scientific experiments, technology and computerized information. Looking back on our past, we belong to the Greek tradition in which this spirit emerged as ferment of the Western civilization.

Where, in this picture—or caricature—of the "enlightened" genealogy, is the place of Western Christianity? It is degraded to the status of an intermezzo, whose vitality and influence has faded away because autonomous reason and scientificity have taken over the functions of a basic framework for meaning. But can rational thought and scientific discovery take the place of the most basic and ultimate foundation of human existence? If not, then how do they and how should they relate to a more fundamental and ultimate framework?

Neither a Christian nor even a marginally informed intellectual can believe that the history of Israel, the Bible and its enormous influence, the life of Jesus and the birth of the Church, the contemplative literature of the Fathers, the medieval geniuses of thought, and the poetry from Francis to Dante are mere expressions of decadence or clumsy announcements of modern insights. If blindness calls the Middle Ages dark and if superficiality mistakes the summits of speculative thought for obscurantism, Christian self-understanding must pity such ignorance. Faith, however, recognizes a life-giving Spirit in the Gospels and the writings of Paul, John, Augustine, Bernard, Gertrud, Thomas, Bonaventure, Teresa, Cusanus, and myriad other mystics, contemplatives, philosophers, and theologians. Who can build his or her existence on science after having discovered "the depth and the height, the width and the length" of that Spirit? Modern secularity is bleak in comparison to the Christian breakthrough as unfolded in a civilization of two millennia. True, the Middle Ages were no paradise: violence, hatred, murder, injustice were not absent from a culture that proclaimed the ideal of universal charity; but who can brag about modern justice and compassion after the carefully planned slaughters of millions of innocents on all continents of the modern world? A Christian genealogy does not despise any epoch or culture; it does not ignore the weakness and propensity to sin which neither Christians nor non-Christians can escape; but it recognizes true inspiration wherever the Spirit blows: in Jerusalem or Athens, Rome or Assisi, Paris or Princeton or anywhere else.

From a Christian perspective, Western history looks very different from its "enlightened" reconstruction. As Christian scholars, we continue the tradition of biblical thinkers and Church Fathers, twelfth-century monks, thirteenth-century theologians, fourteenth-century poets, sixteenth-century mystics, and beyond. The wealth of our heritage is overwhelming, but it also provides confidence. Rooted in faith, we do not want to give up full participation in the scientific pursuits of our culture, but we cannot agree with the widely accepted explanation of its foundation. How then should we assimilate the academic culture without betraying our loyalty to the Christian community? The answer is: by transforming scholarship into an expression of Christian inspiration. But how?

Christian Scholarship

Some disciplines seem to lend themselves more easily to a Christian transformation than others. There is no Christian mathematics, but in the context of this book "Christian theology" sounds like a pleonasm. A theologian explains and demonstrates the meaning and the coherence of the Christian faith, relating it to other elements of the prevailing culture. It seems easy to combine being a faithful Christian with being a teacher and researcher of this same faith. However, even theology can lead away from faith, for example, by replacing it with philosophical doctrines that testify to the fashions of a certain epoch, rather than to the inspiration of Jesus, Paul, and John, or—on the contrary—by identifying faith with a literalist repetition of archaic formulae. A still more fundamental danger of theology lies in its "logical" or theoretical character. Because theological considerations thematize, question, objectify, analyze, explain, and try to understand the "objects" of faith, they cannot, at the same time, address themselves *to* God, like a prayer. Some

classical texts of theology, such as Augustine's *Soliloquia* and Ansel,
logion, are prayers, but they are interrupted by theoretical conside   ,
which turn the attention of writer and reader from God to questions *about*
God. The tensions between the theoretical attitude and "the spirit of prayer"[2]
can be illustrated in many ways. In his novel *L'imposture,* for example, George
Bernanos shows their radical difference through the scenario of a specialist in
Florentine mysticism who is no longer able to pray. He needs the help of an
unlearned but holy woman to say the Lord's Prayer before he dies.

Thinking, teaching, and researching have become ever more objective,
distanced, "skeptical," scientific. The contemplative tradition, in which reading and meditation were integral parts of a praying life, has been lost, except
in a few monasteries where its relation to modern culture continues to be a
source of difficulties. Is it at all possible to make objective thinking flow naturally toward God? Perhaps some analogies can evoke the beginning of an
answer to this important question.

There are many ways to think about someone you love, but a scientific
analysis of the other's body or mind feels awkward unless it is integrated in
a context of mutual concern. In teaching or in an address, we may care for
others' lives and needs, while thematizing aspects of their very existence.
Thinking-about can, thus, be integrated into a concern-for or a devotion-to.
The movement toward another person does not exclude objectifying considerations, but these must be embedded in dedication. Science should be inspired, not only by its own excitement, but by an existential spirit of devotion.
The *logos* of theology and other kinds of theory must be supported by the
deeper movement of faith *in* God (*credere in Deum*), a movement that is not
expressed by any "faith" or "belief *that* God . . ."

Such a unity between faith and scholarship does not leave the latter indifferent. It is demonstrated in the ways that devout scholars practice their
jobs: in the tone, the mood, and the style of their basic attitude towards others, history, and life as such; in their acceptance and admiration or horror in
the face of the facts; in their ways of addressing students and colleagues; in a
radical form of gratitude and hope, and, as their faith grows, in love of God
and humanity. To see *how* that unity is shown, it is sufficient to compare the
dryness of most theological manuals with the radiance of, e.g., Origen's *Commentary on the Song of Songs,* Gregory's *Life of Moses,* or Bonaventure's *Travel
Guide of the Mind to God.*

The idea of an osmosis between faith and reason seems antimodern.
Modernity has preached the autonomy of *reason* and democratic access to

the basic *experiences* on which truth must be built. It has thereby denied that certain uncommon phenomena, such as mystical experience or growing wisdom, can contain truths that science is unable to discover. It has also denied the necessity of *katharsis* or purification,[3] through which superficial and corrupt experiences may become more authentic. Reason has been proclaimed capable of being transparent to itself, and human individuals have wanted to occupy the highest vantage point by sharing in that transparency.

Postmodern thinkers no longer believe in modern dogmas; but only a few have concluded that the dimension from which all beliefs emerge is the dimension of religion, even if it is the religion of an atheist or agnostic.[4] However, the recognition of basic connections between science and faith is a condition for both the urgently needed renewal of the university and the unfolding of faith into its own postmodern intellectuality.

The tasks that are implied in these claims concern all academic disciplines. In literature, for example, the meaning of death, love, suffering, loneliness, education, courage, greed, liberation, pride, and prejudice is everywhere present; but how can real Christians meditate about them without associating the novels and poems they study with the biblical tradition in which those topics are central? In psychology, behaviorism has been shown to be totally inadequate because we cannot recognize ourselves in its picture of human existence. If it is true that a human being is distinct from an animal not only by being *rational*, but also in its specific "animality," and, on a still deeper level, as a praying animal, this truth must have consequences for the entire universe. The same is true of the practices that belong to social work or nursing. In addressing themselves to other persons, practitioners show their motivation and inspiration through undefinable but real gestures of attention and concern. And since true love of the neighbor is equivalent to love of God, their activity must express the same spirit as prayer and contemplation.

Returning to mathematics as an example of those disciplines that seem to contradict the thesis of an insoluble bond between Christian spirituality and scholarship, I would argue that, although "Christian mathematics" may be a meaningless expression, "Christian mathematicians" makes sense. Let me try to make this clear through two brief remarks.

First, mathematics seems to be so abstract and formal a discipline that it can be studied in isolation from all questions of content and existential meaning. However, as intellectuals, mathematicians cannot avoid reflecting on the relevance of their mathematical work for the totality of theoretical pursuits and for the meaning of their own and other human lives in various communities and history. The personal union of life and mathematics does not allow us to make a clearcut separation between the meaning of calculus and the meaning of human space and time. Though mathematics is able to generate complete agreement in its own dimension, this dimension is only one aspect of human space and time, which is experienced differently by Christians and believers of another faith.

Second, teaching and research in mathematics is done through communication with other humans in one and the same world. This communication is not confined to mathematical operations; it engages a wider understanding of the world and a specific style of approaching other individuals. A Christian approach is charitable; it includes the belief that true love of neighbor coincides with loving God and it is the main criterion for the authenticity of the latter. As a member of the Christian community, a mathematician, like any other scholar, develops a characteristic style of speaking, feeling, and behaving. Virtues like benevolence, care, generosity, humility, and patience follow from such membership. Consequently, there is a typically Christian style of devotion to mathematics.

These arguments can be applied to the entire field of scholarship: the *content* of all academic disciplines is linked to the Christian interpretation of the human condition, while their *form*—in a broad sense that includes their social aspects—involves them in a charitable style of communication. "Christian scholarship" is an ambiguous expression, however. It should not suggest that the proper methodology of any science be commanded or vetoed by the Gospel; but as an indication of scholarship that is integrated into a wider context and mode of behavior, it points to people whose scholarship is not isolated from the rest of their lives and the faith in which these lives are rooted.

Ethics and Faith

To conclude this chapter, I would like to indicate a danger inherent in emphasizing some of the virtues that came to the fore above. To begin with, let us not make the mistake of reducing Christianity to an ethics of virtues. The moral aspects of faith are certainly very important, but they lose their Christian inspiration if they are cut off from the central mystery of Creation-Incarnation-Passion-Resurrection.

Not all kinds of ethics are good; many are un-Christian or anti-Christian. In any case—as Paul repeats over and over again—establishing ethics as the highest criterion for human dignity is a denial of God's grace. Rather than expressing it, moralism undermines authentic faith. The Homeric ethics of excellence and shame, the Aristotelian ethics of human beauty, the warrior's ethics of Germanic tribes, the Kantian ethics of absolute duty, the bourgeois ethics of social respectability, and so on, present admirable possibilities of human existence; but none of them can replace the spirituality that emerges from the mystery of Jesus Christ, which generates in every culture and period appropriate patterns and codes of action, emotion, imagination, and thought. No culture can encompass the full meaning of God's revelation, but each and every culture, with its moral and theoretical customs, offers characteristic possibilities for faith's concretization. The leading virtues of a specific culture (for example, fairness, hospitality, or courage) can be accepted by the Christian community, but they must be transformed into expressions of the Spirit who unites humanity with God in the love of Christ. The decisive element in Christian ethics is charity, graciously given participation in God's trinitarian love. This generates, inspires, guides, and "forms" all virtues and actions.[5] Only this source, the source of creation, incarnation, passion, and resurrection, can recreate human beings by calling them to a timely retrieval of the old tradition. Scholarship is neither the only nor the most important dimension of such a renewal, but it has an enormous impact on the formation and information of young and old, and therewith on the future of humanity. To be a Christian *and* a scholar is to repeat in learned ways Christ's passage from birth to death.

On the Relationships between Life, Scholarship, and Faith in a Catholic University

In its vision statement, titled "Building a Bold Tomorrow: Vision 2005," the University of San Francisco describes itself as inspired by "a passion for learning." I would like to take one passage of this statement as the point of departure for a meditation on the tasks that a Catholic university today needs to accomplish.

> Challenging our students to develop the knowledge, skills, and flexibility necessary *to gain wisdom* constitutes the most significant element of our identity and mission.... Our interactive *learning community* recognizes that university education occurs both *inside* and *outside* the classroom. [Emphasis in original.]

These two sentences contain an entire program for higher education. The passion for learning, to which education and self-education respond, demands the best available academic teaching and professional training, but it cannot be confined to the classroom. Since all learning serves the desire for a meaningful life—a desire that cannot be satisfied without at least some degree of wisdom—the aim of all education is integrated wisdom. Information, research, and training are meaningful insofar as they contribute to the kind of insight that conditions a good life. In declaring that "gaining wisdom . . . constitutes the most significant element of [its] identity and mission," a university acknowledges the necessity of a kind of learning that goes beyond academic professionalism; a specific unity of knowledge (*epistēmē, scientia*) and wisdom (*sophia, sapientia*) is then its goal. How can this goal be realized? Allow me to approach this question in a somewhat personal way. I would like to begin with some experiences that I hope we share, in order to ask how we can make such experiences fruitful for the (re)orientation of a Catholic university.

Interdisciplinary Integration

My experiences concern primarily philosophy and theology, but I assume that they parallel similar experiences in other disciplines. If I may start from my own discipline, I would like to draw attention to a basic difficulty that students in philosophy have to cope with: they are confronted with several very different methods of thought, which tend to ignore one another and are rarely brought into a discussion. The situation is complicated, but the standard account simplifies it as a rift between so-called analytic philosophy, which emphasizes the relevance of scientific objectivity, and so-called continental philosophy, which stresses the importance of history and hermeneutics. Not only beginning students, but even most professors feel themselves incapable of overcoming the opposition between these tendencies and unable to synthesize the valuable insights of both. Consequently, the discipline remains divided into different schools without much interchange.

The situation is even worse in theology. Not only does it parallel philosophical pluralism, but theology is additionally scattered into a variety of scientific disciplines—from archaeology and Aramaic to hermeneutics and bioethics—the integration of which seems to demand superhuman efforts.

The specialization of scholarship and fundamental disagreements regarding methodology have caused a general fragmentation of the ensemble that was once unified as a system or an encyclopedic whole and could be taught to anybody who was bright enough and willing to devote time to study. But if it is already difficult to master the different styles and directions within one's own discipline, how much more difficult will it be to bring various disciplines together into one body of knowledge? Should we then abandon the idea of an integrated academic culture?

In response to the fragmentation of scholarship, most institutions for liberal education provide some kind of interdisciplinary program. Students are encouraged to adopt various perspectives and methods according to the subject matters and approaches practiced in different fields of scholarship. Often, this task is entrusted to a core curriculum at the college level. This is, of course, a good antidote against the tendency to obsessive fascination by a single subject. However, the juxtaposition of different courses does not automatically generate an integration of the information provided. Integration demands a unifying perspective, but how is such a perspective discovered? Can we ask students to achieve what we ourselves are reluctant or unable to accomplish? Classes team-taught by professors from different departments are helpful, though they offer only a partial remedy. Perhaps the problem of interdisciplinary integration cannot be resolved unless we also organize some kind of *core for professors*. Are most teachers well-informed about the generally relevant subjects taught by their colleagues? Even more important: do we know how to develop a unified perspective for "interactive" learning? Do we perhaps need an interdisciplinary forum where scholars from all departments regularly inform and discuss with one another the relevance of their discoveries? It would certainly help develop and promote an integrated core. If students could participate in such discussions, these would constitute an exciting experience for the academic community as a whole.

Integration of Life and Scholarship

Another form of integration is even more necessary than the interdisciplinary one. This concerns the relations between our academic pursuits and the lives we live.

It is an old complaint that academia is barely in touch with the real world, the real lives we live, and the reality of the existential struggles of real people in concrete situations. Each of us probably remembers moments when we, as students, asked ourselves what certain classes had to do with the important questions of human life. Did the books we studied give us guidance for living meaningfully? Did they indicate how the available knowledge related to the questions that seemed most relevant for us?

Soon after I started teaching philosophy, several students wanted to involve me in their attempts to bridge the gap between the instruction they received and the life experiment in which they, as adolescents, were involved. They appealed, for example, to Plato's Academy to stress their demand for mediation between theory and practice. Perhaps disciplines like philosophy, psychology, education, and theology attract more students with these kinds of questions than do other disciplines, but I surmise that most professors recall similar experiences.

At first, my reaction was based on a clear distinction between academic and existential questions. I insisted on my academic function and on the necessity of overcoming subjectivistic perspectives through generalization, analysis, abstraction, universally valid statements, and so on. I maintained that objectivity and interpersonal validity, participation in the society, and a scholarly attitude demand distance from personal issues. In this vein, I tried to convince my students that I was a professor, not a spiritual leader. However, my conscience was not wholly at peace, because professors too must ask and answer similar questions for themselves, and students may expect that their teachers, having already struggled with such questions, are in a position to give them some advice. In fact, their challenge is a reminder to professors that, even in their teaching, they should not forget the connections between academic knowledge and existential wisdom.

In an attempt to be more honest, my response to similar demands has changed over time. In a second phase, I responded to the students' demands by reflecting with them about the intrinsic links that connect theoretical endeavors with the pursuit of existential meaning; but I still wanted to stress the distinction between the university as a scholarly enterprise and the more subjective dimensions of personal life. I decided therefore that students could find me at home, but not in my office, in order to talk to me about personal issues, including the problem of how to make their studies fruitful for their lives. This decision led to a regular gathering at my house of about ten to fifteen students who discussed various kinds of philosophical, literary, and religious texts from the perspective of a common desire for existential insight. It was an experiment in uniting academic skills with a search for spirituality, on which I look back with gratitude.

In the meantime, however, I have become convinced that the university itself must embrace the task of showing how scholarship can be made fruitful, as an integral element, in the pursuit of wisdom. For where else can we learn to understand the relevance of old and new knowledge for the meaning of human life?[1]

Under different names and from different sides, the relation between academic education and the formation of a good life is drawing renewed interest. I will here mention two examples: Jaroslav Pelikan's *The Idea of the University: a Re-examination* (Yale University Press, 1992), which is a retrieval of Newman's classic *The Idea of a University,* and Martha Nussbaum's *Cultivating Humanity: A Classical Defense of Reform in Liberal Education* (Harvard University Press, 1997). While Pelikan follows Newman in proclaiming that knowledge — which is more than information and less than wisdom — is the goal of the university,[2] Nussbaum does not focus on *sophia,* not even in its Platonic or Aristotelian sense, but rather on the idea of a liberal, cosmopolitan, and democratic person who has learned how to reason independently. Though she calls this ideal Socratic (in opposition to what she considers Plato's undemocratic philosophy), I cannot discover in it anything more than an Americanized version of the eighteenth-century tradition that still dominates most universities, especially those that are completely secularized. Instead of a "reform," her book is a straightforward expression of the assumptions that dominated the epoch of the Enlightenment. As for Pelikan's much broader scope of knowledge and thought, I would like to suggest that while knowledge should certainly be desired and practiced for its own sake, it can never be isolated from human practice and emotion, or from the kind of faith in which these are rooted.

To discuss the relations between knowledge and wisdom in our time, we must be aware of the "enlightened" assumptions that still permeate most scholarship. The modern alliance of autonomous thought with the ideal of scientific objectivity has generated a theoretical culture in which subjective desires are left to the private feelings and choices of individuals, restricted only by the fundamental equality of all individuals from the perspective of their rights. All assumptions that have not been demonstrated to be true are considered void, and all statements that do not clarify a well-defined matter are unscientific. Subjective experiences are not acceptable in scholarship unless they are defined in behavioral terms. The ideal is a qualifying approach that allows for calculation.

Since modern scholarship has not been able to prove all its basic assumptions, however, it has become clear that authority and tradition do play a decisive role. The ideal of autonomy seems more utopian today than it did in the seventeenth century. "Objectivity" has become a name for existentially uninteresting topics, because any involvement of a subject muddles the outcome of observation. The triumphs of four hundred years of modernity are dazzling from a technological perspective, but disappointing for those who seek wisdom. In response to this result, there are, on the one hand, those who continue to emphasize the methods of good old modernity, while gladly accepting the divorce between scientific rigor and personal wisdom, and on the other hand, those who, out of unrequited love, have become skeptical with regard to meaning and truth. Is it possible to walk a middle path between naïve enthusiasm and skeptical despair, while hopefully reconnecting with the thinkers of ancient and premodern times?

Meaning

At this point, I must return to the passion for learning. Why "*passion*"? What makes us passionate, and not merely curious or eager, to acquire education and knowledge? Which desire motivates us in the university? It must be a desire that was awakened in us before we entered and that will continue once we have left the university to employ or apply our knowledge in the adventure of a busy but also reflective life.

One popular answer is that we desire knowledge because it is useful for the satisfaction of our needs. The utilitarian framework expressed in this answer regards human beings as ensembles of needs that seek fulfillment. Since needs may conflict with one another, something called liberty or freedom should decide how to prevent or resolve such conflicts. Choosing is the human activity by which our decisions are initiated and effectuated. Freedom is thus understood as the capability of choice and as the deciding factor in an economic structure.

This conception of human freedom ignores the fact that we desire more than satisfaction: what we desire before and above all the things we need, is *meaning*. Satisfaction can be meaningless. The most pleasant comfort leaves us empty if our lives are neither good nor noble, beautiful nor admirable. To enjoy the things we need is not the end for which we live. We illustrate this statement, when we risk our lives for great causes or admire such sacrifices. Heroism, suffering for the good of others, perfect devotion illustrate a freedom other than that of a choice between contrasting needs. Desire transcends the economy of needs by orienting us toward a meaning we cannot do without: a human life must succeed in becoming *good*, not only pleasurable. The decisive or ultimate meaning of a human life is not one of the "values" competing in the economy of exchangeable satisfactions. The meaning of a human life is absolute: if you fail to realize it, your life, as a whole, is a failure.[3]

All civilizations have tried to discover how the meaning of life as a whole can be realized, expressed, thematized, and combined with all the other ends we need or want. In the Western tradition, it was the central concern of sages, preachers, philosophers, theologians, and masters of spirituality. Whether its name is *eudaimonia, makariotēs, beatitudo,* blessedness, well-being, human perfection, or happiness, all individuals are moved by a profound passion for succeeding in the art of living humanly.

The contemporary culture provides a broad variety of answers to the question of ultimate meaning, but a serious discussion among the protagonists seldom occurs. The two most popular schools in ethics avoid the question by circumscribing their discussions within the boundaries of (1) respect for human rights and (2) the satisfaction of finite needs, while theories about (3) eternal beatitude are most often excluded as outdated or theological. Moreover, many scholars act as if the question of ultimate meaning is a private question that hardly allows for a public, and even less an academic, debate. Yet, it is the most important question of real wisdom.

The difference between the economy of needs and the most profound human desire can be transposed to the theoretical dimension of human life. In our pursuit of knowledge, we must distinguish the study of phenomena and events that compose the fabric of the universe from the discovery of something that does not have a place or function *within* the universe, because it is ultimately and originally responsible for the meaning of the universe and all that exists within it. From Plato to Hegel, philosophers have taken this distinction very seriously; but some of the postmodern philosophers have condemned it as "metaphysical." The so-called "proofs for the existence of God" were endeavors to transpose the question of life's ultimate meaning onto the level of logical and ontological reasoning, and this connection explains why postscholastic and modern philosophers attached so much importance to those proofs. In his discourses on the university, Newman, for instance, regarded this part of philosophy, traditionally called "natural theology," as fundamental to the idea of the university. Today, however, many or most listeners would shake their heads at such discourses and give up listening. Their aversion to such "proofs" might be justified, but the intuition behind them deserves more consideration than it receives.[4]

Here, I am not going to defend any proof for the existence of God; I will not even elaborate on the meaning of the words "God" and "existence" or on the epistemological difficulties lurking in the clear-obscure of all discourses on infinity. To briefly indicate my own position, I will only say that I neither accept the deducibility of God nor sympathize with a fideistic leap that despises reason. What I want to emphasize, however, is that no one can escape the necessity of taking a stance with regard to the ultimate or absolute. Whether one is a Christian or a Buddhist, a theist or an atheist, a believer or an agnostic, everyone's life is governed by a basic orientation and conviction with regard to the overall meaning of his or her life. I would like to characterize this stance and this conviction as a *faith* in the broadest and most neutral sense of this word. Anyone who is not utterly desperate has a kind of trust in the existing reality as it is. Somehow at least some meaning is possible. Even if a life is full of doubts or experienced as a very shaky wager, it follows some line of its own in some sort of desire and faith and hope and attachment to an—albeit experimental—orientation. No one can deduce the thesis I am defending here because it expresses the most basic or primordial mode of existence and movement that rules individual lives. I can only appeal to the most authentic experiences generated by the fundamental and all-encompassing experiment in which all humans are involved. Somehow, in a way only partially known to us, we are not only moved, but also led by something ultimate.

"Religion," again in a very broad sense of the word, can be accepted as a name for any attempt to concretize the ultimate meaning in words, images, rituals, feelings, practices, concepts, etc. "Religion" then not only encompasses Buddhism, but also those kinds of atheism, agnosticism, skepticism, and nihilism that testify to a passion, a stance, a deep conviction, and a style of movement similar to the ones that are operative in Christian, Jewish, or Muslim faith. Taking "religion" and "faith" in these broad senses might facilitate the dialogue among adherents of different "faiths," including those who do not belong to any institutional religion. However, such a dialogue is doomed to failure if the partners do not in any way accept that there is a dimension of the absolute in every human life.

Faith

One cannot profess a religious faith without agreeing that it is highly relevant for all the key issues of one's life, including familial and social relationships, the education of one's children, and the motivation of one's work. The osmosis between faith and daily life is not always ideal, and all ways of believing require purification, but a religious community provides its adherents with a fundamental orientation that can be developed into an elementary form of wisdom. Personal realization of wisdom is not easy, it demands many religious and secular conditions; but scholarship is not a necessary requisite: few saints were learned, and rarely is a scholar also a prophet.

Although the wisdom of a faithful life is different from accomplished scholarship, they appeal to one another. Scholarship needs faith to overcome its indifference toward the most interesting and decisive questions of a life, whereas faith needs scholarship to become "real," i.e., socially and culturally concrete. Theology, for example, is a translation of faith into the imaginative and conceptual language of a particular culture. But theology is not enough; the entire culture—including its social and economic mores and its ideas about power, rights, sexuality, mortality, communication, and art—is called to express the spirit of a fundamental faith. This call cannot be fully obeyed or even clearly heard in a world where the State is inspired by a faith of its own in contradiction with the faith(s) of its inhabitants. The conflicts that emerge from such a divorce cannot, however, silence the fundamental demands that the citizens must fulfill in the name of their double loyalty to both their religious *and* their political community.

Scholarly Wisdom and Faith

What do these demands imply for a Christian who is involved in academic scholarship? How can we blend the most rigorous scholarship with loyalty to our religious community? How is it possible to be respectable members of academia without obscuring the glory of God?

Before trying to answer this question, let me share an amazing experience I had at Loyola University Chicago. Some years ago, I wrote a short paper on the question of whether we could and should try to revitalize the ancient and early Christian meaning of *philosophia,* understood as a search for integral wisdom.[5] When I asked some colleagues from philosophy and theology to give me a critical response, they brought still other faculty into the discussion and within a few weeks more than ninety professors from all disciplines had shown interest in discussions on the relations between Christianity and academia. The amplitude of this shared interest led to a series of meetings in which about forty or fifty professors participated each time. We always focused on the same question: What is the relevance of the Christian tradition for your academic pursuits and what is the relevance of your academic work for Christian life in the contemporary world? After two years of discussions, the time seemed ripe to establish a center for the study of the relations between Christian faith and the contemporary culture, which would focus our reflection by organizing interdisciplinary seminars and research groups on the mutual relevance of Christian faith and secular knowledge.

From this experience, which parallels similar experiences in other universities, I learned (1) that many scholars have a profound interest in overcoming the divide between their search for faith-oriented wisdom and their professional devotion to the ideals of modern and postmodern scholarship, but also (2) that the answers to our questions ought to emerge from the new situation that is ours. We cannot postpone the search for a good answer, because we cannot flourish without unifying our two loyalties. Neither as believers nor as scholars should we remain naïvely divided between a secular world and a realm of "supernatural" beliefs. The latter would become more and more mythological, while our scholarly pursuits would be confined to a completely profane and ultimately uninteresting, if not profoundly boring world. The real presence of faith *in* the real world demands the integration of worldly knowledge into the perspective of grace and ultimate meaning. Scholars cannot stop thinking about their own personal union of faith and scholarship.

It would be a fatal misunderstanding to interpret the mutual integration of religious and secular meaning as a unilateral obedience to the theories and imperatives of ecclesiastical theologians. In the first place, theology is not identical with faith. Faith is a gift of grace; as trust in God, it can never be completely transparent; though very certain of itself, it remains an incomprehensible mystery. Theology, on the other hand, is a historically and culturally conditioned interpretation of faith, which depends on old and new insights of philosophies, sciences, literature, habits, and opinions. Furthermore, just as all academic disciplines must ask themselves how they relate to the most profound questions of human life, so theology must reflect critically on its own double fidelity to the earthly rootedness of life, including its allegiance to recent scholarship, and to the part of wisdom it owes to faith.

As a community of free and responsible researchers, the university cannot accept external guidelines without first testing them critically. Within academic boundaries, faith cannot be the criterion of scholarly truth, but scholars ought to recognize that scholarship itself cannot be the ultimate foundation of a good life. If they do contend that only scholarly knowledge can lead to wisdom about the truth, they thereby proclaim a particular belief. Though popular in nineteenth-century positivism, only unwise universities can pledge allegiance to such a faith.

The university of the new century needs an explicit and generalized discussion of the connections between the many beliefs and scholarly disciplines represented within its schools and departments. A Catholic university may insist on the importance of its Catholic perspective, if it does not discriminate against other profound convictions, just as secular universities can emphasize their beliefs without forcing Catholics to accept the rules and rituals of their faith. It is a myth that secular institutions are neutral with regard to religion. By altogether excluding religion from their affairs, they offer a God-free environment and education; but in doing so, they at least *suggest* that humanity or nature—or other gods—are self-sufficient grounds and ends and that faith in God is a superfluous, or even superstitious, addition to thorough education and cultural maturity.

The Catholic Scholar

Scholars who happen to be Catholic, i.e., Catholics who happen to be scholars, find themselves confronted with the task of integrating their twofold allegiance. Most scholars, Catholic or not, have adapted the criteria and goals of their academic work to the demands of the secular, enlightened university. A total identification, however, would risk a gigantic loss of memory: if the long-standing traditions of premodern *philosophia* and contemplation are forgotten or treated as primitive attempts to become as smart as "we" moderns are, we have lost a wealth of insights, tasteful refinement, meditative enjoyment, and purifying practice. The great traditions from Homer to Racine and from Plato to Pascal cannot be ignored unless humanity could create a future without past. Since the Gospel, Catholic wisdom has tried to baptize all truth and beauty that was discovered within and without its horizon. However, since the beginning of modernity, the Church seemed to betray its own catholicity by refusing to welcome the modern sciences and the awakening of emancipated individuals to their inborn rights. The conflict took several centuries, but it remains our task to assimilate all the good of modernity, which in the meantime has evolved into a polyvalent culture.

When I was a student at the University of Paris, the history of philosophy between Plotinus and Descartes (a history of thirteen hundred years) was ignored by otherwise well-informed professors. One professor read some texts of Saint Thomas, but medieval philosophy did not figure in any official program. The separation between church and state still manifested itself in crass ignorance about the spiritual life that had nourished the slow emergence of Europe from antiquity. The situation was somewhat better at the "Higher Institute for Philosophy" at the Catholic University of Leuven in Belgium, where I had obtained my licentiate in philosophy. There, the study of medieval philosophy, represented by Thomas and Scotus, was obligatory, but all the theological elements of their thought were carefully silenced. The professors, all of whom were Catholic and most of whom were also priests, maintained a strict separation between philosophy and theology; they even refused to discuss fundamental questions about the relations between autonomous knowledge and religious faith. One would think that the philosophers of any Catholic university would see it as their special task to clarify and answer these questions, but in Leuven one had to agree with the ideé fixe of a strict separation.

Philosophy departments at most American universities are still very much dominated by the "enlightened" prejudice that there is no "real" (i.e., emancipated, objective, scientific) philosophy between antiquity and its reinvention by Bacon, Hobbes, and Descartes. Until recently, the Church has responded by insisting on St. Thomas's system, but every scholar knows that the Catholic tradition in no way can be restricted to his thought, whose monumentality does not destroy other monuments. From Clement and Origen via the Cappadocians, Augustine, Dionysius, Maximus, and Eriugena through the school of St. Victor and the giants of the thirteenth century to Nicholas of Cusa, innumerable thinkers have mediated in their own ways between faith and human thought, thus leaving us an inspiring and challenging heritage. In many respects their utterly sophisticated search for integrated wisdom offers better paradigms than the standard positions of modern or postmodern thought.

If I focus here on the relations between faith and philosophy, this is due to my familiarity with this discipline and theology. It is true that ancient and medieval thought does not offer a similar wealth of insight to contemporary scholars outside philosophy or theology. Yet, every Catholic who is a serious scholar is also a kind of philosopher and theologian. As soon as scholars realize that not only their students but they themselves are puzzled by the interpenetration of faith and thought in their own persons, they cannot avoid investigating the conditions and the consequences of this interpenetration with the same seriousness they devote to the problems of their specialty.

Their reflection will then produce a theory that clarifies the unity of revelation and research, of faith and reason, of Christianity and culture. To prevent this theory from remaining naïve and biased, they certainly need exchanges with philosophers and theologians, just as philosophers and theologians need exchanges with scientists to prevent them from forwarding absurdities. If such exchanges continue, all Catholic scholars who think that their work is somehow relevant for a meaningful life, will find themselves engaged in an interdisciplinary pursuit of Catholic wisdom.

Justice and Compassion

To illustrate what an alliance between Catholic orientation and down-to-earth scholarship could mean, I would like to finish this meditation with some remarks about an issue that the Jesuit order has made its device for dealing with the contemporary world: the issue of social justice and solidarity with the poor.

Obviously, an academic approach to justice demands the cooperation of many disciplines. Not only economics and law, but also theology and Scripture, sociology, politics, psychology, cultural anthropology, history, education, social work, nursing, medicine, and philosophy are needed for a full insight into the nature, the context, the demands, and the available possibilities of realizing justice. Decisive factors for the success of such an interdisciplinary program are its overall framework, the mentality of the participating researchers, and the spiritual climate of the promoting institution. Here, Catholicity makes a profound difference when compared to traditions that are motivated by mere recognition of the mutually limited rights of private individuals. The utilitarianism of a society ruled by individual claims can certainly clarify some aspects of justice, but there is a great difference between such a world view and one inspired by Israel's prophets, Jesus's beatitudes, the suffering of saints for others, the thought of the greatest theologians, and the mystical texts of Christian spirituality.

If compassion is God's reason for engaging human history, devotion to social justice is infinitely good. The modern struggle for human rights and against all discrimination deserves unreserved devotion. The historical reluctance of ecclesiastical authorities to join this noble struggle was a great sin against the Church, for which we owe sincere apologies, even though consolation can be found in the remembrance of innumerable true Catholics who, at all moments of history, have served the persecuted and the poor. They showed not only that rights are absolutely to be respected, but also that the goodness of the just goes much further than righteousness. The alliance of scholarship with faith produces charity, and no social justice is possible without it. If it is true that the glory of God shines in concretized compassion, *philosophia,* as the wisdom of love, is an integral part of that glory. The cooperation of disciplines in this spirit requires the backing of a great and passionate spirituality. That is why a faithful and enlightened retrieval of the Christian tradition is a normal part of any education in Catholic universities.

The Future of Christian Philosophy

FOUR

Professors and students who are involved in both philosophy and Christian faith belong to two communities: as Christians, they participate in the communion of saints; as philosophers, they belong to a republic of thinkers. Both communities are concretized in particular institutions, which, in my case, are the Roman Catholic Church and the American university. The combination of faith and thinking is also practiced in other contexts, and not all Catholics who work in the American university are models of loyalty. Moreover, most institutions are mixtures of excellence and mediocrity; their pursuit of perfection is interwoven with deficiencies. However, to be as concrete as possible in the following meditation on the future of philosophy in a religious context, I will appeal mainly to Catholic and American experiences that I share with many of you.

Christians have been educated in particular versions of faith in God as revealed in Jesus Christ. Though their faith does not depend on any specific culture, it cannot realize itself without appropriating the representations, customs, and symbols of a particular place and epoch. However, the cultural opinions and customs faith adopts change over time, because the God in which we believe embraces all places and times. To be alive, faith demands up to date expressions. The variety of cultures in which it invests itself in different spaces and epochs constitutes a complex and varied tradition in which it remains true to itself, while its cultural expressions may undergo many transformations. The constant reshaping of faith in loyalty to its purest sources is the task of prophets, saints, poets, and faithful men and women, including their leaders and intellectuals. These people will not succeed unless they are inspired by both a genuine "sense of faith" and familiarity with the surrounding culture. Since faith cannot be isolated from all cultural versions, it is not surprising that there are many concretizations of it, even within the parameters of one universal Church. The purity of the Gospel does not impose a uniform expression, but each and every expression must be purified in the name of the one true faith it tries to concretize. The criteria for such a purification cannot be found through a so-called "literal" return to the oldest sources, for not only do these present us with a puzzling plurality of dated interpretations of God's revelation, their original sense also demands much commentary and mediation to be understood in our age. Although historical study can decipher the meaning of early interpretations, only an inspired retrieval can bring them to life time and again. To present faith as genuinely as possible, we must thus express it in linguistic and other symbols that are recognizable as meaningful here and now (but not as less shocking than in the beginning!). How are we able to do this? How can we know the pure core of faith if it is only given in historical, changing, and sometimes distorted forms? Spirituality and theology have developed several devices for the "discernment of spirits" that is needed here. Without entering into this difficult subject, I want only to emphasize that, according to one of the fundamental devices, true faith is neither an exclusively, nor a primarily theoretical affair. More than knowledge, we need here an acquaintance that is the fruit of a right "sense" or attunement, good practice, trust, and prayer.

What, however, has philosophy to do with these remarks about the relation between faith and culture? This question can be answered in several ways. In the first place, we want to remind ourselves that it is not sufficient for an epoch, nation, culture, or institution to call itself Catholic or Christian to guarantee its loyalty to Jesus Christ. The Crusades and the Inquisition, papal condemnations of essential human rights, and episcopal blessings of cruel tyrants did betray the Christian message. The same is true of silly sermons and fundamentalist fascinations. We might even feel inclined to maintain that most concretizations of faith—in the first place our own—are impure and that the Church is an *ecclesia semper reformanda*.[1] In a philosophical or metaphilosophical reflection on the relevance of Christian faith, we must therefore be well aware of the danger that we ourselves or others amalgamate it with some of its travesties or caricatures. Christian faith is accompanied by the sad knowledge that Christians, too, are sinners and that the "corruption of the best is worse than all other corruptions."[2] The real question, however, is whether genuine faith, if realized according to its own demands, is admirable, true, liberating, and enjoyable.

A second reason why philosophers should be aware of the relations between faith and culture lies in the fact that they cannot separate their philosophizing from the basic conviction of their lives. For Christians who philosophize this means that they cannot adopt the deepest convictions of non-Christian colleagues as their own, although they may be able to reproduce them imaginatively through some sort of empathy. With regard to themselves, however, we must state clearly that such *Christians cannot avoid reflecting on the mutual relevance of their own faith and their philosophy (including their own metaphilosophy)*. It is no secret that *all* philosophers are guided by some unproven convictions that can be called "faiths" in a broad sense of this word.[3] If philosophy is a radical form of thinking, the faith of a philosopher cannot remain naïve. Consequently, a philosopher who is also a Christian would not be reflective enough or not sincere, if he did not think about the relevance of his faith for his philosophy.

Christian and Philosopher

Before analyzing the union of faith and philosophy in one person, this union should be made somewhat more concrete.

If the entire Law can be recapitulated in the undivided love of God and the neighbor, this love is given by the Spirit of grace, who liberates us from egoism and its violence. Grace, love, and peace are granted in Jesus Christ, whose passion shows how humble, compassionate, patient, and generous God is. To be a Christian is to be inspired by the Spirit of God as lived by Jesus. Grace makes us gratefully patient and generously humble in joyful hope that this Spirit may prevail over sin and death.

This summary is one way of appropriating—or being appropriated by—the consoling message that was announced to the historical community of God's people. If faithful updating of the meaning of that message demands a situated retrieval of its authentic tradition, intellectuals—especially philosophers and theologians—will propose their own versions of such a retrieval, while submitting them to the judgment of the Spirit who guides the community of saints.

The meaning of a profession of faith does not become clear until its generalities are applied to the moral, legal, economical, political, scientific, and artistic aspects of the world shared by Christians and others. The difference between a Christian and other forms of life and thought then becomes obvious, even if some of these other forms likewise call themselves Christian. To characterize the relevance of authentic Christianity for an American and Christian philosopher who lives in the twenty-first century, we could begin with a diagnosis of modern philosophy in its relation to Christianity.

The Spirit of Modern Philosophy

Contemporary philosophers have been educated in Western, masculine, and modern kinds of philosophy. Their modernity is particularly obvious in two characteristics: (1) belief in the autonomy of reason, and (2) awe for the sciences. Here, I will not dwell on the second characteristic, but concentrate on the first.

In one of their first lessons in philosophy, most students are told that philosophy is distinguished from other disciplines, and especially from theology, by its *autonomy*. It does not rely on opinions or dogmas; instead of beliefs, a methodically conducted combination of common experience and reason is sufficient for discovering how things are and how we should behave. Many students have responded to this message with enthusiasm and joyful hope. Like the leaders of Enlightenment from Bacon and Descartes to Voltaire, Kant, and Hegel, they received it as a message of liberation. A promise was made: philosophy will teach you to be free and your own master, in knowledge, choice, and behavior.

The contrast between that promise and today's philosophical reality is striking. Instead of beginning with obvious facts and logical principles in order to gradually unfold a complete system of truth, the professors confront their students either with a bewildering diversity of unfinished projects and fragments, disputed questions and doubts approached by a variety of authors from different perspectives, or with the ongoing discussions of one self-sure school that ignores all other schools but struggles on along its own lines of inquiry. Handbooks and instructors tell the students, in an authoritative way, which texts are important, how they have to be interpreted, how we today should think, which schools and philosophers are outdated, good, or trustworthy, and so on. Rarely does a teacher show, however, how one can reach truth without unproven assumptions. And yet, the modern dogma about autonomy demands to be tested on the basis of empirical evidence and rational insight alone. What at first is known in the form of mere opinions, should be proved in a purely rational way. That such a reconstruction takes time and cooperation is natural, but if it does not even partially succeed in the course of four or five centuries, the autarky of philosophy becomes unbelievable, more wishful than truthful. The idea of a self-sufficient philosophy might still be a regulative and productive though unattainable ideal, but it can no longer be declared a real possibility, because such a possibility is neither an immediate truth nor a very plausible hypothesis, and the results of modern belief in it are poor, to say the least.

In the past, the ideal of enlightened autonomy has generated several attempts to develop a complete system. Spinoza's *Ethica* and Hegel's *Encyclopedia* unfold the idea that the universe can be reconstructed in theory, but even these monuments of thought are full of gaps and unwarranted assumptions. All systems remain sketchy or fragmentary and most post-Hegelian philosophers have abandoned the ideal of a self-sufficient system. Even in scientistic versions of philosophy, the impossibility of absolute autarky is acknowledged. Skepticism and relativism, and, in any case, deep suspicions with regard to "metaphysics" and "speculation" have become the rule. However, while autonomy is still venerated as a bulwark against religious dogmatism, a host of philosophical, scientific, and literary stars are greedily quoted as authoritative guides for an enlightened treatment of the real world.

By proclaiming philosophy autonomous, the classics of modernity emancipated the European culture from ecclesiastical domination. Religion as such was not immediately attacked and for many years the old traditions of Christianity remained influential. After Hegel, however, the struggle against infantile and mythical accounts of reality was extended to a dismissal of all faiths in God. The belief in divine transcendence was perceived as a threat to human freedom, because "God" was understood as the name for a powerful highest being that alienated humanity from its proper tasks and destiny, while freedom was seen as complete self-mastery. Thanks to the removal of such a superpower, man could and should (re)create a fully human world by positing himself at the origin of a universal reconstruction. Instead of beliefs, rational planning and engineering would govern the course of things. The dream of possessing and ruling the world as human property seemed a real possibility.[4] Humanity would finally become its own providence.

The human subject was henceforth understood as an originary and encompassing Ego—not the empirical ego of an arbitrary subject, but the universal I that all individuals share: a rational subject that sets the standard for all choices and thoughts of individuals. To realize this dream, one had to show how that universal Ego contains all that is true and good. Individuals would then recognize their own true self in Ego's conquest of the universe.

The result of this project was disappointing. Rational deduction has become more and more formal, while experience has become more problematic. "Reality" does not tell us anything if it is not interpreted, but too many interpretations are defensible, and who is able to save the best ones or combine them into an overall synthesis? The very idea of a superior and impartial perspective has become a chimera. If "autonomy" implies that all "metaphysical" approaches, and especially all attempts to reintroduce an ultimate unity, are forbidden, the impossibility of universal truth seems to be inevitable.

With some simplification, the actual situation can be characterized as one in which we must choose between an extremely formalistic conception of philosophy and a renewed attempt to develop plausible interpretations of human existence and its universe. If we could assume that form and content can be kept apart (an assumption that is debatable), the temptation is strong to withdraw from any search for wisdom in order to concentrate exclusively on the formal aspects of reflection. But philosophy would then lose all impact on the reality of human life.

Another option leads to philosophy as an attempt to clarify and (perhaps only partially) justify a determinate position with regard to the main questions of our being in the world. As a way of acquiring at least some existential understanding, it joins the search for meaning that is also pursued in poetic, religious, and commonsensical attempts. If this kind of philosophy is confronted with Christian faith, we cannot avoid the question of their cooperation. Although it may fail at establishing a system of genuine wisdom, it can still serve as a laboratory where interpretations are produced and tested. Insofar as various interpretations are plausible without being the only acceptable ones, their character comes closer to literature than to science, especially when metaphysical questions are not dismissed. In fact, all radical and encompassing interpretations contain a profound but unproven conviction and are in this sense rooted in a kind of faith.

If philosophy has become a critical assortment of plausible interpretations, it is in danger of losing its passion for wisdom. Have philosophers, like anthropologists, become collectors of views and visions? Then philosophy has become a museum in which we can stroll from one sophisticated opinion to the next.

Philosophy and Inspiration

A friend of wisdom is engaged in the search for a well-argued position with regard to the truth of things. As long as such a position is not found, one struggles, passionately, patiently, courageously. Indifference or cynicism are enemies of wisdom, while skepticism is fatigue and defeat. But how do we overcome the pluralism of plausible theories? If empirical and logical means alone cannot convince us to prefer one theory over the others, how can we overcome our indecision?

Adherence to a particular philosophy is not based on perception and intelligence alone. The thesis that the world is created, for example, is not the outcome of mere argumentation. Besides epistemological elements, it involves a basic mindset, a mood and an overall attunement of the person who defends it. Belief in creation touches more deeply than any theory; it situates a person's base and core in the universe. It expresses itself in radical gratitude, a mood that needs neither philosophical nor theological explanations, although such are generated by it in all self-aware believers who have learned how to think.

In groping for a position of our own in the labyrinth of philosophy, we are led by Desire. Plato and Saint Augustine are right: experience and intelligence are driven by *erōs,* desire, love.[5] All metaphilosophy should begin here. The origin of our theoretical and practical experiments is in the heart. Toward which horizon or end is this oriented? The question is difficult because we cannot objectify what precedes all thematization. But we live our desire, and the question of its orientation is solved by taking it on as a personal destiny. Reflection may play a role in finding out *how* we should correspond and adjust to the dynamism that drives us, especially if we are philosophers; but *erōs* is deeper, stronger, less manipulable than thinking thinks. Although it can listen to thought, it has an inspiration of its own.

What inspires and orients our desire? The answer is a wager. Is it true that our heart is restless until it finds rest in God?[6] Is the Infinite itself the unique desirable that moves us from the beginning by being loved?[7] Is God in the end the only Good? If saints have recognized the desire for God as the most "natural" of all desires, how did they understand the word "natural" and who was the God to whom their "natural desire" was referring?[8]

Is Desire, as transcendence beyond the finite, inherent to our common human nature? If so, philosophy should make it the basis for all investigation. The literature of ancient Greece does not support the idea that all humans naturally, essentially, and inevitably desire union with God. Except for a few extraordinary passages of Plotinus,[9] such a desire was rather seen as a form of hybris. *Mēden agan!*[10] The tragedy showed what trespassing the limits means. Many twentieth-century philosophers, too, recognize themselves in the finite constellations of Seneca or Martha Nussbaum, rather than in medieval descriptions of the height and the depth, the length and the breadth of an infinite desire that loves all good and beautiful beings but cannot stop at any of them. Who are capable to establish what humans as humans, essentially or naturally and inevitably, desire? The answer is, of course: those who are most authentically human and have the purest self-knowledge. This answer implies that there are various degrees of authenticity and purity in being human and in the knowledge of what that means. If we assume that people can make progress or regress in authenticity, it also implies that the truth of desire is best known by those who are very sincere and advanced in desiring. As ancient and medieval thinkers knew, all emotions must pass through several purifications to be radical enough to orient our understanding. The theoretism of most modern philosophers has forgotten this fundamental truth, but a reawakening to the importance of emotional therapy is underway and the illuminating powers of the heart are being rediscovered.[11]

The statement that only God is the ultimately or absolutely desirable and the always-already-desired, is quite "natural" for a Christian. Does this mean that Christians have a more profound sense for the ultimate than most contemporary philosophers? Does it mean that a Christian heart is more genuine than a heart that does not care for infinity? Are Christians wiser than others about the restlessness that bothers the core of their lives?

In asking such questions, we are not quite sure whether we are doing philosophy or theology or just examining the tonality of our moods. We find ourselves driven to a field of questioning that lies somewhere between the prosaic exercises of antimetaphysical philosophers and faith-guided Christians. If we call this middle field "metaphysics," we could risk the formula that metaphysics can mediate between faith and philosophy. But many misunderstandings lie here in wait.

In the first place, we must clearly exclude the idea that a purely philo-sophical discussion—even enriched by new insights in the powers of the heart—can prove Christianity to be the truth. Faith opens another dimen-sion than thought, although there is no essential contradiction between them. However, as I suggested for Desire, we are not sure where the border-line lies between a "natural," "purely philosophical," thought and a life that is shaped by grace. "Human nature" is an abstraction; not the name for a con-crete form of life. Any concrete life is an individual version of humanness marked by a particular faith that gives it a position and a style of its own. As we said before, we cannot separate the "natural" or universally human elements of a particular life from the basic faith that has penetrated all its facets. Nobody, not even an atheist or agnostic, can therefore speak in the name of a faithless or "natural" humanity. When Christians try to do this, they are attempting to show what constitutes the humanness (or "human nature") of all humans, and, more specifically, that the God of Christian faith fulfills the most genuine Desire that all humans share. However, their concepts of humanness and "natural desire" are colored by several layers of Christian initiation and history. Even the most innocuous of daily experi-ences is different for atheists and Christians. Since the latter believe in cre-ation, they perceive the God-given character of reality as its most profound characteristic, whereas the perception of an atheist is concentrated on a very different, finite light. The attempt to bracket grace in order to first discuss what is common to humans as such can only be an exercise in provisional ab-straction. It does not allow for a description of concrete experiences. More-over, is there a middle ground between experiences whose horizon is infinite, and experiences that are confined to finite frames? Is there any horizon that is neither finite nor infinite? Is there such a thing as "naturality," if creation is permeated by grace from the first to the last moment of its existence? "Incar-nation" would be the answer, but this leads us straight into theology.

Second, Christian revelation cannot be used to solve philosophical doubts. In revealing God himself, and therewith revealing who we are, faith teaches neither astronomy, nor biology, history, or philosophy. To treat Reve-lation as a stopgap for our theories would degrade it to be a cultural phe-nomenon without perennial importance. A "perennial philosophy" is an inner contradiction if "philosophy" is taken as a synonym for some doctrine or system; but faith in Jesus Christ is the same "yesterday and today, tomor-row and in eternity."[12] Even though it needs the changing wealth of historical cultures in order to be operative in the real world, faith can never be identified with any particular philosophy or theology. A comparison with politics and art might help: the attempt to prove a particular theory on the basis of the Gospel can be no more successful than a proof that democracy is the best form of government or that realism is *the* model for all painting.

Third, some philosophical interpretations of reality are incompatible with Christian faith, while others are sympathetic to it. When confronting Christianity with existing philosophies, we must distinguish the network of their theses from their spirit. Some theses cannot be integrated into the thinking of Christians, such as the thesis that one must kill or enslave people who have committed crimes. Even though such a thesis is not explicitly prohibited in any source of revelation, it is obviously in contradiction with the spirit of evangelical pardoning without limit. The spirit of a philosophy—its inspiration and orientation—is more important than the explicit statements in which it unfolds its attitude.

If we want to maintain our loyalty to both the Christian and the philosophical community, we cannot avoid a critique of the mentalities that rule each of them. The continual (re)conversion to God that is practiced by genuine Christians acknowledges the necessity of such a critique. In philosophy, however, less attention is paid to the spiritual climate that dominates any discourse than to its logical rigor; the spirit of a thought is seldom questioned. Yet, it is necessary to discover by what kind of mentality one is guided when following the guidance of, for example, Kant, Hegel, Nietzsche, Heidegger, or Lacan. Kant's moralism has facilitated a new sense for the sacredness of law and duty, but it has also occluded the dimension of religion. Hegel's *Te Deum* to the Spirit has fused and confused God with world history and philosophy itself. It is difficult to say which spirit animates Nietzsche's multifarious universe, but a fascinating seducer deserves a special vigilance. Who is at home in Heidegger's Hölderlinian polytheism? Can it be baptized, like Hellenistic or German gods that once were converted into Christian saints? Cynical, morbid, bitter philosophies exist. They are welcome candidates for conversion.

Some other philosophies seem more open to the Christian message. Perhaps *all* philosophies are open to conversion insofar as they yearn for truth, even if they explicitly abhor the Christian institutions. Many Church Fathers thought that Plato's generosity, his awe for the Good, and his hopeful acceptance of death, were a good preparation for belief in the Gospel. Plotinus's ascent to the One and his sense of purification were greeted with sympathy by many Christian mystics. Aristotle's contemplation of being was welcomed into the medieval theology of creation. The spirit of those Greeks was not exactly the Spirit of Jesus Christ, but the difference did not annul deep affinities. Do postmodern philosophies offer similar affinities? Most of the famous ones are clearly post-Christian; although they preserve some elements of the Christian heritage, their basic tonality does not feel familiar to a Catholic. Others are openly hostile, but they might in fact be closer to Christian traditions than it seems or than they know. Only a few express a mindset that seems close to or familiar with the climate of a Christian community. Gabriel Marcel, Paul Ricoeur, Emmanuel Levinas, and Jean-Louis Chrétien come to mind. Though all of these see themselves as philosophers, they neither deny nor obstruct the communication between their professional allegiance and their deepest convictions. However one may evaluate their philosophical strength, their search is undeniably genuine. Intent on the most authentic expressions of their tradition, they seek to clarify their experience, without mutilating it, in a reasoned language that can be understood by anyone. If philosophy is experience in search of understanding, they are genuine philosophers. What distinguishes them from those who separate their philosophy from the faith that guides their lives is their willingness to take experience as concretely, entirely, and profoundly as they can.

My praise for Marcel, Ricoeur, Levinas, and Chrétien must not be understood as a plea for some scholasticism in their trail. One might think that Kant, Hegel, Nietzsche, Heidegger, or Wittgenstein are greater philosophers and that we, Christians of the twenty-first century, must do with one or more of them what Origen, Augustine, Bonaventure, and Thomas did with Plato and Aristotle. They converted the soul of the ancients' works and transformed elements of it into elements of the Christian tradition. It might be possible to do something similar with the thinkers of modern history, but all conversions demand considerable efforts. The rethinking of Hegel's experiential and conceptual oeuvre, for example, generates familiarity with the spirit that permeates his system. To confront this spirit with the Spirit of Jesus Christ leads to a struggle in the style of Jacob's fight with the angel.[13] There is no guarantee that Hegel's thought will not be limping afterwards. In any case, its arrogance will be humiliated; but what position will emerge from such a submission? Similar considerations concern the conversion of Heidegger's thought. Too many gods dwell here; should they be converted into angels? In any case, all exorcisms presuppose that the performers are sanctified in their own experience and thought.

The time of retrieving pre- and post-Christian philosophies is usefully spent if it familiarizes us with the different experiences and perspectives of fellow thinkers, but the main task to be achieved is the search for a genuine elucidation of our own inspiration. Despite much skepticism, the epoch is good for a new start in Christian thought. On the one hand, a worn-out dogmatism in theology has faded away, on the other hand, essential questions of life neglected in modern philosophy have returned to the main scene. To answer these questions, Christian philosophers can reconnect with premodern philosophies and theologies, though, of course, they must rethink them within the horizon of a very different present and future. Three questions especially seem to be most urgent: (1) the question of desire, (2) the question of intersubjectivity, and (3) the question of God.

It is not difficult to show that *Desire* is central, explicitly or implicitly, in the works of Nietzsche, Marcel, Scheler, Heidegger, Lacan, Levinas, Derrida, and many others; but it even more obviously dominates much of the reflection from Plato and Aristotle to the end of the Middle Ages. With the declining interest for affectivity in the course of modern philosophy, desire has less and less been treated as a main topic, but little analysis is needed to show its hidden impact on the systems of Descartes, Spinoza, Leibniz, Malebranche, Kant, Fichte, and Hegel. The entire history of Western philosophy can be interpreted as a history of *erōs* in search of self-understanding. How could Christian philosophers today neglect the relations between human desire and the conviction that Christian faith contains the promise of a desirable ultimacy?

Intersubjectivity has never been the central topic of Western philosophy, but since Feuerbach, many have pointed to it as a most basic, yet forgotten, experience. In our century, several philosophers have approached the subject, but even after Buber, Marcel, and Levinas, there is an enormous amount of work to be done. The importance of this issue for the understanding of Christian love is obvious. If grace and charity coincide, there is no more relevant subject than the relations between you and me and her and him and all of us.

Finally, God is, of course, *the* issue. To what extent is the philosophical situation new in this respect? An answer to this question would take more than one book. Only one remark: whatever we argue for in philosophy, we no longer can conclude by saying: "and this is what all people call 'God'";[14] for it has become sufficiently obvious that no image or concept or name of God is universally recognized, though there might be a hidden convergence of all the manners in which individuals and cultures refer to the ultimate.

"The God of philosophy" was an absolute that received many names and shapes in Western history: the Good, the unmoved Mover, Pure *Energeia*, Thinking of Thinking, the One that is not *Nous*, supreme Being, being itself, the Infinite, Substance, highest Judge, absolute Spirit, and so on. A Christian knows that all these pseudonyms express very little of God or even distort his Name. The task of a Christian philosopher cannot lie in defending the God of Aristotle or Kant or any other philosopher; instead, we must answer, with philosophical means, to what extent the God of Christian faith can be understood as response to human Desire and how those pseudonyms are related to the One whom Jesus Christ called "Father."

Does Theology Have a Role to Play in the University? A Philosophical Perspective

Does theology have a role in the university? I propose to reflect on this question along the following lines. After a brief reconnaissance of the academic situation, I will ask how theology can respond to it and what kind of strategy such a response demands for the near future. One part of my answer suggests that theology requires the cooperation of all the branches of academic scholarship, and that all these branches require the cooperation of theology. I will then illustrate this thesis by indicating some connections between theology and the discipline with which I am best acquainted: philosophy. The subtitle of this paper contains a warning: though I am not wholly ignorant of theology, the character of this paper will be mainly philosophical.

The Situation of the University

Let me begin with a statement on which, I believe, most scholars agree. The specialization of academic disciplines has led to separation and mutual ignorance, even within these very disciplines. Specialists in inorganic chemistry no longer understand the research performed in organic chemistry; specialists in mathematical psychology have little communication with clinical psychologists; few analytic philosophers understand the works of Heidegger or Levinas, and so on. Though often taken for granted, this compartmentalization of scholarship has also generated a call for interdisciplinary work, but attempts at achieving this are still rare and timid, while the results are modest.

Theology is not one of the disciplines that is frequently called upon in this context, even in universities that are proud of having a department of theology. This fact can be explained as an effect of the modern conception of science, according to which the object of a science cannot exceed the boundaries of a specific form of experience, while thinking is limited to autonomous reflection along the lines of a particular logic. The modern, enlightened university is not interested in God, humanity's relationship with God, the presence of God's glory in all things, the mysterious character of spirit, and so on. Suspicion about such subjects prevails. What Plato, Augustine, Thomas, Cusanus, or the mystics experienced as pure light is treated with contempt and dismissed as subjectivistic, and their interpretations of world and history are classified as unwarranted beliefs.[1]

Yet, modern scholarship cannot do without synthetic interpretations of the human universe. Indeed, it does not require much intelligence to see that the meaning of particular theories and partial truths depends on the manner in which these have a subordinate place within the entire constellation of acquired or tentative truth of which they are elements. Isolated statements, arguments, and theories have only a provisional meaning, as long as they are not integrated in higher syntheses. Particular theories cannot assess their own relevance for the encyclopedia of insights we would like to possess. Still less do they know what role they should play in the search for a meaningful life of their authors and the human community. Chemistry, for example, cannot answer the question—it cannot even formulate the question—of why a person should study or enjoy it. Similarly, the method of history does not reveal how the historian should use the insights obtained by it for a reflection about the lessons of history for life. Some scientists, for instance in physics or linguistics, have presented their own specialty as a universal discipline, while trying to apply their methods to all questions deemed relevant. The result has been a failure. Some of them have forced the human mind into the narrow categories of their own disciplines; others have declared that all questions that surpassed the limits of their specialty were meaningless or essentially unanswerable. Some mathematicians have tried to show that their

ιe universal method sought; but they cannot deny that their for-
s many questions about the ontic character of reality. Moreover,
u.~   cannot be purely formal because it is restricted to the spatio-
temporal aspects of the existing reality.[2]

Insofar as academic scholarship does not relinquish its demand for a unified conception of human knowledge, it looks toward philosophy, which, in
modern times, has replaced the integrative role theology played previously.
This appeal to philosophy is qualified, however, by the axiom mentioned
above with regard to the particular disciplines: it must be free from religious
considerations and divine forces.

In the early period of modernity, philosophy was still convinced that it
could and should show "that" and "how" the phenomenal world was linked
to God in a universal onto-theo-logy. However, the evolution of the last two
centuries has imprisoned the philosophical imagination in a self-sufficient
world by declaring that human intelligence must be satisfied with the un-
mysterious prose of finite phenomena. Atheism — methodical or real — is the
rule; but philosophy cannot give up its drive to create order and unity in the
diversity of discoveries with which we are confronted.

The modern emancipation of philosophy from its obedience to religion
and theology was favored by a theology that divided the human universe
into a merely "natural" realm with its own laws and rationality, on the one
hand, and a "supernatural" domain ruled by God's grace, on the other. Philosophy conspired with theology in splitting the universe into two worlds:
one in which modern scholarship was autonomous, and another, above, on
top of, or behind the first one, which was the exclusive domain of religion
and theology. For a while, the two worlds coexisted in a fluctuation of polemics and suspicious truces, but via deism and positivism, contempt for the
theological "*Hinterwelt*" became the rule of academe. Faith became marginal
to emancipated scholarship, and theology was tolerated as an atavism or removed from the company.

My simplifying summary of a complicated history does not begin to do
justice to the actual situation, but it might still help our orientation. The same
may be said about the following sketch in three points of the relations between theology and the rest of academic scholarship.

1. Theologians form a ghetto; their impact on other scholars is minimal
because their expertise does not touch the latter's "real world." The traditional role of theology is now taken over by philosophy, the theory of science, a general methodology, or the ensemble of particular methods worked
out in various departments.

2. When scholars are Christians and eager to understand what they believe, their understanding is naïve and unscholarly, if they have not supplemented their knowledge by some study of the best ancient or contemporary theology. Many Christian scholars are thus learned persons whose acquaintance with their own most basic and intimate convictions is vague and amateur, sometimes even infantile and primitive.

3. Theologians are necessarily hobbyist in many fields of modern scholarship, although they cannot abandon the task of interpreting the entire universe of creation and history in light of an all-encompassing revelation.

Is the university then a breeding ground for hybrids? Has modern scholarship generated scholars who are good in one or two specialties but primitive in most other fields, especially in the most important of all: that field where the coherence of all scholarly disciplines and their relevance for a meaningful human life is contemplated? If theologians are hobbyists in most disciplines, how then can they still be relied upon when talking about God's plan for the modern and postmodern world?

How Should Theology Respond to this Situation?

The answer to this question depends, of course, on many presuppositions concerning the nature, the task and the method of theology. I cannot discuss all of these here (although they guide what follows), but I can try to defend a few statements that seem to be basic and well-founded.

1. Theology is the scholarly aspect of faith-in-search-of-understanding. This search includes an investigation of the essence and the modes of faith, but it is not "autonomous" in the modern sense of the word, because it emerges as a need and desire of faith itself. This faith is neither a hypothesis nor an axiom, but rather the most basic of all kinds of trust and rootedness. Theology is thus radically different from religious studies and cannot be pursued by atheists, unless these are able to imaginatively and affectively reproduce the experience of faith from which the desire of universal intelligence springs.

2. As a scholarly interpretation of God's Word, theology illuminates the meaning of human existence in this—the only—world. All talk of two worlds or of a separation between heaven and earth must be given up in order to show how God's grace and glory is present everywhere in the only real world in which we live. This unique universe of human involvements and words—where mountains throne, dogs bark, birds and crickets sing,

while splendid and horrible events occur—is the only place and time where God reveals what all of it means by involving Godself in its greatness and misery and by commanding us to do the same. A theologian knows that the universe speaks of God and that a nontruncated experience is aware of God's omnipresent grace. This distinguishes theology from all modern scholarship, whose postulates ignore such experiences.

3. As a science in the Greek and medieval sense of *epistēmē* and *scientia,* theology does not directly thematize God, but rather focuses on our asymmetric relationship with God, who does not fit into any theme or topic or concept or image or question or statement or syllogism or theory. Even the relationship between God and creation is not directly accessible in theoretical reflection. Theological thematization remains lateral or marginal with regard to the prior alliance and commerce constituted by God's addressing "the soul" of individual believers and their community and the soul's responding to God in gratitude, trust, hope, and prayer. Theology therefore dies when it loses its links with prayer.

4. By clarifying the bond between God and humanity, theology does a service to the community of faith from which it emerges. It is neither equivalent to faith, nor to the contemplation that operates through affective, imaginative, and intelligent appropriation of faith. As an epistemic and scholarly discipline, theology is more rigorous and less profound than the mystical element of that contemplation; but in a reflective culture, it expresses the intellectual presence of the Spirit whose grace transforms all facets of civilization.

———

Having boldly stated these theses about the essence of theology, I will try to answer the question of how theology should respond to the academic situation sketched above. My answer can be summarized in five points, which I will explain somewhat following their statement.

1. An ideal theology gratefully welcomes all serious scholarship into its orbit.

2. It encourages other scholars not to mistake an aspectual or partial explanation of the universe for an absolute and radical one.

3. It integrates all disciplines, insofar as these are theologically relevant, into a theory of its own.

4. It relativizes its own achievements, including all its attempts at synthesis, as mere signposts on the way to existential contemplation and love.

5. It shows how theology itself and other disciplines fit into a C existence that does not testify only to intellectual excellence, but also to emotional and practical holiness.

Let me try to explain these points.

1. It is clear that modern scholarship has been welcomed by most departments of theology, given the broad array of disciplines that are practiced within them. Archaeology, geography, philology, interpretation of ancient texts, Semitic languages, Greek and Latin, cultural anthropology of the Middle East, exegesis, hermeneutics, literary criticism and comparative literature, phenomenology of religion, history, philosophy, astronomy, physics, chemistry, evolution theory, genetics, psychology, and sociology are represented in the study of the Bible; the history of Judaism, Christianity, and other religions, Church history, fundamental, dogmatic, moral, and pastoral theology constitute their own programs. With some exaggeration, we can say that theology has reproduced the entire proliferation of modern disciplines within its own domain. Theologians have become very skilled, even exemplary, in several academic disciplines, such as philology, hermeneutics, and history, which thus are no longer confined to other departments. The reproduction of so many nontheological disciplines within theology expresses the conviction that their modern developments must be integrated if theologians want to be up-to-date. It also indicates that theological research cannot be isolated from the discussions that go on in departments and associations of ancient languages, literature, history, and so on, if it wants to be supported by valid exegesis of biblical and other texts. Similarly, a dogmatic theologian cannot write about creation without at least some knowledge of philosophy, astronomy, and evolutionary theory. However, if various theological disciplines cannot be practiced in a scholarly way without professional qualification in nontheological disciplines, it is obvious that (a) nobody can be up-to-date in all of the disciplines needed in theology—so that, in this sense, no one can be an all-around theologian, and (b) cooperation with professionals in other disciplines is imperative to prevent theology from producing naïve or superficial discourses. A consequence of this situation is that theology mirrors within itself the scattering of disciplines that is characteristic for the modern university.

But what about the interpretation of the existing universe and its history in light of their relations to the one God of creation and incarnation, sin, suffering, and eschatology? Or is this not the main task of theology? A grand synthesis, albeit experimental and provisional, is necessary, not only for the reasons already mentioned, but also for the theological reason that theology is the intellectual element of faith's quest for ultimate and universally valid wisdom. Although some people are impressed by trendy declarations about the end of all great stories, their credulity is misplaced. Nobody can live without traditions and genealogies that underpin one's belonging to a basic community, and theologians should be the last to believe that creation and salvation do not allow for overall interpretations.[3]

If theology itself, as a modern or postmodern *universitas scientiarum,* became fragmented—such that, for example, a systematic theologian would regularly misuse texts that a specialist in literary criticism or exegesis reads according to the reconstructive devices of contextual interpretation—or if biblical and patristic scholars would not see it as their task to show the relevance of their discoveries for Christian scholars of the twenty-first century, then theology would have fallen victim to the same fragmentation as the entire university. If theology cannot overcome this fate, its task will be taken over by a more naïve mode of speaking about the mystery and plan of God. This mode can be authentic, as Francis and Teresa, for instance, show; but in less holy persons it is extremely vulnerable to the influence of fundamentalist, trivial, trendy, or sensational prejudices.

2. If theology cannot unify its own subdisciplines, it will also be unable to point out how the nontheological disciplines complement one another within the universe of truth. Each theory has a tendency to exaggerate the relevance of its own perspective and method. This is the scholarly expression of a basic temptation to arrogance that accompanies our narcissism. Theology should be equipped with generosity and prudence to recognize the full but limited importance of all theories without and within its own domain, and to reconcile them as possible parts of one integrated vision.

3. Only theology is capable of achieving such an integration, if it is true that the highest, central, and universal perspective is not just one perspective, but the Word without competition, which is the light of the entire world. In doing so, theology relativizes its subdisciplines by putting them in their place (together with the secular elements they borrow from other departments), while transforming them into organic members of one overall constellation.

4. If such a theology is possible—and it must be possible if theology still has a future—it must resist the temptation to consider itself the only theory that could be proclaimed to be fully and uniquely true. First, the truth cannot be captured in any theory, but theories are friends of the truth insofar as

they orient our minds toward it; and, second, the truth of faith is so fundamental that conceptualization can only reach out to it by pointing beyond its own borders. In this sense, theology—even the most profound and synthetic one—offers only signposts on the path to truth. The mistake of defining faith as a doctrine easily results in treating it as a theoretical system, whereas it is, first of all and even without theory, a humble attachment to listening, gratitude, and hope. Conceptual translations of faith turn into arrogance when they do not realize that the underlying attitude is inspired by a spirit of grace. Faith precedes and goes before and beyond any analysis or synthesis, but authentic attempts at outlining the core and horizon of faith offer guidance or reorientation to our desire for that before and beyond. The best aspect of a well-oriented and rigorous thought is that it points beyond itself toward that which is "greater," "deeper," "longer," and "wider" than any representation or synthesis, because it transcends all human possibilities except the most nuclear of all. This possibility is called "prayer," "being in grace," "*obedientia fidei*," "love," or "inspiration." In any case, theology is neither a supreme view of God's kingdom nor an exhaustive explanation of dogmatic definitions; its reflection is enveloped and sustained by the asymmetric relation to God that is the core of devotion.

5. If theology succeeds in thinking the coherence sketched above and its connections with the life of faithful Christians, it will overcome the separation between systematic and practical theology by taking its lead from the spirituality that precedes any scission between doctrine and mystical experience. The modern relationship between mysticism and theology mirrors the contrast between a naïve experience and a rationalistic conception of thinking that gave birth to modern philosophy. It is one of our tasks to overcome that scission by retrieving the premodern discussions about the vocation of all *scientia* to become *sapientia*.

To prevent misunderstanding, but without giving up my plea for an overcoming of fragmentation, I would like to insist on two reasons already given, and add a third reason why theological syntheses, though necessary, cannot be final results, but must again and again be replaced by new attempts. Any success in the direction of a coherent theology must be relativized from three perspectives: (1) no synthesis can coincide with faith itself; (2) no synthesis is the only true and salvific one, because even the best synthesis is only an approximation of the truth, which is much too overwhelming to be possessed in thought; (3) as bound to the particular language and cultural situation of its author(s), any theology is an historical phenomenon that has its proper place and time. Keeping in mind the historical, finite, and referential character of all theologies, without denying their necessity, will protect theology against totalitarian pretensions and remind it of its loyalty to the community of believers in search for a better, though always deficient, understanding of the incomprehensible mystery.

At this point, I should ask whether I have provided an answer to the question announced in the title of this chapter. I have argued that theology needs other scholarly pursuits to perform its own task and that it cannot accomplish this task if it does not integrate what other disciplines offer, together with the fragments produced by its own subdisciplines, in an encompassing yet humble theory. But what about the needs of the university with regard to theology? The answer to this question has remained implicit. It is necessary to make it explicit.

The University Needs Theology

If the object and method of a particular discipline confine it within specific limits, satisfactory knowledge about the universe and its history cannot be found in any particular discipline. Only philosophy, if it is indeed all-inclusive, could compete with theology for the integration of all scholarship into one whole. Scholars who are neither philosophers nor theologians, but know everything in their own field, can be like children concerning the fundamental questions that regard human life, the universe, and world history in general. When such scholars try to determine how their knowledge should be connected to the rest of their lives, most often they turn to a commonsensical, intuitive, or "philosophical" view. Such a view may be excellent, even better than the views of professional philosophers or theologians, but it does not reach the level of academic inquiry of which our culture is so proud. If we want to approach the most important questions of human individuals and communities with the rigor required by modern scholarship, we are referred to philosophy or theology. Therefore, the question of whether the university needs theology is, in the end, a question about the rivalry of philosophy and theology.

It would be too cheap to proclaim that for religious people theology is superior to philosophy, while establishing philosophy as the royal road to salvation for nonbelievers. For so-called nonbelievers are equally supported by a certain trust or faith. It is simply impossible to live a human life without belonging to some community with its own fundamental trust and history, tradition and authority. Enlightenment, liberalism, and conservatism, for example, are powerful alternatives to Christian (or, for that matter, Muslim or Hindu) faith. Their genealogies and wagers are different but no less prejudiced and authoritarian. The myth of an unprejudiced, autonomous, and independent point of departure, proclaimed and believed by most modern philosophers, has never been realized, and it has been abandoned by all great philosophers since Hegel's death. That it is still taught only shows how slowly attractive fictions die.

Yet, even if it is acknowledged that a presuppositionless beginning is impossible, many philosophers will hold on to the thesis that philosophy is a better guide for scholars than theology. The following are two of their arguments.

1. Whereas theology takes for granted a particular, not universally acknowledged belief, philosophy replaces all particular beliefs with experiential and conceptual elements that every normal person can check and test; it thus speaks a universal language and appeals to common experiences of all human beings. Good philosophy is universally valid, autonomous, controllable, democratic and nonauthoritarian, while the validity of theological statements depends on the truth of a particular claim that cannot be proven: the claim that what it calls "revelation" is true. As universal *epistēmē*, philosophy is better suited than the doctrine of Christian theology to synthesize the specialized knowledge of the modern university. Theology should not impose its unproven particularities on nonbelievers or adherents of other religions. The only concession that philosophy can make in this context is to maintain a certain tolerance with regard to theological instruction of those scholars who freely ask for it out of need, interest, or curiosity.

2. A second argument is shared by an outdated conception of philosophy and an outdated theology. It presupposes that philosophy explains what our natural intellect can discover, while theology adds its supernatural truth to it. Philosophy would then contain the truth everybody can recognize as such, while theology would be reserved for believers. Wrongly appealing to Aquinas, the modern theory of a *natura pura,* to which the order of grace would relate as a *superadditum,* has often been defended by quoting the famous adage "*gratia supponit naturam,*" while the more originary truth that "*natura supponit gratiam*" is frequently forgotten or ignored. And yet creation is the effect of God's grace; not the other way around.[4]

If God's grace is first, it is operative in all things, especially the human mind. But how is it then possible to isolate nature from grace? As an abstraction — not a concrete and complete entity, but rather a *moment* or element of grace — human nature cannot be defined unless the definition includes its reference and "excedence" toward God's spirit. That's why a human being is not a mere *animal rationale,* but rather an *animal orans,* whose nature and rationality are marked by transcendence.

From a philosophical perspective, we must affirm that most philosophers from Parmenides to Hegel have recognized human transcendence, although their interpretations vary widely. Agnosticism and atheism have become popular rather recently, but in all cases where "God" is invoked as ultimate intentum, we must ask *which* God is affirmed or rejected before we ask questions about God's existence and the possibility of arguments for affirming or denying it. Pascal's remark about the difference between "the God of the philosophers" and "the God of Abraham, Isaac, and Jacob" is often quoted to show that theology can no longer appeal to the proofs of our "natural" intellect. Even if these proofs were valid — the argument goes — their conclusion would be useless for an authentic discourse on the God of Christian faith. While the "God of Abraham, Isaac, and Jacob," whom Pascal opposes to the God of "the philosophers and savants," is for him also the "God of Jesus Christ," many authors of our century who quote the text of Pascal's *mémorial* stop at Jacob, thus emphasizing their allegiance to the Jewish tradition over against the Greece of philosophy. However, it seems to me that the God of Jacob is not quite the same as the Father of Jesus. If you reply that Jacob's faith is included in Christian faith, I would not contest that, but ask whether, in that case, certain aspects of Aristotle's and Plotinus's God could not also be retrieved in "the Father." I am not so sure that the God of a thorough philosophy contradicts the God to whom Christians pray, but I am fairly sure that few intellectuals of our century realize what the great onto-theo-logies from Plato to Cusanus show about our transcendence toward God. When Scotus, for example, calls God *primum principium,* we do not easily hear in this expression all the echoes, resonances, and assonances that make it for him an appropriate summary of the original mystery from which the universe emerges and to which it constantly refers. Even less does the One of Plotinus enflame many modern or postmodern hearts, but Dionysius and others understood it as a pseudonym for the excessive generosity of infinite and "super-essential Love." If our thinking were able to follow the steps and distinctions of the great metaphysicians, we would be filled with awe for the dimension to which their rational arguments lead the willing mind. I do not deny that classical ontotheology needs to be criticized, but it must first be understood. Its weakness does not lie in its metaphysical character, but instead in its clumsy conceptualization of the personal and interpersonal relations within the finite universe and consequently in its inability to articulate God's manners of speaking and listening, giving and loving, suffering and enjoying. If philosophy could show that the "principle" or "cause" of all human personality and goodness "speaks" and "loves" in an infinitely lovable way, "the God of philosophy" would not contradict but would rather "prefigure" the God of Christian theology.[5]

Will philosophy be able to do this without converting to Christian faith and theology? Perhaps, but this is a question for the future, because contemporary philosophy does not offer such an ontotheology. The general trend is agnostic and uninterested in questions about God, skeptical with regard to the possibility of a unified theory, averse to metaphysics, and incapable of retrieving the great ontotheologies of the past. *Fin de siècle?* Fatigue? Resentment toward a misunderstood religion? Arrogance or true faith behind a façade of philosophical autarchy?

A diagnosis of the secular faith that is expressed in the prevailing philosophy can show how its agnosticism and disinterest are linked to the restrictions that modernity has imposed on the breadth and depth of experience, affectivity, intuition, and thinking. Limiting itself to empirical and logical material that any sufficiently intelligent person can control, philosophy has replaced the necessity of sensitivity, perspicacity, imagination, good taste, growth, and purification with a "democratic" and primitive concept of perception and vulgar kinds of rationality. Lacking unity, philosophy has developed in different directions: for example, it identifies with one branch of scientific inquiry, abandoning itself to naturalism or historicism, or it restricts itself to a formalistic metatheory, or it despairs and surrenders to its own fragmentation.

Perhaps this picture of philosophy is too unilateral and somber, but it is not wholly untrue. Among modern philosophers, Spinoza, Kant, and Hegel stand out as heroes of metaphysics, but even their works testify to a truncated experience. Nietzsche's passionate accusation of all theology and of the very idea of truth can be interpreted as the expression of a new search for "the unknown God," and there are attempts—especially among Calvinist philosophers—to show that philosophical discoveries about God are possible; but all of these exceptions are not enough to entrust philosophy with the guidance of scholars in their search for existential meaning.

Is theology capable and ready to take on this task? It is, if it can bring its own subdisciplines together as members of its own corpus. For then it will have discovered how to integrate representative parts of the *universitas scientiarum* into an overall interpretation of the human condition. It could then even extend the range of its expertise to the disciplines that are not yet represented in its own department. An interdisciplinary gathering is not possible, however, without the mediation of a rejuvenated philosophy that is open to theology as well as to the particular disciplines. Therefore, theology must engage itself in a conversation with philosophy, challenging it to ask and answer the most relevant questions of meaning and to seek a coherent understanding of the human universe. In turn, philosophy must critically respond to the theologians' use of categories, argumentative structures, and descriptions of the earthly realities that have been the philosophers' speciality.

Against this program, two objections can be raised:

1. Nobody is capable of mastering the entire field of theology, along with philosophy and all other disciplines; and

2. non-Christian scholars are not served by theology.

To answer the second objection first, Christian theology offers itself as a discussion partner not only to other theologies, but also to the expressions of the fundamental kinds of trust (or "faith") that underly the deepest convictions of irreligious scholars, including skeptics, agnosticists, and atheists. The most fundamental discussion that emerges when the latter respond to this invitation relates the participants to one another through their differences and affinities in a dimension that precedes and supports their shared scholarship. There is no neutral thought, but the various theologies and "a-theologies" refer to a common source from which their agreements and differences spring. This source, hidden but present in their struggle for mutual understanding, holds them together and might lead them to greater affinity.

The impossibility of gathering all knowledge in one person, who then, as a new Origen or Aquinas, could write the new *summa*, points to the necessity of exchange and dialogue. Scholars will be obliged to simplify and translate for nonspecialists what they have learned in their own specialties. Interdisciplinary knowledge and discussion is paid for by simplification and a loss of precision, but this price is not too high for growing communication and the emergence of tentatively shared visions and narratives. The search for truth is no longer an individualistic adventure of some heroes of thought. The *locus veritatis* is neither a judgment nor a particular theory, but the community of investigation.

The call for dialogue has almost become a slogan today, but one cannot say that it has given birth to a brilliant practice. The privatization of scholarship has in fact intensified, making the call for synthesis at the same time more and more utopian. In this respect, too, we must state that dialogues between theology and the other academic disciplines will be successful only if theology conducts an exemplary conversation on its own ground.

Indeed, there are good and bad conversations. Their quality is determined by quite a few intellectual and moral conditions. For example, a good exchange among scholars is not "democratic," because some participants are more knowledgeable than others. As a scholarly discipline, theology is neither democratic nor autocratic, because the Spirit has been given to the Christian community. A worthy and fruitful conversation presupposes many virtues, such as genuine love of the truth, loyalty to faith, respect for the interlocutor (especially for a hostile one), detachment from one's own fixations, and a good ear for others.

The community of theological discussants is based on their union in faith. The *scholarly* expression of this union is not to be found in a monolithic theory, however. For, as a *logia*, theology is not the *immediate* expression of faith; its reflective language cannot replace the Word itself. The metaphorical and conceptual discourses through which theologians situate the truth of faith in the culture of their epoch cannot capture that truth; at best, they refer to it as the hidden secret that can save the adherents of any culture that allows faith to convert them.

The belief that any theology can coincide with faith itself is a dangerous form of idolatry. No theory is equivalent to the life that is expressed in it. This thesis is true of all academic disciplines, but especially of the most universal and "totalitarian" ones: philosophy and theology. As approximations of the lived truth, they cannot be monopolized by any system. For even if the perspective from which they are developed is fundamental and very wide, it is still too particular to comprehend the truth. Even the most encompassing and profound theories are only viewpoints; the hiddenness of the central mystery grows with every elucidation of its illuminating presence. A plurality of systematic theologies testifies to the profundity of that mystery, if they indeed remain loyal to the preconceptual attachment that is

/e of the community of faith. The unity of theology does not lie in
theory, but in the linguistic, conceptual, and metaphorical variety
of th... ugh meditations.

Accordingly, the unity sought by theologians within and without their
own domain is radically different from that of philosophical systems in the
style of Spinoza or Hegel. By humiliating the autonomy of *all* theory before God, theology frees the mind for a direct access to the center: God as revealed in Jesus Christ crucified and resurrected. This center invites all individuals to recognize the truth about their own bodies and souls. Scholarly
theories are helpful, but gray in comparison to the existential questions and
demands implied in this mystery. However, sensitivity, good taste, self-critical
experience, affective and imaginative purification go beyond the grayness of
any theory. Gratitude for three thousand years of wisdom—even if that wisdom was mixed with errors—generates hope: professors, too, can be touched
by inspiration.[6]

From Philosophy to Prayer and Vice Versa

Philosophy—Religion—Theology

This chapter is a (meta)philosophical attempt to clarify the theoretical practice called "philosophy of religion." It proceeds in stages. (1) Beginning with
a very broad definition of "religion," it claims (a) that the religious dimension
is not only a necessary and basic topic of philosophy, but also its source, and
(b) that *all* philosophers, in the practice of their lives, rely on a basic "faith."
If this is true, the question arises as to whether they can abstract from their
faith in practicing philosophy. (2) The existing "positive" religions concretize
the religious dimension, but this dimension is universally realized and expressed, even in atheistic and agnostic attitudes and convictions. All humans
rely on a basic faith. (3) The modern self-conception of philosophy as autonomous thought rests on the assumption that it can claim independence
with regard to the lived existence from which it springs. This conception is a
dream that has not been and cannot be realized. It must therefore be replaced
with a metaphilosophy that respects the faith-based essence of philosophy.
(4) Religion (the religious dimension and its concretization in a faith) is united
with philosophy not only as its object, but also as the basic condition of the
philosophical (re)search. (5) Philosophy is a *relatively* autonomous element
of the self-aware and self-critical life of concrete philosophers. Its language is

simultaneously particular and universal. As an attempt to think in the name of and for all humans, it continues its traditional task. Insofar as it is performed in the service of a religious community, it is a particular faith in search for understanding, including an understanding of itself. As a faith that seeks understanding, all philosophy includes a philosophy of religion. If the faith in which a philosophy is rooted includes belief in God, this philosophy includes a (philosophical) theology. In its universal function, however—as a thought for and in the name of all—philosophy brackets its theological character, though it neither can nor should repress it. (6) The union of religion, including its faith and theology, and philosophy is attested by all the connections mentioned in (1)–(5). Lacking an Archimedean standpoint, philosophers of religion should concentrate not only on the religions that are their particular subject, but also on the radically religious dimension to which they owe their inspiration. Philosophy of religion is a learned mode of being religious. It cannot master what it enlightens, but it can express its own mixture of dependence and independence in conceptual language.

Religion

From an existential perspective we can use the word "religion" to indicate the deepest dimension of human life in which all other dimensions are rooted.[1] This very broad definition of religion points to the basic fact that human individuals and communities feel more or less at home in the world and its history. Instead of "feeling at home in the world," we could also say that the religious dimension is the dimension (or the level) where the question of decisive or ultimate meaning is asked and answered—at least tentatively and in an embryonic, albeit half-unconscious, form. All living persons accept their existence as somehow and to some degree meaningful, despite the many doubts, frustrations, rejections, and rebellions that may assail them. Insofar as the meaning that is found or presumed in the universe is fundamental, supporting human existence as a whole, it permeates and colors all other dimensions. As such it decides about the meaning of human lives.

The definition of religion proposed here implies that all concrete (or "positive") religions can be interpreted as symbolic, ritual, and practical enactments of specific modes of being at home in the universe, aware that existence is not absurd, but virtually meaningful. It also implies that modes of inhabiting the world without religion, such as agnosticism or atheism, are likewise "religious," insofar as their acceptance of the universe expresses (or even confesses) that existence in it must have a meaning. Materialists, biologists, and historicists, for example, may locate meaning elsewhere than in a realm of God or the gods, but they, too, believe in a basic meaning of existence.

The self-awareness that belongs to the deepest dimension of human lives is a pre-predicative and pre-propositional, rarely self-conscious experience with a primarily affective character: the dim awareness of a fundamental attunement, a basic "mood." We feel more or less at home in a specific mood. The universe can inspire awe, admiration, gratitude, anxiety; we can feel threatened, safe, secure, content, frustrated, nostalgic, and so on. Being affected by phenomena, we react by affectively responding to them. How we respond depends on the openness and refinement of our sensitivity, our character, the story of our life, and many other conditions. So long as we continue to live, however, there is always some sort of basic consent and trust, even if these are hidden or overwhelmed by anguish and temptations of despair. Somehow we remain attached to our existence and confident that it is better to be than not to be. Even suicide cannot be preferred without, for the time being, approving and using the tools and actions needed to assure one's own disappearance.[2]

Trust, confidence, or "faith," taken in a sense as broad as the basic concept of "religion," implies the affirmation that existence (including the entire universe insofar as one has to deal with it) has an overall meaning. Even if it is not *full* of meaning, it must be more meaningful than nothingness. This affirmation is lived, rather than pronounced or thought. It is the element of consent in our moods, the basic mood that grants us the possibility of having a position and an attitude with regard to the universe and our existence in it. It grants us a "stance." This stance is not statically fixed. An originary desire keeps humans on the move. As propelled by desire, a stance does not only trust the present (despite all threats), it also moves forward in search of meaning. Although, on this level, a clear answer to the question of life's meaning is not available, desire anticipates that it must be possible to discover it and that it is already operative in the search. "Faith" is thus linked with hope. If it includes attachment and the will to continue, it is also animated by a basic form of love, which, at this stage, still may be confined to love for oneself.[3]

A reader of the preceding pages may have become suspicious: is this chapter an attempt to read the three "divine virtues" of Christian theology into the originary dimension of human existence, encompassing even such areligious or antireligious ways of life as atheism or agnosticism? Or is it perhaps an attempt to reduce the Christian religion and its theology to existential categories that fit all human beings so well that religion in any normal sense of the word and the differences between religions no longer matter? Not exactly. However, it does attempt to identify a universal level or dimension that feeds all forms and ways of life. At the same time it remains well aware that such an attempt cannot be undertaken from a completely neutral, Archimedean perspective. The universality of the religious dimension is always approached from the perspective of a particular attachment (faith, hope, and love); but such a perspective no more prevents a discussion with other particular perspectives or approaches than the difference between French and English or Chinese and Russian prevents a dialogue about language as such.

Autonomy

By proclaiming its own independence, philosophy has positioned itself as a rival of all moral, religious, literary, and political authorities. No longer in awe of the authority of dogmas or traditions, philosophers had to reinvent the universe on the basis of self-evident facts and principles. Their task was no longer ruled by powers other than thought itself; instead of serving states or churches, from now on they would speak in the name and for the benefit of humanity as such.

The modern emancipation necessitated a separation of thought itself from all the particular features of communal, historical, and individual life. None of the idiosyncratic or epochal elements involved in human existence should play a role in the constitution of universally valid truth. In their great variety, factual religions should either be interpreted as a series of variations on one general "religiosity" (not a "positive," but a "natural" religion) or seen as approximations of one universally valid philosophy, or even as failed attempts to capture the truth, which is in any case the monopoly of philosophy.

Descartes thematized the necessity of a clear separation between his life in the world and the philosophical abstractions on which he wanted to thoughtfully rebuild the world and his own humanity,[4] but his successors have paid little attention to the radical split between theory and practice he proposed. They have accepted or varied his theoretical program without showing the possibility of a thought that could be wholly free from existential particularities.

The history of modern philosophy has demonstrated with utmost clarity that none of its systems is self-sufficient and that all philosophers have remained heavily dependent on the questions, discussions, conceptual frameworks, methods, and terminologies of predecessors and traditions, even when they succeeded in their revolutions and transformations. The best philosophers appropriated their past in an original way, thus transforming their inheritance into new beginnings, but none of their systems can be understood as a creation founded upon indubitable evidence and crystalline logic. All of them are rooted in some hidden faith, even when their authors were not aware of it.

In order to separate their philosophy from their lives as they live them, philosophers must find a freestanding perspective outside their own worldly and historical existence. Only then can they form an objective and universally valid judgment about the universe, including their own functioning within it. This standpoint is sought in thought itself. Thinking thus becomes the activity of an extra-existential, suprahistorical, and supraterrestrial thinker, either in the form of a transcendental consciousness or as a transhuman or superhuman subject whose thoughts must be revealed by a human interpreter. As a hermeneutic or prophetic service to humanity, philosophy must reduce the entire variety of cultures and stories to general forms and structures that could be verified everywhere. A formal universe is then (re)created which must be filled in by the real diversity of individual lives and communal histories.

Philosophy and Religion

How does religion fare in the context of a philosophy that claims to be autonomous?

If religion, like art and morality, is an essential phenomenon, it cannot be excluded from philosophy. For within philosophy all exclusions are arbitrary—or rather, they are impossible, because the horizon of philosophy is unlimited. If religion is not a genuine phenomenon, philosophy must show which more genuine dimension hides behind its masks. If it is genuine and irreducible to anything else, philosophy will have to confront the rivalry that emerges from this fact. An autonomous philosophy necessarily submits religion to its own perspective and principles. If philosophy is indeed autonomous, it takes itself to be the highest tribunal for questions of meaning; if not, it remains open to the possibility that the ultimate judgment might come from another, deeper or higher realm. If there is such a realm, philosophy would have to accept the subordinate, relative, and provisional character of its "autonomy," whereas in the first case, it is philosophy that knows the meaning of religion *and more:* the reason why religion is meaningful or not, the extent to which different religions represent different degrees of truth and meaning, and so on. Hegel's reduction of the religious phenomenon to an imperfect presentation of philosophical truth is a consummate example of this reduction, while the subordination of philosophy to religion is asserted or assumed by all those philosophers who see themselves as primarily religious.[5]

Is the expression "primarily religious" a pleonasm? Can one be religious, i.e., engaged in a religion, without being aware that religion *founds and encompasses* the entirety of human existence? Is it inevitable that the thought of religious persons either fits into their faith, or else put it to the test, which might then result in the believer turning away from it, modifying it, or reinforcing it with philosophical considerations?

The crucial question is where a thinker stands when observing and thematizing others' or her own religious involvement. Thinking from the stance of religion (which I have called the basis of lived existence) *ipso facto* relativizes philosophy as a stem or branch that cannot separate itself from the tree it serves. How could the branch claim the final judgment about the meaning of the tree? Thinking from an Archimedean standpoint is either an abstraction—and to that extent only a provisional or hypothetical enterprise until it find its place in the whole of a life—or it is indeed *autarchic,* but then it expresses another faith: the faith (or the "religion") that identifies autonomous thinking with the truest and deepest dimension of life. The main task to which existence calls humans is then nothing other than thought, and all other tasks, such as art, morals, rituals, sport, and love, are subordinate to it. Philosophy itself is then the true religion. It is not difficult to show that the God of this religion must coincide either with a grounding and all-encompassing thinker whose existence is imaginary as an unrealized ideal, or with a transcendent or transcendental consciousness whose truth is revealed in the finite messages of the philosophers.

If the autarchy of philosophy is in fact rooted in its own philosophical faith, the principle of philosophical autonomy implies a rivalry with concrete religions. Then philosophy necessarily competes with religions for the right to present the basic and decisive answer to the question of ultimate meaning. In the name of its autonomy, philosophers must then claim that they presuppose nothing that is not obvious to all people, while looking down on religions as a variety of particular beliefs that are neither empirically nor rationally warranted. These beliefs might be interesting (i.e., they might respond to existential interests or even be of interest for an epistemology of the connections between belief and truth), but their meaning is subordinate to the overall interest and the ultimate meaning of the philosophical enterprise. The stance and the faith of philosophy puts the faiths of religions in their place and relativizes their interests.

The claim of autonomy obscures the faith-driven passion of modern philosophy. The pretention that it is led by universal reason alone falsifies its dealings with religion by interpreting its relationship to the latter as a relationship between universality (reason) and particularity (faith). If, on the contrary, philosophy recognized its rootedness in its own faith, it would recognize the particularity of its own bias. This bias does not necessarily preclude the task of speaking in a universally recognizable way, but it entails the awareness that it cannot do this in a nonparticular language. Neither natural nor conceptual languages are universal. All of them are particular perspectives on the universe. Moreover, the individuals who express their thoughts in them give them a personal twist.

Philosophy as Religion

Dedicated philosophers are aware of a double impetus: though fascinated by the task of formulating universal truths (e.g., the truth about the religions, their own included), they are primarily interested in their own destiny (and its truth) and that of others. If their existential and theoretical interests coincide, philosophy is nothing other than the theoretical side of their existential endeavor. Thought and life are one, though a distinction is still possible to the extent that existence encompasses more than thought. If faith or "religion," in the broad sense, is fundamental for existence, the religion of a thinker permeates his thinking, but when he speaks to those who do not share his faith, he will look for common ground and shared assumptions in order to make a discussion possible despite fundamental differences. If we reserve the name "philosophy" for the level of universally shared assumptions, we abstract from all the real and possible differences in faith. Such

a universally valid philosophy does not represent the concrete (and therefore existential) thought of its author, because it is only an abstract element
of it. Modern philosophers have believed that this element could be emancipated and proclaimed as something independent, while denying that such
independence presupposes another kind of existential rooting and another
kind of trust than the faith from which self-thinking was liberated. This conviction explains why modern philosophy saw itself as the universal and highest perspective; but its faith in itself as the supreme way of finding meaning
puts it beside, not above, other religions. Philosophy, in its modern self-
interpretation, is the religion of Enlightenment; it is a "form of life" rather
than an abstract element that, thanks to its abstractness, fits into a more deeply
rooted engagement with existence. The real relation between philosophy and
religion depends on philosophy's conception of its own practice. If philosophy tries to be autarchic, it is a rival of other religions, claiming for itself the
same kind of ultimacy, universality, and authority; but if it confines itself to
being the thinking element within a religion—as conceptual understanding and clarification of the universally relevant meaning of that religion—
it gives up its autarchy by adopting a more authentic, albeit limited, relative,
and subordinate, independence.

The religious character of autarchic philosophy is shown by its appeals to
particular traditions and authorities, by the rituals it develops, by the standards and the forums through which it protects its orthodoxy, by the scholasticism of its questions and answers, and by its excommunication of dissidents.
Originality and revolutions soon develop into chapels of heterodoxy if they
are not domesticated by integration into the mainstream. The stories that
philosophy tells about its past—e.g., in their Kantian, Hegelian, Nietzschean,
or Heideggerian versions—are as simplistic as other all-encompassing myths,
and the practice they recommend is ruled by the law of celebration and repetition. Conferences are dominated by endless monologues and controlled by
judges who screen the thoughts of the newly initiated. For those who profess
the autonomy of philosophy, there is a church in which they can feel at home.
What is more tempting than the promise of a free, all-judging thought, especially when it is authorized by the fame of stars!

The freedom of the enlightened faith on which modern philosophy
thrives necessarily rivals the inspired freedoms that are enacted in Jewish,
Buddhist, Hindu, Christian, or Muslim faiths. But rivalry is a kind of enmity
as long as each faith is convinced that it must triumph over the others. Such
a triumph can consist in an *Aufhebung* or integration, by which other faiths
are judged and subordinated. Hegel's philosophical integration of the reli-

gions or Origen's integration of Platonic and Stoic elements are examples of such conquests.

Are hostility or submission the only alternatives or is a friendly coexistence, perhaps even a sort of fraternity, between philosophy and religion possible? If philosophy is an autonomous and secular "religion," its coexistence with Christian faith (and its theology) is comparable to the coexistence of Christianity with Judaism, Islam, or Buddhism. Peaceful coexistence between religions cannot be established by giving up one's own faith, but only by mutual respect. But how can one maintain a wholehearted adherence to one faith without dogmatism, relativism, or syncretism with regard to other faiths? Respect, on this level of ultimacy, presupposes shared recognition of a fundamental and ultimate truth and meaning. How can recognition of other faiths avoid relativizing one's own faith insofar as it contradicts the others? Recognition—and the mutual respect that ensues from it—is not possible unless the various faiths, despite the contradictions that seem to drive them apart, are experienced as somehow pointing to and converging on a truth that, though darkly and differently revealed in respectable religions, does not let itself be captured completely by any of them. Such truth must then be deeper and "more ultimate" than faith and religion themselves.

Even this hypothesis does not undermine the possibility of a firm adherence to one's own religion, because such an adherence does not deny that other religions, in their aporetic or contradictory ways, point toward the same hidden God.

One formulation of the nonrelativistic relativity intended here is the Christian conviction that in heaven there are neither sacraments nor ecclesiastical structures or dogmas. Even religion itself should not be made into an idol; it should always be lived as referring to the first and last itself.

Must the modern project of an autarchic philosophy be saluted by other religions as an alternative form of salvation? Is its *gnōsis* one of the religions through which human beings open up to the ultimate truth of their existence? If receptivity, listening, acceptance and thanksgiving are characteristic of religion, modern philosophy does not strike us as characteristically religious. Its obsession with the "I" that thinks and masters, uses, acts, concludes, and enjoys seems too humanistic to allow for much mystery. But perhaps its indefatigable and self-critical questioning betrays a genuine desire for something greater than itself, which could grant it a freedom other than the narrow one of self-identity. Perhaps even this philosophy points to an inconquerable dimension of absolute transcendence. From where does its passion for the truth come and what justifies its hope? Would it really be satisfied by conceptual transparency or would that put an end to all hopes? Even Descartes desired wisdom more than knowledge; and who would prefer clarity over a good life? If philosophy, even in its modern version, has always been a passionate search for the union of ultimate truth and goodness in the form of a partly given, partly conquered wisdom, it, too, is a religious enterprise. But then it can and must also be understood, evaluated, respected, and dealt with from the perspective of other religions.

The recognition of modern philosophy as one among many religions would restore its existential seriousness, but at the same time it would rob it of its metaphilosophical monopoly. Philosophy could no longer claim to be the highest court for questions of meaning and truth, because it is only one (respectable, but particular) way of engaging in the essential quest. Even intellectuals could not proclaim its supremacy unless they could demonstrate that its conceptual language is more trustworthy and encompassing than the symbolisms of other religions. If the reverse is true, or if both have their own strengths and weaknesses, a more brotherly or sisterly relationship might be possible, unless one or more religions could correctly claim that it encompasses all true philosophy. But why should the latter be the case? Can't we become what we have to be without conceptual mastery? To see such mastery as the summit of wisdom would make us Hegelian or Spinozistic; but it is exactly such kinds of faith that we are questioning.

Philosophy of Religion between Philosophy and Religion

Which consequences concerning the philosophy of religion follow from the (hypo)thesis defended in the preceding pages? If philosophy is autarchic, it must summon all (other) religions and judge their identity, structure, truth, and meaning in the name of its own standards, which it regards as the highest and ultimate standards of truth and meaning. The identity and essence of the religions are then *a priori* adjusted to the patterns and restrictions of the judge's logic. All the elements that do not fit into the observational or conceptual framework of such a philosophy must then be considered irrelevant and meaningless—extrarational. A certain form of contempt, inherent in all judgmental attitudes, then characterizes the philosopher's stance.

If an autonomous philosophy itself is a kind of religion, the situation is different. Instead of being the highest tribunal before which the other religions must legitimize themselves, it must allow other religions to identify and evaluate this philosophy (and its thoughts about religions both in general and in particular) from their own religious perspective. In the trial that ensues, philosophy must justify its faith in reason and its exclusion of certain elements considered essential by other religions but rejected as irrational, superstititious, irrelevant, or false by any autonomous philosophy. At the tribunal of truth, a religious judge will question the claimed neutrality and universality of such a philosophy and ask what credentials it has for revealing a way to existentially relevant freedom, wisdom, salvation, goodness, and truth.

To be understood, so that philosophy can defend its own endeavors, including its judgment about the religions, the judging religion must speak a language that philosophy can understand. It will therefore borrow thoughts and terms from the philosophers that are available in the culture of the time. Many examples of this procedure can be found in Jewish, Christian, and Muslim thought from the first to the fifteenth centuries. While adopting Platonic, Aristotelian, and Stoic elements of Greek and hellenistic cultures, Philo, Origen, Augustine, and many others used them to distinguish their own way of existence from the philosophical forms of life that belonged to their epoch. Their appropriation certainly transformed the philosophies that had emerged in another context, but even so they tried to remain comprehensible to differently inspired philosophers. The result of their attempt was a multitude of theologies for which they often used the title *philosophia* to show its affinity with the Greek endeavor. Aware of the impossibility of existential and noetic autarchy in any rigorous sense of this word, they tried to translate their faith as much as possible into a renewed kind of philosophical language, while remaining convinced that such an enterprise could never reduce the mysterious character of their faith. At the same time, however, they did not doubt that human reason was enlightened enough to engage in a rational dialogue with other philosophers, many of whom recognized their own religious allegiance.[6]

The relationship between Christian or Jewish or Muslim "philosophy," on the one hand, and philosophies that claim to be autonomous, on the other, can be transformed from a trial into a dialogue when both the judging and the judged parties agree to deal with one another as respectable partners in a discussion about wisdom and the ultimate meaning of human existence. Valid observation and logical clarity are necessary conditions for such a discussion, but they are not sufficient, because the radical dimension in which they are rooted and the faith that guides their existential engagement cannot be reduced to conceptual or empiricist claims and arguments.

It is difficult for dedicated philosophers to give up the conviction that all things in heaven and on the earth have to be probed by philosophy, but it is more truthful to recognize that the universally valid judgment they expect from philosophy is either too abstract to be true or too proud to be good. However, a similar judgment is true about theologians who, longing to be modern and respected by secular thinkers, adopt philosophical autonomy as one of the principles of their own work. Instead of revering philosophy as a separate realm of universal truth, they should integrate and thereby transform the meaning of that realm, which thus can show its theological virtuality. As a limited clarification of faith, theology is a self-conscious philosophy of religion. It tries to understand how its own thinking can throw light on religions (including modern philosophy as grafted on a typically modern faith). As a faith in search of understanding, philosophy (even in its explicitly theological versions) does not entail dictatorship, because its arguments should not be mistaken for faith itself, while faith can only be authentic if it is and remains free. The free consent of trust guides both philosophy and theology because neither of them is radical enough to be original. Thus, both are at the service of an orientation that originates and carries them, and this orientation constitutes the essence of human existence.

Universality?

To conclude, just a remark to prevent misunderstanding. What happens to the universality that modern philosophy has loudly proclaimed to be the distinguishing mark of its validity? If philosophy itself is a *faith* in search of understanding, must we then abandon all hope that universally valid truth can ever be found and communicated?

Instead of answering this question here,[7] I will only indicate that the conception of universality these pages imply is more akin to the universality that conditions the sharing of "identical" thoughts in different languages. All translation presupposes a silent, prelingual commonality. Would this not be a necessary presupposition for human universality? Perhaps the assumption that universality can be enclosed in the form of judgments is itself an idol that should be discarded, if we want to be true to religion and the origins of philosophy.

Retrieving Onto-Theo-Logy

"Religion after onto-theology" was the title of a conference held in July 2001. It summarizes the conviction found among "continental" philosophers that onto-theology is outdated, while religion still (or again) has enough meaning to be considered in philosophy. Of the questions such a title triggers, one has puzzled me more than others: to what extent can we declare that ontotheology (or onto-theology or onto-theo-logy)[1] belongs to our past, either in the sense of a definitively closed period or as a heritage that is still alive and for which there might still be a future? It is the polysemic word "after" that bothers me most, but if we want to discuss it, we should first try to agree on the meaning of "onto-theo-logy."

Perhaps I am naïve in asking "What should we mean by onto-theology?" Anyone who has followed the American development of "continental philosophy" should know the group language of its adherents and not doubt their basic conquests. If this is the right answer to my question, I am afraid that "onto-theology" has become one of those code words that characterize a regional language through which one version of continental philosophy fences off the ignorant, i.e., those who do not agree with the basic tenets proclaimed by the recognized stars. That similar fences are inevitable in all learned discussions might be true (although some philosophers are widely understandable, even for nonprofessional philosophers); but should we not be alerted when the fence is made of a whole range of keywords which by themselves are not clear enough to convey an insight in the news they summarize? All of us know examples of such words. Most of them have at least two meanings according to the context in which they are used. As elements of the everyday language, they are perfectly understandable by anyone who is familiar with idiomatic English, but as elements of the regional language in which "onto-theo-logy" is used to characterize the past, they restrict their meaning to a particular interpretation of their use in characteristic contexts of a particular philosophy. Such double meanings are found, for example, in "presence," "subject" (cf. "after the subject"), "foundation," "violence," "transgression," and "impossible," while examples of *philosophical* words whose meanings have become different from their *historical* meanings are "cause," "ground," "idea," "metaphysics" and "metaphysics of presence," "ethics" (cf. "against ethics"), "modern" (cf. "postmodern"), "Plato," "Platonism," and "Neoplatonism."

The difference between the peculiar meanings that many words have within the language of a certain postmodern school, and their meaning in "ordinary" or historical use has struck me most when studying such classical authors as Plato, Plotinus, Aquinas, or Hegel. Often I did not recognize their works in interpretations whose orthodoxy is not contested by many members of that school.[2] Their "readings" might be interesting in themselves and point at hidden promises of the interpreted texts, but do they facilitate our discovery of the latters' meaning? This question becomes even more critical when certain "postmodernists" try to justify their anti-onto-(theo)-logical position by biased or false interpretations of the best metaphysical texts. When such interpretations are accepted by those who skip a personal fight with the classics, their access to the past is blocked—but then also their access to the present, insofar as this lives on the capital of its heritage.

If certain concepts, such as "presence," "metaphysics," "grounding," and "founding," are used to summarize and outdo entire oeuvres, they prevent or distort direct study, and if a new orthodoxy wins over serious confrontation with those oeuvres, philosophy has become a scholastic enterprise. Appeals to hermeneutic authorities, repetition, simplification, arrogance and trivialization then imprison thought. Scholasticism not only blocks originality, however; it also blocks the possibility of transforming the past into a future. By condemning twenty-six hundred years of "metaphysics" and "ontotheology," we waste a heritage that could have been promising, if we had not been insensitive to its wealth. By thinking of ourselves as "after metaphysics," or "after ontotheology," we might have already lost one of the most promising promises.

Onto-Theo-Logy according to Heidegger

If the word "onto-theo-logy" is used to characterize a certain past as closed and no longer inspiring, what exactly then lies behind us? It cannot be the logical element in ontotheology that irritates us if we want to continue using some sort of logic in our meditations. Does the *theos* or the *theion* bother us? But why then is there still "religion" after all? Or does religion not imply some reference to the divine, the godly, "the God or the gods"?[3] We will come back on the latter question, but let's focus first on the "*on*" (beings) in onto-theo-logy.

I will do this in a while, but by way of preparation it might be necessary to consider the particular interpretation of the word "onto-theo-logy" that has become a shibboleth for those who use it to distinguish their own thought from an allegedly obsolete past: the interpretation given by Heidegger in "The onto-theo-logical constitution of metaphysics."[4] Since we cannot indulge here in a close reading of this intricate text, I limit myself to a succinct summary of the passages that are immediately relevant for our purpose, from which I then will draw a few conclusions.

(1) Heidegger criticizes the entire onto-theo-logical tradition as irreligious insofar as it is "perhaps" (*vielleicht*) further removed from the godly God than "the god-less thinking that must give up the God of philosophy, the God as *causa sui*."[5] I take the word "perhaps" in the quoted phrase as a rhetorical formula of politeness, because the next sentence firmly declares: "This means here only: It [the god-less thinking] is freer for the godly God than onto-theo-logic likes to acknowledge."[6]

(2) The phenomenological criterion Heidegger offers for the recognition of a godly God is that humans can "pray and sacrifice to him," "in awe fall on their knees," and "make music and dance for this God."[7] This criterion fits many religions, especially the Greek one (think, for instance, of Homer's description of the funeral rites for Patrokles). Applying it to the philosophical tradition, which has always been an onto-theo-logical tradition, Heidegger concludes that those religious activities are not possible with regard to

the God of philosophy. I interpret this to mean that the latter does not invite or inspire music making, dancing, sacrifices, and prayers as appropriate answers to his emergence from the philosophical tradition.

(3) Heidegger declares that the quintessence of the onto-theo-logical God lies in his being a "cause of himself" (*causa sui*). Without analysis or presentation of the relevant texts, he refers here to a name of God that is found in modern, mainly Cartesian and Spinozistic, texts.[8]

(4) Heidegger comes to this result of his survey of Western onto-theology by insisting on the "grounding" (*gründen*), "founding" (*begründen*), and "finding out" or "fathoming" (*ergründen*) that, according to him, have obsessed the tradition. He apparently thinks that the philosophers could not stop their quest for grounds once they arrived at God, whom some of them called the first or ultimate "cause" (*archē, aitia, causa*).[9] Without paying attention to the historical polysemy of the word "cause" (including the meanings of *eidos, idea, morphē, forma, ousia, telos, hylē, materia, esse, existere,* and *essentia*), Heidegger declares that "the most originary *Sache*" itself has been thought to be not only the ground of the being of all beings, but also the ground or *cause* of *itself.* This, he writes, is the appropriate or pertinent (*sachgerechte*) name of God within philosophy (insofar as it has been a *founding* discipline). He thus states, but without proof, that the philosophical tradition has been blind to the question of a groundless beginning or origin.[10]

In response to Heidegger's text I can only summarize, in the form of counterpoints, what I see as theses guaranteed by the best historical scholarship, most of which I have checked within the limits of my own struggle with classical texts of the philosophical tradition.

For a fair assessment of (4) Heidegger's diagnosis, and especially of his view that the ontological framework of Western philosophy is permeated by the logic of a grounding thought, a full retrieval of all the great classics would be necessary. That would demand (a) a full rehabilitation of those thinkers that are excluded from Heidegger's history of philosophy, namely all post-Aristotelian "Greeks" (i.e., all thinkers from 300 B.C.E. to 600 of the Christian era), most Christian thinkers from Justin and Clement (200) to Cusanus (1500), all Jewish and Muslim thinkers, all English and American thinkers, all French thinkers except Descartes, and some other geniuses such as Spinoza, Jacobi, Marx, Freud, Blondel, and Bergson. From my perspective, Heidegger's circumvention of the entire period of what Enlightenment's ignorance called the Dark Ages is particularly ominous. If we want to know how philosophy of religion might be possible, shouldn't we learn from those who were highly skilled professionals not only in philosophy, but also in religion?

(b) Such rehabilitation would also demand the recognition that the classics have not submitted God to the question: What is the ground of God? On the contrary, all of them—and most clearly the Neoplatonists—have insisted on the abyss that separates *all* caused causes and connections, as integral parts of the universe or the *Nous* (spirit), from God as the One who cannot be caught by any categorical or conceptual grasp.

With regard to (3) the third point, concerning God as *causa sui,* I claim that a close reading of the passages in which Descartes, Spinoza, and Hegel call God *causa sui* shows that this name, in conjunction with the other names they use ("the infinite," *substantia, Geist*) does not justify Heidegger's interpretation. Heidegger ignores or hides the stubborn resistance of most thinkers from antiquity to the end of the Middle Ages against the theological use of the expression *causa sui.* No great philosopher has ever maintained that God is the cause or ground of his own being and even Spinoza and Descartes did not and could not think that, because it is unthinkable, a pure contradiction.[11]

As for (2) Heidegger's appeal to his own criterion for a godly God, it is remarkable that, for example, Bonaventure, whose profound involvement with religion cannot be doubted, did not have any problem with an ontological approach to God. In the fifth chapter of his *Travel Guide of the Mind to God,* Bonaventure refers to God as *esse ipsum* in a specific, infinite (and therefore utterly obscure, but supremely meaningful) sense, but he subordinates this rather Aristotelian onto-theo-logy to a more Platonic and Dionysian evocation, while integrating both traditions in his theological version of God as revealed in the life of a crucified man.[12]

As for (1) Heidegger's suggestion that a godless thinker or a godless time might be closer to the authentic God than "the philosophers" (and thus very close to authentic mystics), this question cannot be decided by a general statement or an individual testimony. I gladly agree that certain atheists can be more religious than certain Christians or Jews, and that certain experiences and expressions of the practical and theoretical atheism of our time might have mystical aspects, if indeed we take religion on its deepest level; but I do not see why the ontological program as such would be an obstacle to approaching God, and I am sure that Heidegger has not proved that. Whether it is the *best* way for a thinker to reflect about religion as a communitarian and individual dimension of life remains to be seen, however.

Besides, is onto-logy not a correct translation into Greek of Heidegger's own *Denken des Seins*? And if we take Heidegger's Hölderlinian religion seriously, may we not characterize his meditation on the gods of that religion as an onto-theo-logy (or perhaps rather an onto-theio-logy)?[13]

Does Onto-Theo-Logy Have a Future?

If the onto-theo-logical project that has fascinated the great minds from Parmenides to Hegel (i.e., if a tradition that has catalyzed the religious contemplation of so many intellectuals from antiquity to modernity) is not destroyed by Heidegger's critique, and if no pre- or post-Heideggerian thinker has given a more convincing refutation, we must ask whether that long tradition still can be retrieved in a way that allows for the recognition of a "godly" or a "Godly" God. The question itself implies that we know what "godly" and "Godly" mean, but is that not precisely what we want to discover? As a criterion that might guide our search, I choose only one word from Heidegger's description of authentic religion: *prayer,* though I am not sure whether I understand it in the same way as Heidegger does.

What religion is and how it can be lived in authentic and inauthentic ways, cannot be stipulated by philosophers independently; it is lived religion itself that decides about this. Just as art cannot be constructed by philosophy, religion has its own criteria for authenticity. True, some or even many requirements of philosophy coincide with the requirements of religion, but religion has its own origin and orientation, and its attitude differs from the philosophical attitude.

It is obvious that nobody is able to talk in the name of religion as such, because religion, just as art, exists only in concrete varieties, and no one represents all of them in an authentic way. What we can do, however, is to state clearly what, after having lived and experienced a particular religion, we believe to have discovered as a core without which no religion would be possible, though each religion has its own version of that core. The unfolding of that core and its self-critical evaluation might need or invite philosophical skills; it might thus generate philosophical and/or theological discourses and texts, but no religion would recognize itself—and certainly not its most authentic version—in a "religion" that is independently construed, deduced or imagined by philosophy. My own experience of Christian life has led me to the conviction that religion in its full, corporeal, communitarian, historical, individual, and spiritual (i.e., charitable and contemplative) sense can be summarized as trust or faith in God, if we include in this expression gratitude and hope, grace and peace. All these words simultaneously veil and reveal one unique "relation," which can also be expressed in the word "prayer," if this is understood in its deepest and simplest sense, that is, as the most originary and all-permeating responsivity of an existence in devotion to the creative, all-permeating, and healing God.

It seems to me that "prayer," of which I venture here a clumsy description, can be recognized as a summary of religion by the faithful adherents of all religions, though, of course, its unfolding into communal traditions, practices, liturgies, laws, and beliefs shows many apparently irreconcilable differences. Whether philosophers can recognize their own philosophical faith in "prayer" (for philosophers, too, have a faith) depends on many factors, but that at least some form of prayer is central to all religions, can hardly be denied. If my statement may be accepted not only as a "subjective" impression but as a (hypo)thesis that deserves to be considered, we can simplify our problem by asking how the onto-theo-logical project can be related to the possibility and actuality of prayer. As I hope to show, this question is fundamentally a question about the relation between two basically different attitudes. But before we come to that, we must ask ourselves why the God to whom Abraham, Isaac, Jacob, Moses, David, and Jesus prayed seems to be forgotten or even contradicted by "the God of the philosophers." According to an answer this question has often received, the God of the philosophers is not interested in human history or nature; this God is not inspiring, protecting, compassionate, creative and recreative, saving and consoling. Is he even a person?

I allude here to the view of those who oppose the philosophical God to the God of their faith, as an impersonal to a personal God. However, can they explain what it means to conceive of God as a person? What we know about persons concerns a multitude of individual and finite human beings, but God is neither finite nor an individual. Can we, by thinking, free the concept of a person of its individual and finite constrictions? Can we think an infinite Person? If we can, this would not be enough to approach God, because God is not only the infinite Other, he/she/it is also that in which "we live and move and have our being" (Acts 17:28). But let us reserve the latter thought for a later moment of our investigation.

Though I am not convinced that the God of philosophy (e.g., Plato's Good and Plotinus's or Bonaventure's One) is necessarily cold and impersonal, I do agree that *modern*, and to a certain extent *all*, concrete attempts at ontology and ontotheology have (at least partially) failed because they were not capable of clarifying *what and how persons are.* If you will permit me a sweeping generalization for the sake of clarity, I would like to say that Western philosophy, since its beginning, has remained a reflection about things, *res, realia,* reality, the cosmos, *physis,* nature, the world, entities that can be objectified, posited, put in place, set, caught in theses and antitheses, thematized, treated as pieces, parts, or moments of a cosmos, an overseeable totality, a panoramic whole. The paradigm in light of which philosophers have considered being was not beings (*to on, onta*) as such, but *thematizable,* and in this sense *objectifiable,* beings. In this light, human beings were treated as special sorts of things (*res*). Their *essentia* was treated as a *realitas* different from but wholly connected with other parts of the world.

Persons

We find the clearest example of such treatment in social philosophy. From Hobbes to Hegel human beings were thought of as moments of a system, parts and participants of a world whose structure could be reconstructed *ordine* and *more geometrico.* The thinker was an engineer who not only analyzed the existing community as a complex system but also ventured to construct a better system, called utopia, while puzzled by the fact that the existing social systems did not work so well as the system of nature.

An obvious objection against the thesis that even modern philosophy did not develop a philosophy of the person, is found in the overarching importance of the *Ego* that thinks, the birth and growth of psychology in all its varieties, the thorough analyses of self-consciousness, and so on. However, contemporary behaviorism shows how little humanity can be found in a discipline that focuses on human existence. Phenomenology has reminded us that material objects do not guarantee an appropriate perspective for their "formal" treatment. As I will argue further on, modern philosophy was not able to discover the quintessence of human personality for two reasons: (1) it did not develop a theory of intersubjectivity as distinct from sociality, and (2) its attitude and method do not allow us to encounter and fully perceive what is proper to persons.

Other objections against my (hypo)thesis can be made through commentaries on Kant's and Hegel's theories of subjectivity and intersubjectivity. As for Hegel, I would like to refer to some of my studies on Hegel's practical philosophy,[14] but with regard to Kant, I recognize that the basis of his ethics shows a sense for the extraordinariness of human personality, insofar as the basic *fact* to which he appeals (the "fact of reason") includes a dignity that is irreducible to any impersonal value or economy and thus differs radically from all thinghood or *res*-like "*reality.*"[15] However, his explication of this fact (humanity in myself and others is not a means, but an "object" or "end in itself"), though fitting well in his framework, does little justice to the phenomenon that he tries to describe.

A third response to my (hypo)thesis could be that Heidegger has given us something like or something better than a philosophy of the person in his phenomenology of *Dasein* as temporal and historical being-in-the-world-with-others. Again, a long discussion would be necessary to come to an agreement about this claim. My strategy in such a discussion would be to stress the following points.

The Relevance of Levinas for Onto-Theo-Logy

Heidegger's *Sein und Zeit* can be read as a partial fulfillment of the ontological project. Initiated by Aristotle, this project emerges from the impossibility of thinking "being" in a univocal way. While maintaining that "being" is all-encompassing, it recognizes various modes and dimensions of being, which cannot be understood as species of one genus. Heidegger has followed the injunction implicit in Aristotle's "*legetai pollachōs,*" insofar as he shows against those who reduce all being to *Vorhandenes* and *Vorgestelltes* that *Zuhandenheit,* worldliness, and *Dasein*—including its *Existenzialia* such as *Jemeinigkeit, Geworfenheit, Mitsein,* and *Zeitlichkeit* are differently or otherwise than the being of things and objects. But, however groundbreaking and splendid his descriptions are, the horizon of his enterprise remains within the orbit of the modern egology, according to which all beings are there for (or given to) a center whose awareness encompasses all of them within the total but finite horizon of its universe. This explains why Heidegger's philosophy of inter-subjectivity is reduced to a very general indication of *Mitsein* and some wise, but unconnected remarks about *Fürsorge.*[16] The human other is one of the beings that belong to the wider world in which *Dasein* is involved; he or she can leave the scene as soon as the massive importance of such collective phenomena as *das Man, das Volk,* or the *schicksalhafte Gemeinschaft* is discovered.

At this point, the lessons of Emmanuel Levinas interrupt the Heideggerian phenomenology of *Dasein's* "being-in" (*Insein*). To a certain extent, the phenomenology deployed in *Totality and Infinity* can also be interpreted as a partial fulfillment of the ontological project, but in its realization something dramatic happens that makes a rethinking of the entire project necessary. In his first *opus magnum,* Levinas's wavering between an ontological and a meontological language is remarkable.[17] The reason for this wavering lies in a certain indecisiveness with regard to the question of whether "being" should be accepted as the absolutely all-embracing word or rather reserved for all beings except God. In an ontological language, one could express the abyss between the totality and God as the difference between the universe of finite beings and the only one infinite being; but it is obvious that "being" then cannot be understood as generically encompassing both. The difference itself between the finite and the infinite is infinite; God is not *a* being and therefore not a highest being, either. And why should we use the same word for two "realities" that are infinitely different?

The only alternative seems to lie in finding a neither ontic nor ontological word for God, while continuing to use "being" for all finite beings. The word "infinite" could be tried out to name God, as Scotus and other thinkers have done, but Levinas uses this word (for reasons we will see) also for the description of the human other, which makes that word ambivalent. Already in *Totality and Infinity* Levinas appeals to Plato's difference between *ousia* (being or essence/*essance*) and *to agathon* (the Good) as names for the world of beings and God, respectively. The Good or God is neither a being, nor an essence, nor being (neither *ousia,* nor *einai*) as such. However, with regard to religion, Levinas's main thesis holds that the relation to God (which I have named "prayer") coincides with the relation to the other human person. In order to retrieve Levinas's thinking about religion, we must therefore pass through his phenomenology of the human other. His approach to God and his philosophy of prayer cannot be separated from his analysis of interhuman proximity, but for the sake of clarity, we can provisionally focus on the latter aspect.

Presupposing your acquaintance with *Totality and Infinity,* I here review some of its main points insofar as they are relevant for a possible retrieval of the onto-theo-logical project. In doing so, I will use the language of phenomenology, although Levinas has progressively replaced this language with another language that tries to avoid such expressions as "phenomenon," "appearance," "manifestation," "experience," "being," and even "consciousness."

Someone who looks at me or speaks to me cannot be seen or understood as a part or moment of the world. In a face-to-face relation, you do not belong to me who is settled in the world. Levinas does not claim that Heidegger is wrong in showing that we are involved and always already engaged in the world—on the contrary, in both *Totality and Infinity* and *Otherwise Than Being* he gives his own phenomenology of our worldly or "economic" mode of being—but he denies that this worldly involvement, as still dominated by the centrality of me, Ego, is the absolute or ultimate horizon of life and thought. The appearance of a human other disrupts this horizon; he or she is "a hole" in the world's being, an exception and contestation of the economic universe ruled by laws of interest and exchange. As a codename for our being-with(-one-another), *Mitsein* resumes our sharing one world within which *we*, as much as everything else, are exchangeable. The social context in which we are involved by birth and inculturation is basic for a hermeneutical perspective on our being-there. Levinas recognizes and stresses its importance for our hedonic, interested, civil and political dwelling, working, and thinking. However, the Other who speaks to me or looks at me urges and obliges me to respect and esteem her existence—not by what she says or does, but by the fact of her meeting me. Presentation imposes obligation. The Other's face or speech or gesture cannot be treated or conceived of as one of the exchangeable things or events that populate and compose the "world"; they do not fit the economy of values and equivalences, as Kant already firmly stated. Another human neither is nor has a value. While Kant states that a person has dignity (*Würde*), not a value (*Wert*),[18] Levinas affirms that the Other has "height" (*hauteur*). In comparison to all the interchangeable elements of "the world," this height is absolute and "*infinite.*"

Levinas chooses the word "height" to describe what phenomenologically distinguishes the emergence of the Other "in" and "from" the world, for two reasons. (1) The first reason lies in the *fact* that the Other's existence before me is experienced as simultaneously and indivisibly being a command: the Other's existence, as present before me (or rather turned toward me), obligates me. The scission between is and ought is not pertinent in this "case." Theory and practice, violently separated by Descartes and his followers,[19] are bound together in the Other's face and my appropriate perception of its demanding factuality. That I experience the Other as commanding me does not have anything to do with a difference in social (or other worldly) *roles*, such as those of master and valet or husband and wife. As a radical and "quasi-transcendental" (or, as Levinas says, "pre-original" and "an-archic") "fact," the Other imports a presocial and prepolitical, prescientific and pretheoretical perspective into my being-in-and-belonging-to-the world. Thus it becomes clear that Levinas responds to the modern question of how we can understand intersubjectivity: the presuppositions that the Other is *primarily* an *alter ego,* and that ethics must be grounded on non-normative and value-free facts are false. A freer and more adequate description shows otherwise.

(2) The second reason for using the words "high" and "infinite" for a characterization of the Other lies in Levinas's thesis about the coincidence of ethics and religion. The only possible contact with God, "the Most High,"[20] who cannot be seen or felt, lies in a fully appropriate response to the presence of human Others. Religion is charity. The two main commandments are one. Those who recognize here a long biblical tradition and accuse Levinas of translating his faith into philosophy seem to suggest that one cannot be a serious philosopher if one shows phenomenologically that certain convictions can *also* be approved—at least in part or approximately—from the standpoint of philosophy.

If Levinas is right, many implications can be made explicit that shock the foundations of modern and postmodern philosophy, probably even of the entire philosophical tradition of the West. I would like to dwell a while on one of these implications.

If Levinas recognizes, on the one hand, that we are in the world,[21] while, on the other hand, the Other disrupts my worldly life, it is obvious that he must combine both perspectives by subordinating the world (or the totality) and our economic, social, political, and scholarly involvement in it to the moral dimension opened by the Other's facing and speaking. I, the subject whom the Other obligates, am steeped in the economy of a world that we share, the world of our *Mitsein,* but the face-to-face shows that you—but also I as facing and speaking to you—are rooted in another dimension than the worldly one. The world of *Mitsein* does not form the ultimate and absolute horizon; the moral perspective disrupts and pierces that horizon and shows its relativity. The Infinite refutes the pretensions of the totality to be the ultimate. But if the totality, and therewith the horizon and context of the universe of beings, is not the ultimate, is philosophy itself then not dethroned? Not if philosophy itself can recognize, produce, or accept the infinite difference between the totality and the Infinite. That is, if the Platonic difference between the being of all (finite) beings and the Good can still be retrieved.[22]

At this point, I would like to make a metaphenomenological remark with regard to all Levinas's statements about the human other as a hole in being, as coming from on high, as disruption of the world and interruption of the economy, and so forth. Such statements can be justified only if the life of the speaker or writer himself is involved in the relation expressed by those statements. In other words, the perception of the Other is possible and true only if it is achieved in the first person: me.

This is the condition of all basic experiences in ethics and religion and ignorance of it has caused many false and superfluous problems. That all philosophy must ultimately be based on the *immediacy* of surprising phenomena has been known since Aristotle's epistemology, and phenomenology has elaborated this insight in its descriptions of the intuitive elements of all acquaintance and understanding. Less attention has been paid, however, to the extent to which the first-person perspective of an involved speaker is a necessary component of many statements whose truth cannot be "seen" by outsiders.

If, for example, "the Other" is nothing else than person B who is seen by person A (while I, the speaker, am the Cogito that reflects about the universal genus "persons"), it seems foolish to say that B is not equal but higher and commanding in relation to A. The main speaker is here the outsider who, from the height of a panoramic overview perceives A and B as instances of a universal genus "persons" or "the person" (or "the essence of a person").

Everything changes, however, if I, the thinker, ask myself how you, whom I meet as a phenomenon that surprises and confronts me, appear and what you are. When you face me, you not only surprise and amaze me; your facing provokes me to a response, which I cannot refuse (turning away or keeping silent is also an answer). My unavoidable response involves me in a specific relation with you, but this relation is preceded and triggered by your being-there. The question "Who and what are you?" is now an element of an existential involvement. As part of my life's involvement with you ("the Other"), philosophy itself, including the basic perceptions to which it must appeal, becomes (again) an existential enterprise.

What I formulate here in terms of a first-person perspective plays a constitutive role in Levinas's distinctions between (1) "the Other" and "the Same," (2) the Other and the third (*le tiers,* all others), and (3) the Saying (*le Dire*) and the Said (*le Dit*). Without entering the difficult discussions of the many complicated problems these distinctions carry with them, I will try to indicate in my own terms to what extent a phenomenological epistemology should be concerned about the difference between an involved speaking and the speaking of the "uninvolved onlooker" (Husserl's *unbeteiligter Zuschauer*) who was the hero of modern philosophy and early phenomenology.

If later phenomenologists have replaced Husserl's transcendentalism with a hermeneutical involvement, only Levinas, I think, has given the personal involvements of the speaker and the listener (or of the face that looks and the face that responds) its full significance.

Toward a Postmodern Onto-Theo-Logy

If we acknowledge Descartes' *Discours de la méthode* as paradigmatic for the basic position or stance of the modern philosopher, the following features are obvious. One of the first decisions to be made consists of the separation between the practice of life, especially in its utilitarian, interhuman, poetic, moral, and religious aspects, on the one hand, and the intuitions, principles, and scientifically permitted moves of pure theory, on the other. This decision immediately assigns a particular position to the philosopher: it places him outside all involvement in corporeal, worldly, and historical affairs, reducing his thinking to the most uninvolved movement of intellectual elements. Since the task of this purely theoretical movement lies in a metaphysically and scientifically justified (and possibly rectified) reconstruction of the real world in which all of us (including the philosophers) live, the philosophers have a superior standpoint from which they must recreate the world, including the praxis in which they always already have been involved. Philosophers thus study the natural and human universe from a distance. In order to be complete, they must have a panoramic standpoint, which they find in the Cogito itself. Since their only access to the Cogito lies in their self-consciousness, they themselves are or participate in the highest possible viewpoint from which the totality of all things (*ta panta*) becomes visible.

We know that Descartes failed to achieve the task whose phases he designated in his metaphor of the tree.[23] Only Spinoza and Hegel, and to some extent Leibniz, succeeded in fulfilling the great program. Most modern philosophers followed Descartes' advice to adopt a purely theoretical—neutral, panoramic, and universalistic—perspective in order to justify the principles of the existing universe, but almost all modern works show weakness in those passages where the original union of theory and praxis and their promised reunion become a problem. Thought has left life behind and, despite a few existentialistic revolts, ethics and religion continue to lead a marginal and unjustified subsistence. For the question of you and me this means that, in this kind of philosophy, you and I can be perceived and treated only as instances of "the I" in general (well known by, but not quite identical with, the philosopher who studies it) or as hardly different varieties of human subjectivity. The human subject has been studied by idealists and empiricists under the species of "the mind," "consciousness" and "self-consciousness," or "the I," but *you* have disappeared from the scene. It did not seem necessary to focus on you in philosophy, since you, as another I, were equal to me in all essential aspects. A good illustration of this viewpoint and the attitude that is expressed in it, is found not only in the literature about "other minds" but also in the basic postulates of Fichte's, Hegel's, Husserl's, and Scheler's attempts to deduce a multiplicity of (self)consciousnesses, subjects, and egos from the ego's mind.

As for the stance of postmodern philosophy, several of its basic presuppositions notably differ from the axioms of modernity, but with regard to the Cartesian position sketched above, it wavers. Though conscious of the erotic, social, cultural, linguistic, and unconscious forces and contexts that codetermine our thinking, the view from the outside and above and the superiority of autonomous judgments are maintained, while the possibility of universal validity—at least in theory—is given up. In practice, however, the postmodern scholasticism, signaled above, combines peremptory judgments about impossibilities and necessities with numerous appeals to the opinions and authority of its own stars and traditions.

Everything that can be seen and said from the standpoint of the modern *Ego Cogito* becomes necessarily a part of the panoramic universe that the philosopher tries to systematize. "The Said" (*le Dit*) indicates the economy of this ego's world. Then, your provocative speaking and my response can no longer be heard differently than exchanges within the universal context of a world-constituting economy. From this perspective, my, the surveying philosopher's, involvement in our conversation is only one of the many exchanges between the innumerable, essentially indifferent persons that make up the various groups, communities, peoples, nations, continents, and so on. Sociology and social philosophy in the modern style take over, whereas interpersonality and individuality vanish from the scene. The old dicta *De individuo non est scientia* and *Individuum est ineffabile* are then confirmed again. The divorce between philosophy and *real*, i.e., not only individual but unique, *lives* is then "justified."

However, if philosophy is nothing else than life's own stylized and refined reflection upon the surprising universe in which it since long has been involved, the Cartesian approach cannot be justified. The theoretical neutralization of life, including its affective and practical determinations, cannot be more than an abstractive experiment in unbiased searching for elements that can be recognized by many, perhaps all, other people who remain engaged in life while thinking about it. If reflection remains as close as possible to the experiences of life that can be shared by many, it cannot deny its dependence on the "first-person perspective" from which the most important adventures are perceived and digested. Before I can oversee and analyze the phenomena that amaze me, they have already provoked, affected, and engaged me. One of the most originary affections I have always already undergone is the encounter with some "you's," who have prevented my death by greeting me at birth and educating me, listening to me, befriending me, accepting me as a colleague, and so on. "The Other" in Levinas's emphatic sense is a philosophical pseudonym for some neighbors with whom I have become personally acquainted, and, by extension, for all others whom I should listen to in light of such closeness as befits the other who, by existing, demands my esteem. The secret of the stance that allows for Levinas's language about the other as revealed in the other's speaking, lies in my willingness *not* to separate my observations from my commitment to the other who addresses me. Speaking is in the first place speaking *to* another—*in response* to the other's emergence; speaking "*about*" another can be done only afterwards. Responsivity, involvement, commitment, and devotion *to you* precede all that can be said *about* you. To reduce you to an object, a theme, or a problem, is the beginning of murder.

Let us now return to the question of whether Levinas's phenomenology of the Other might be accepted as a contribution to the project of a transformed onto-theo-logy. I have said that the onto-theo-logical project perhaps can be renewed if we are able to finally produce a complete analysis of the different but related and mutually referential dimensions of being. The last step we have sketched involves us in a debate on the essence of another human being in its twofold appearance of (1) the Other, as facing and obligating me here and now (you, my neighbor or *proximus*), and (2) the Other as sharing with me the world (i.e., the "third," each other, all people, including myself). If we can finish this debate, we might come close to answering the question asked above of how one or more *persons* appear "in general." However, a phenomenology of the Other is only a first step in the direction of a philosophy of the person. While and after discovering how other humans, as *you, he, she, we, they,* and *all of them,* should be respected within philosophy, we should also rethink the essence of *me*. Levinas has attempted to renew the philosophy of the I in *Otherwise than Being,* but perhaps his emphasis on certain aspects of the relation between the other(s) and me has obscured other aspects that should not be forgotten in a retrieval of the tradition about the ego.[24]

Only a phenomenology of the person in its multiple versions as you, me, we, all of you, he, she, and they, can give us an idea of personality, but such an idea is *neither adequate nor sufficient* for an understanding of prayer, religion, and God. Though it brings us closer to the "being" or "essence" of God, it also blocks the ascent by imposing an inherent finitude on any mind that tries to think of God as "a person." We do not have a concept of non-finite personality—the predicate "infinite" that Levinas uses to describe the extraordinary essence of the Other cannot mean that the Other does not have limits—and we cannot conquer such a concept by trying to extend the limits or take them away, because of the *absolute* distance between the finite and the infinite. After exploring the possibilities contained in the concept of a person to direct our mind to God, a phase of negative theology is thus necessary to overcome the finitude of this concept.[25] However, in this essay, I will leave the necessary negations implicit; instead I will briefly point to another aspect of our referring to God, which presupposes God's not-being-a-person.

To approach God *in philosophy* we need more or better than a philosophy of personality. We need at least two transitions: (1) one from the "reality" of things to the personality of persons—God as a person to whom one can look up and pray is already better than a cold Object, but not sufficient for true religion—and (2) a second transition from God's being "like" a person or quasi-person to being that "in" which we live as in a "context" and "horizon" which contains in some infinite way all that is given in the finite totality of beings and their different dimensions. Especially in the texts of mystics and very good theologians we find many expressions in both directions: God is not only the Face to whom we direct our prayers; God's presence is also the horizon and the "*all*" (*omnia—esse ipsum?*) in which we move and participate, the fire of which we are sparks, the spirit to whom we owe our breath. These statements are sketchy, but they are supported by a long tradition of religious and theological writing. Their unfolding would demand thorough discussions about the intricacies of analogical and apophatic language, especially if we want to learn from the ways in which learned mystics described the quintessence of the religion to which they were devoted. At stake here is the question of creation: if God can be approached through the metaphorics around persons and personality, on the one hand, while God's infinity invites us to appeal to an analogically transformed "being-in" and "participation," the entire network of categories related to efficient causality crumbles. Medieval philosophers knew that the full meaning of "grounding" cannot be reduced to *poiēsis* and even less to the causality of modern science, but neither of their causes fitted the relation between God and the universe adequately. Some of them tried to think of God as a "quasi-form" (*causa quasi-formalis*) of the created totality, but not only is this expression obscure (as all predicates that are attributed to God), it must also be defended against accusations of pantheism.

If onto-theo-logy still has a chance, and if the sketch presented here makes sense, the realization of such a project demands much thorough thinking, perhaps too much. The most extensive and subtle discussions about the questions I have briefly indicated can be found in the Muslim, Jewish, and Christian philosophies of the Middle Ages. Most of them were written by authors who were committed and devoted to God through the affective, imaginative, practical, liturgical, institutional, and intellectual possibilities that their religion offered them. Their reflection was supported and animated by a religious experience for which the mystery that caused their (onto-theo-)logical problems did not appear as impossible. In their prayers, the otherness of God and their unity with the embracing quasi-totality of God's presence was experienced as quite appropriate to the only non-idolic God, although any formulation of this contradictory union remained clumsy and enigmatic. What became obvious in lived devotion broke through the limits of their reflection, because devotion reaches farther than reflection. The latter is tempted by exaggeration and reduction: deism sticks to God's otherness and separation, whereas pantheism exaggerates the identity without being bothered by the abyss. Both have a partial conception of presence, while atheism prefers to stay within the walls of a finite totality.

Wonderment and Faith

EIGHT

Christians who have the good fortune to be philosophers cannot avoid attempting to understand their own personal union of faith and philosophy and the consequences this union has for the character of their philosophy and their Christianity. Unless they are completely naïve, in which case they cannot be good philosophers, they will want to discover how their thought and their faith influence one another.

Can the relation between faith and philosophy be understood as a specification of the more general relation that connects philosophy with those nonphilosophical or prephilosophical elements that support and partially determine its form and content? After Kant and Hegel, philosophy has become so metaphilosophical that this kind of question has become standard in the contemporary discussion. It is uncertain, however, whether faith can be ranged among such elements as language, pathos, the unconscious, economic structures, and so on. Faith is unique, but in a very formal sense it too precedes philosophy.

The question of the complex relationships between philosophy and faith concerns the essence of philosophy, but it does not reach the essence of faith because philosophy is not a necessary element of the latter, although educated

Christians can hardly avoid asking scientific and philosophical questions about the content and validity of their faith. Given that insight into these relations presupposes at least some understanding of faith, their thematization inevitably presupposes a theology—albeit an embryonic or implicit one. All philosophers who accept the possibility of a faith more radical and more ultimate than philosophical thought, whether Christian or not, must accept the possibility that faith influences philosophy and that such influence cannot be ignored in any serious metaphilosophy.

Let these remarks suffice for now to suggest the horizon within which I will thematize some aspects of the relation between revelation and philosophy.

Grace and Nature

The question of the relationship between philosophy and faith has often been treated as a question about two domains of human knowledge: "natural" knowledge, which human beings can acquire on their own, and a kind of "supernatural" knowledge, which is given by God through authoritative signs and words. "Natural" in this context points to the abstract and universal "nature" or "essence" that constitutes all humans, or, in other words, that which remains when we bracket the history of grace. Most often, however, this "nature" is identified with the totality of possibilities that are seen as human by modern, Western civilization. Theologically, it is obvious that all concrete people share a history in which grace plays an essential part. But then it is impossible to separate *in concreto* what is due to nature and what is due to grace. If grace is operative always and everywhere, it might very well be included in what humans seem to be capable of on their own. Is the desire of being united with God, for example, a natural desire—in which case it would be surprising that no ancient Greek ever considered such a possibility—or has it rather been widened and implanted by grace?

If revelation is operative "since Abel,"[1] we might surmise that all expressions of human existence contain at least some elements of grace. Even if the concept of a *natura pura* ("mere nature") remains necessary for explaining the difference between creation and divinization, we must abandon the illusion that we can insulate a non-"supernatural" reality from history. Besides, would not such a reality be the same as hell? But hell is not nature. *Tout est grâce*,[2] and *assumption precedes creation*.[3] What humans *au fond* and from the beginning of creation are, is revealed in the birth, the life, the passion, and the resurrection of the man Jesus Christ, but this man is a divine mystery.

A Christian cannot deny these truths, not even in philosophy, if it is true that philosophy claims to think about the most radical questions. But how then can Christians converse with philosophers of different faiths, or with those who claim not to believe? Is the solidarity among philosophers and their ideal of universality disrupted by differences in faith? If nonbelievers could monopolize the word "philosophy," Heidegger's strange characterization of Christian philosophy as "wooden iron" could perhaps be defended, but why should such a monopoly be granted?[4] Christians who agree with Heidegger on this point must either abandon their philosophical aspirations and elect faith alone, or adopt some form of nonthinking theology (if such a round square is possible). If being a Christian does not exclude participation in the history of philosophy, are we nonetheless forced to philosophize within parentheses? Does philosophy itself then not become an abstraction, the provisional truth of which must be checked, and eventually transformed, by theology? Or can we still take "philosophy"—with St. Augustine and others—to mean the encompassing discipline in which the true *sapientia et fortitudo Dei,* Jesus Christ, is thematized as the illuminating center and symbol of all creation?[5] Philosophy would then coincide with theology.

For several reasons, mainly practical, we might prefer to maintain a distinction between philosophy and theology, but even then we must maintain both that theology, as a thinking discipline, is in need of philosophy and that the philosophy of a Christian, as a conditional and provisional discipline, cannot ignore its existential and essential connections with faith and theology. *In any case, it is a mistake to make the philosophy of nonbelievers the standard for philosophy as such.* Their perspectives are equally motivated by prephilosophical convictions about the ultimate questions. If philosophy were autarchic, it would be the unconditional horizon and basis of all human knowledge. If it could overcome agnosticism, its result would be a form of absolute knowledge, which in turn would be able to explain all nonphilosophical convictions, including all true and pretended revelations. If, however, philosophy as such can neither replace nor absorb Christian faith, and if this, instead of being a decorative *superadditum,*[6] is "the one thing necessary,"[7] then we must acknowledge that nonbelieving philosophers are rooted in something similar: some kind of radical trust or wager, a sort of philosophical faith, some "Yes" or "Amen," as Nietzsche would say, thanks or due to which they bless or condemn, accept with sadness or joy, the world in which they are at home. Thinking is more than just thinking insofar as it emerges from a fundamental disposition, stance, and inspiration. A radical attunement to the world, life, history, and language orients every search and conditions all theses.[8]

The modern attempt of Western philosophy to make thought completely independent is the exaggerated result of a tradition that began in Greece by proposing that the practice of *theōria* as a way of life could ensure *eudaimonia*. Much less scientific than their modern heirs, Plato and Aristotle propounded a mode of existence that combined political, ethical, and aesthetic elements with theoretical ones, but their contemplative perspective was preponderant. The entire Western tradition has been heavily dominated by the contemplative ideal, especially during its first two millennia; and philosophy has never ceased to be more than a scientific enterprise. In comparing the philosophy of a Christian with other philosophies, we must therefore not neglect the dimension to which each philosophy owes its characteristic stance and orientation.

A large research program in metaphilosophy could be unfolded at this point, but here I only give an example that would fit into such a program. I want to emphasize, however, that theology cannot be barred from participation in such a project; for how would a "strictly philosophical" metaphilosophy determine the relevance of revelation, grace, and faith if it excluded them? The contribution of this chapter to that program lies in comparing two modes of philosophizing which, while radically different, are nevertheless both born from a disposition that goes under the Greek name for wonderment: *thaumazein*.

Wonder

Thaumazein means to wonder or to marvel, to be amazed or astonished, and sometimes to admire or to honor. Although the verb is not used very often in the texts of Plato and Aristotle, both authors state the primordial importance of wonder for *philosophia*. The use of the word *thaumazein* in the New Testament points in another direction. Amazement here does not introduce us to philosophy in the Greek sense of the word; rather it confronts us with a very different, twofold possibility: faith (*pistis*) or disbelief (*apistia*). Both the philosophical and the biblical modes of wonder are primordial, but they open different realms. Can they be combined without radically transforming one or both of them? Can a Christian be a Platonist or an Aristotelian? Can a Platonist (or an Aristotelian or a Stoic) be a Christian? Is Christian Platonism, is Christian philosophy in general, a *contradictio in terminis?*

Thaumazein *and Philosophy*

In the *Theaetetus,* Socrates guides a young man in the unfolding of the apparently contradictory elements of a certain issue. Trapped in an *aporia,* Theaetetus exclaims: "The gods know, Socrates, that I wonder (*thaumazō*) beyond nature (*hyperphyōs*) what all that might be (*ti pot' esti tauta*) and, to tell you the truth, sometimes it becomes black before my eyes when I look at it." Socrates then pays Theaetetus the compliment, in jest, that his friend Theodorus, who introduced him to Socrates, displayed good judgment about his *physis* (nature and character). "For wondering (*to thaumazein*) is the very *pathos* of someone who is in love with wisdom (*philosophos*). Indeed, there is no other origin (*archē*) of philosophy than this one, and the man who said that Iris is a child of Thaumas, was a master in genealogy" (*Theaetetus* 155c–d). My overly literal translation attempts to render Plato's play on words which, together with "the gods," has disappeared in the translations I consulted. First, the relation between the search for wisdom (or philosophy) and the gods is reaffirmed as the horizon within which the philosophical life is lived. This is expressed not only in the invocation "*Nē tous theous?*" but also in the reference to Iris and Thaumas (cf. Hesiodos, *Theogony* 165). The name of the titan Thaumas can be understood as synonymous with *thauma,* wonder or marvel, while Iris, as Rainbow who links heaven and earth, is the messenger of the gods, especially of Zeus. Philosophy is not an exclusively human enterprise; it mediates between mortals and gods, as is even more obvious in Diotima's discourse on Eros in the *Symposium.* Neither human nor divine, *erōs* is a *daimon* thanks to which heaven and earth communicate, so that the universe forms a coherent whole in and with itself (*Symposium* 202d–e).

Presupposing the decisive role of *erōs* in the philosopher's way of life, Socrates declares that the pathos that commands the search is wonder—not, however, a wondering of pure curiosity but rather an amazement motivated by desire for insight into the truth.

I have found no other texts of Plato in which the relations between *thaumazein* and *philosophia* are thematized, but any reader of his oeuvre will be struck by its climate of wonderment that borders on admiration. In the quoted passage amazement emerges from a specific phenomenon that is already under philosophical discussion, but in general we may safely state that all questioning begins with the startling appearance of phenomena, situations, words, or customs that make us wonder.

Philosophical amazement is a *pathos* oriented from the outset toward understanding. It moves within the horizon of truth as manifestation. The true and the good are perceived as showing themselves, and the setting is theatrical. In their amazing appearance, the phenomena are simultaneously puzzling and splendid or horrible to the eyes of body, heart, and spirit. Beauty (or its opposite) constitutes the horizon within which sensation and thinking move. Wonderment is aesthetic in the broadest sense of the word. Contemplation, *Anschauung*, *theōria*, makes the "seer" delightful (*eudaimōn*).

In the first chapters of his *Metaphysics* Aristotle underscores the importance of amazement within the context of a theory about the nature and significance of our desire for knowledge. The famous first line of the *Metaphysics* states that "all humans by nature (*physei*) strive to know" (980a21). In developing this thesis, Aristotle insists on the self-sufficiency of the desired knowledge, distinguishing it clearly—perhaps too clearly!—from all kinds of productive, practical, and utilitarian knowledge. Sense perception, experience, remembering, and *epistēmē* are desirable in themselves. *Theōria* is both autarkic and liberating because it exists for its own sake, especially in its highest form, the knowledge of the "first" and foremost realities (*ta prōta*) and of the good and best among all beings. As independent and free, theory is a divine kind of *epistēmē*: a knowledge of divine realities that can be fully known only by the God. As neither useful nor productive, theory is the very perfection of human nature.

The function of *thaumazein* is explained in light of this metaphilosophical conception. Motivated and oriented by a natural desire for divine theory, wonder is the origin and ruling principle of philosophy. "Now and in the beginning it is through amazement that humans began to philosophize" (*Metaph.* A2, 982b11–13). Amazement is caused by the surprising phenomena of *physis*. It sparks doubts and questions (did I see this accurately? can such an event be real? how is this possible?) and it generates reflection. When I cannot find an explanation, I am confronted with an *aporia*, but the entire process of surprise, wonder, questioning, and reflection is dominated by the desired *telos:* knowledge of what the phenomena properly are, and why they are as they are and behave as they do.

Speaking of wonder and knowledge (982b7 ff.), Aristotle makes a parenthetical remark about the relation between myth and philosophy: because someone who is at a loss, while at the same time full of amazement, believes himself ignorant, "the friend of myths (*philomythos*) is somehow (*pōs*) a friend of wisdom (*philosophos*), for myths are composed of wonders" (982b17–19). Read in its context, this passage does not mean that the philosopher looks with reverence or expectation to the wisdom of myths; on the contrary, in addition to natural phenomena, the imaginary world of mythology also surprises and amazes the philosopher's mind by urging him to understand what is really going on from the perspective of principles and causes (*archai kai aitia*). That Aristotle is not here professing any preference for the enigmatic or mysteriously incomprehensible is also clear from his explicit statement that "the possession [of *theōria*] must somehow (*pōs*) end in the opposite of what for us is the origin (*archē*) of our search" (983a12–13). Perfect theory abolishes *thaumazein,* but since we mortals are not capable of divine perfection, our knowledge will somehow (*pōs,* in some sense) remain steeped in the pathos of marveling; a *pathos* that leads us to the question of what, how, and why things are such as they are.

———

The meaning of wonder, as thematized by Plato and Aristotle, cannot be severed from its role as the source of a contemplative wisdom that transcends production and behavior. Divine likeness is realized among humans only by approximation to the self-sufficient God, who thinks his own thinking but neither loves, works, nor acts.

In order to take a position with regard to this heritage it would be necessary to see how Plato's and Aristotle's ideas of wonderment have changed throughout Western history. Let it suffice for now simply to point out that the Greek climate of contemplative marvel has been conquered by a more prosaic framework in which wonderful phenomena are replaced by puzzles and riddles which must—and in principle *can*—be solved by humans. Rainbow, the daughter of Wonderment, no longer relates us to the gods. Rainbows do not evoke anything divine; the problems they suggest are solved by calculation of spectral refractions.

Thaumazein *in the Gospels*

The following is a very modest contribution on wonder as it is found in a few passages of the Gospels. Instead of being a scholarly study, it is only an invitation to pay attention to some textual constellations thanks to which *thaumazein* and related expressions show their Christian relevance.

Thaumazein as used in the New Testament never indicates an amazement that is caused by natural phenomena; what amazes is either an event, for example a deed or word of Jesus, or someone's disposition. Most often it is Jesus who amazes other people: his followers, a multitude of people (*hoi ochloi*), or his enemies. In most, perhaps even in all cases, the context is a situation that is critical from the perspective of *pistis* (faith or trust). People are amazed by Jesus because they do not understand his enigmatic behavior. Often their amazement is mixed with *phobos,* the fear of an existence without hope (e.g., Lk 8:25: *phobēthentes ethaumasan*; compare Mt 8:27: *ethaumasan,* with Mk 4:41: *ephobēthēsan phobon megan*).

In several cases where wonder is expressed, the language borders on admiration, but even then it betrays an unresolved question. Wonderment is ambiguous: it can lead to faith (*pistis*) as well as unbelief (*apistia*). As a sign of contradiction, Jesus can either be taken as speaking in the name of God or as a *skandalon.* To be struck by Jesus is to be awakened, shocked, faced with the need to make a decision: shall I accept what this person seems to signify? Shall I put my faith in him as a manifestation of God's saving presence? Or shall I reject his life as incompatible with my understanding of human existence?

The transition from amazement to faith cannot be made without the help of revealing words, but these alone are ineffective if the Spirit does not "open the heart" of the hearer. *Pistis,* however, liberates from fear and converts amazement into glorification.

Most stories in the Gospel relate the ambiguous situation of people who are wondering about Jesus but have not yet accepted him as the word of God. To exaggerate somewhat, we might perhaps say that the entire drama of Jesus's public life is presented as a series of confrontations that are repeatedly met with undecided amazement, culminating in a fatidic rejection by the powers in place and the flight of his disciples. The perspective from which the story is told, however, is that of faith in Christ. As was the case with the wonder that generated Greek philosophy, so too the proper character of the amazement presented in the Gospels depends on its outcome, which now is not discussion and insight, but faith or unbelief.

Let's look at a few examples. When, during a storm at sea, Jesus was awakened by his companions with the words "Save us, Lord, we are perishing," he said: "Why are you afraid, men of little faith (*oligopistoi*)?" "Then he rose and rebuked the winds and the sea; and there was a great calm. And the people marvelled (*ethaumasan*), saying: 'What sort of man is this, that even the winds and the sea obey him?'" (Mt 8:23–27). In Mark 4:40–41 we read instead: "'Why are you such cowards (*deiloi*)? Do you still have no faith?' They were terrified (*ephobēthēsan phobon megan*) and said to one another: 'Who is this, that even the wind and the sea obey him?'" Luke 8:25 likewise combines amazement and fear when he writes: "He said to them: 'Where is your faith?' Full of fear they marvelled (*phobēthentes ethaumasan*) . . . ."

That amazement can lead to rejection is clear from several confrontations between Jesus and his enemies, as for example in Luke 11:14 where we read that the people (*hoi ochloi*) marvelled over Jesus's casting a demon out of a dumb man, but that some of them attributed this to his cooperation with Beelzebul, the prince of demons. Similarly, Jesus's response to the Pharisees' question about the tax law made them marvel (*ethaumasan*), after which "they left him and went away" (Mt 22:22). (Luke 20:26 has here: "marvelling at this answer they fell silent: *thaumasantes . . . esigēsan*.")

A highly dramatic portrait of the way in which initial amazement can be transmuted into enmity is found in Luke's account of Jesus's first appearance in the synagogue of Nazareth, which can itself be read as a summary of the entire Gospel (Lk 4:16–30). After having read the text of Isaiah 61:1–2 ("The Spirit of the Lord is upon me . . ."), "Jesus closed the book, gave it back to the attendant and sat down; and the eyes of all in the synagogue were fixed upon him. And he began by saying: 'Today this scripture has been fulfilled in your hearing.'" While the response initially sounds positive, nevertheless it does not go beyond a mixture of amazement and admiration: "They . . . were amazed (*ethaumazon*) at the gracious words that came from his lips." But then the doubts begin: "Isn't this Joseph's son?" Jesus answers that no prophet is accepted in his home town. "When they heard this, all the people in the synagogue became furious. They got up, drove him out of the town, and took him to the brow up the hill on which the town was built, in order to throw him down the cliff" (Lk 4:28–29). On the other hand, we see a rapid transition from amazement to faith, when Matthew summarizes Jesus's healing presence in the following words: "Jesus . . . went up on the mountain and sat down there. And great crowds came to him, bringing with them the lame, the maimed, the blind, the dumb, and many others; they put them at his feet, and he healed them, so that the throng was amazed, when they saw the dumb speaking, the maimed whole, the lame walking and blind seeing; and they glorified (*edoxasan*) the God of Israel" (Mt 15:29–31).

Even though wonder appears to be a necessary phase in discovering Jesus's significance, several passages seem to suggest that it always includes an element of indecision or disbelief. Towards the end of Luke's Gospel, for example, we find the following: "Peter got up and ran to the tomb. Bending over, he saw the strips of linen lying by themselves, and he went away wondering to himself what had happened" (*apēlthen pros heauton thaumazōn to gegonos*, Lk 24:12). Even during their last encounter with Jesus the disciples were startled and frightened, thinking they saw a spirit. Jesus said to them: "'Why are you troubled, and why do doubts rise in your hearts? Look at my hands and my feet. It is I myself! Touch me and see; a ghost does not have flesh and bones, as you see I have.' When he had said this, he showed them his hands and feet. And while they still did not believe it (*apistountōn autōn*) because of joy and amazement (*thaumazontōn*), he said . . ." (Lk 24:36–41). It is only afterwards, at the very end of the Gospel, that "he opened their minds" (Lk 24:45), the result of which is displayed in the closing sentence of the Gospel: "Then they worshiped him and returned to Jerusalem with great joy. And they stayed continually in the temple blessing God" (Lk 24:52–53).

The meaning of Jesus's amazing existence is revealed by a reference to the revelations given to Israel: "He opened their mind (*nous*) so they could understand the scriptures" (Lk 24:45). A complete study of *thaumazein* in the Gospels should not neglect this hint about the hermeneutical character of revelation. Amazement is converted into an understanding of this person as the word of God by interpreting his appearance in light of the Law, the Prophets, and the Psalms. Jesus himself offered this reading at his first appearance in the synagogue of Nazareth, but he remained alone. Only after his death was his significance as the Word of God accepted by a group of followers. On the one hand, one must already belong to a written tradition, while, on the other hand, the tradition must be reinterpreted in light of a new event, including new words and deeds.

Confrontation

Before we return to the question of the compatibility of Christian faith and philosophy, we ought to compare the two modes of wonder briefly outlined above. We might begin with the statement that both kinds of *thaumazein* are forms of a surprised awareness that confronts us with the question of truth, and that both introduce a way of life in which truth plays a primary role. However, the word "truth" again covers a difference as radical as that between Plato's wondering about the phenomena of the cosmos, on the one hand, and the astonishment of those who hear Jesus's words and see his deeds, on the other.

Motivated by the desire for knowledge, the *thaumazein* of Greek philosophers views the universe from a distance. By means of perception, they let the phenomena show their splendor as marvels that raise questions: What is this? Does this appearance hide a secret, an inner life? How can we discover its core, its root, its ground, the ruling principle from which it emerges as it surprises us? Their perspective was a mixture of marvelling, admiration, and puzzlement, which gave rise to a thematization of wonderful but enigmatic phenomena. *Physis* was one of their central words; even humans (*anthrōpos*) and their productions, such as law and literature, were seen as interesting parts of Nature.

The surprising phenomena around which the Gospels revolve are very different. Rather than observing natural events, people were shocked by a person who involved them in a drama from which they could escape only by rejecting his significance. Amazement was now provoked by someone who claimed to speak the words and do the deeds of the very God they thought they already knew.

When marveling leads to philosophy, it opens a theater in which all beings receive a place and function of their own. The ensemble of appearances, rather than being tragic, displays a harmony in which the gods are no longer jealous; but the final reconciliation with existence continues to be found in spectacular contemplation. Even if he is in some way involved, the philosopher remains an onlooker who keeps a distance not only from the trivial needs and utilitarian concerns of life, but also from the fundamental questions of ethics, politics, and religion. Even in suffering, the philosopher remains the master of the game. *Meditatio mortis* (pondering death) shows the mind's sovereignty over corporeal life.

The drama of the Gospels involves their readers in a history of grace that does not allow them to avoid a decision. To remain a mere onlooker, even if passionately fascinated by the *theatrum mundi,* would be equivalent to indifference with regard to grace. The prevalent moods of the Christian texts are anguish, wonder, admiration, and, if faith prevails, hope, gratitude, and glorification. The neutrality of a sovereign metaperspective is impossible here because the prevalence of a thematic self-consciousness would destroy the challenge and the encounter in which a faithful Christian is engaged. Faced with a human person who is the revelation of God, I cannot treat him as Plato treated Socrates: Jesus Christ is not an actor in a masterpiece; he challenges me in a different way. If he is "the word" or "the son" or "the epiphany" of God, I can only respond to him who addresses me and welcome him as such. Revelation is not *primarily* a wonder that makes me think, but rather an astonishing declaration of love. No theoretical answer to such a declaration is appropriate.

Instead of a desire for pure and incorruptible knowledge, the New Testament provokes another, deeper desire: the desire for saving grace. Rather than being a form of thematic knowledge, the *gnōsis* of faith is the sensitivity to a mystery that does not become less mysterious in becoming more familiar; on the contrary, the more it opens me up, the more it escapes my grasp.

The *eros* of the Greek search for wisdom triumphs in the contemplation of the first and ultimate realities, coupled with the beauty of a virtuous existence. Intersubjectivity is realized in politics and friendship, but perfection is interpreted in terms of the individual. Excellence in virtues leads to blessed immortality. Perfection is symbolized by a unique God who actively thinks his own thinking in splendid self-isolation.

A Christian eye is not primarily oriented toward contemplation. The Christian hand is not *poietic*,[9] but graciously offering. In response to God's facing and speaking to us, our seeing and hearing are aspects of adoration. Speaking is not primarily a form of explanation; it is a form of addressing.[10]

Can a Christian be a Philosopher?

Can we at the same time inhabit Jerusalem — or Rome — and Athens? Without in the least claiming that my rudimentary sketch of the difference between two kinds of amazement suffices for a definitive answer to this large question, it still might give some hints for further exploration.

To begin with, we might ask whether faith abolishes all wonder, even the wondering *pathos* of the philosopher. As I mentioned above, when faith sets in, the pre-Christian wonderment is converted into admiration and adoration. Insofar as we are not yet fully converted, we continue to be moved by "little faith" and superstitions. We recognize ourselves in the pusillanimity of the disciples and in the prayer "I believe, Lord, help my unbelief" (Mk 9:24).

Doubts and questions that continue to amaze us accompany our faith; the element of surprise lives on in praise and confession, gratitude and confidence, pastoral care and religious contemplation. Prayer and *agapē* are obviously central in the practice of faith, but contemplation remains important insofar as the purification that prepares grace has also a cognitive element. Among its various meditative, theological, and mystical possibilities, *reflection*—which includes a critical distance from oneself—is a healthy exercise. It is possible to develop such reflection into a time-consuming part of one's life, but a very pure faith is quite possible without theology.[11]

If reflection completely isolates itself from prayer and praxis, it reverts to the stance of an outsider, thereby losing the attitude that is necessary for understanding faith on its own terms, and thus obscuring its relationship to reflection. When theology dominates faith, it usurps the place of a "faith in search of understanding" (including the understanding of itself)[12] and devolves into "religious studies." In such a case it differs little from an uncommitted study of the Christian religion, except that it might state as truth what a neutral study restricts to hypothetical beliefs.

If philosophy itself is a radical form of existence, emerging from a basic trust, as it was for the Stoics, Plotinus, Spinoza, and Hegel, its *pathos*—operative in wondering and critical questioning—excludes an essentially different kind of basic trust. The coincidence of the ultimate end—call it *eudaimonia* or the meaning of life—with *sophia* makes philosophy incapable of entering the city of God, unless *sophia* is discovered to be the name of a "word" that is surprisingly "spoken" by God. Such a discovery presupposes a radical conversion, and this requires a metamorphosis of the very questions themselves. The question "what is that?" (*ti estin?* or *ti pot' esti tauta?*) does not lose its meaning and validity, but it must somehow bow before exclamations such as the following: "What sort of man is this?" (Mt 8:27: *potapos estin houtos?*) or "Nothing like this has ever appeared . . . !" (*Oudepote ephanē houtos . . . !* Mk 9:33) or " Who is that man that the wind and the sea obey him?" (Mk 4:41: *Tis estin . . .*) If faith philosophizes, the word "is" has become mysterious in a way not known in Greek philosophy. How can we think the unity of the wonderful and amazing *einai* (being) of cosmic phenomena with the amazing appearance of an existence through which God signifies that he loves humans?

Does the contrast between Athens and Jerusalem exclude the possibility of an autonomous philosophy among Christians? If such a philosophy really is ultimate and radical, the answer must be yes. Philosophy must then either replace faith or be broken by it, just as the temples and statues of the pagan gods were smashed by the God of Jesus Christ. However, the columns of Greek and Roman temples, and to some extent their patterns too, have been adapted, reused, and imitated in Christian churches. Similar attempts have been undertaken with regard to the philosophical constructions of antiquity. However, none of these attempts succeeded without a radical conversion of the "spirit" and basic orientation of Greek philosophy into another spirit, which in turn changed the reflexes of the inherited philosophy.

The modern histories of philosophy, whether Hegelian or scientific, have accustomed us to think of philosophy as a neutral discipline that began around 600 B.C. and, slowly progressing to authentic science, liberated itself from all religious and other prejudices.[13] The concept of philosophy that is operative in such histories coincides with the idea of an autonomous and anonymous discipline in which neutral kinds of observation and constructive reason dominate human reflection. This typically modern concept does not fit the Western search for wisdom according to which philosophy, rather than being a science, is a way of life. The neglect with which modern histories treat that search as it has been practiced from Parmenides to Hegel, Kierkegaard, Nietzsche, Blondel, Bergson, Heidegger, and Levinas, shows how little they have reflected upon the metaphilosophical questions that arise when the existential rooting of philosophy is taken seriously. Like ethos, music, and other arts, philosophy is concrete and historical in a radical sense: not only its methods and applications, but also its basic disposition and prereflexive acquaintance with existence change through time. While this statement says nothing new, it upsets modern assumptions about reason's autonomy. Growing insight into the prephilosophical conditions of philosophy—its emergence from desire, language, temporality, and so on—inevitably transforms its practice and its nature. By itself, however, this insight is insufficient for answering our question about the compatibility of philosophy and faith, because faith cannot be understood as just another dimension alongside language, structure, time, or the unconscious.

The central question seems to be whether a kind of philosophy is possible in which wonder and thought are integral elements of the disposition that belongs to faith. Can we question and reflect as well as non-Christian philosophers, when the autonomy of modern philosophy is converted into faithful obedience to a call that comes from a deeper depth and an ultimate perspective? Then, questioning, reflection, analysis, and argumentation are elements of contemplation, and contemplation itself is practiced as a re-

sponse to the revealing Word that addresses us. Such an integration remains
incomplete if philosophy is only transformed into a form of intellectual meditation or theology, because it would not surpass a thought *about* the existence of Jesus Christ as the revelation of God. The primary question is not
whether we should force philosophy to again become an intelligent hand-
maiden of theology. Faith is not primarily a believing *that*, but, as has often
been pointed out, a trust toward or a *credere* in, a confidence that surrenders
to God. The mystery of Jesus Christ *speaks to* us. It can therefore neither be
heard nor understood in the observing, speculative, or scientific mood, but
only in a disposition that is open to being surprised, addressed, invited, and
urged to answer by a cordial response that is radical and total. Theology loses
its inspiration when it tries to become a scientific discipline rather than a *lateral commentary on a decisive encounter.* This was understood by Augustine,
Anselm, Bonaventure, and others who wrote their theologies in the form of
prayers: prayers of confession, love and acceptance, adoration and supplica-
tion. Even negative theology cannot isolate itself from such integration into
prayer. The negations that urge the human mind to reach beyond the being
of beings would provide no direction or motion, were they not animated by
the upsurge of adoration.[14]

Nevertheless, there is something awkward in those writings: in his *Confessions* for example, rather than writing a letter to God, St. Augustine writes
for other Christians who share his faith. Prayers to God alternate with discourses about God in which he talks to readers or to himself, but always
within reach of his readers' eyes and ears. One has the impression that he
regrets not being able to talk to God and human readers at once. But isn't he
in fact doing just that? And isn't that exactly a typically Christian aspect of
our relation to God? God revealed himself in a man who could say: "who-
ever sees me, sees the Father" (Jn 14:9). Moreover, isn't the son of God the
first of many others whose lives, faces, words, passions, and deaths confront
us with the same compassionate God? Doesn't God address us in the words
and deeds of every individual in history who accepted Jesus Christ as *the*
Event? If incarnation is a fact, prayer and fraternal care cannot be divorced.
Even reflective discourse can be equivalent to prayer if it maintains its essential connection with the most immediate expression of faith in God. Such
discourse constitutes a Christian form of friendship: the fraternity of people
who hear and think differently from those who believe that the presence of
Jesus Christ in history need not be understood as God's own revealing word.
The Good is not to be found on the summit of an ideal hierarchy, but rather

in the lowlands of compassion with ordinary humans. But this compassion cannot be separated from the practice of transcendence.

If theology and the philosophy of a Christian are integrated as elements of a faithful existence—i.e., an existence that is grateful, hopeful, prayerful—how shall we think about and practice these disciplines? Like all other components of the contemporary university, these disciplines are no neutral institutions; they have their own, modern, prescientific and prephilosophical motivations and assumptions. If Christians participate in them, they do this in the way St. Paul wanted to be "Greek with the Greeks and Hebrew with the Hebrews." We know how disappointing his attempt in Athens was (Acts 17:22–34). Was his failure due to a philosophical error? Do we hear the echo of his disappointment in his polemics against "the wisdom of the world" in the first letter to the Corinthians (I Cor 1:20)? "The wisdom of God" (I Cor 1:21) cannot simply reject or ignore what centuries of thinking have produced in their search for the truth. But it would be equally mistaken simply to adapt Christian faith to Greek or Jewish modes of existence and thought. The choice that confronts a Christian who wishes to participate in the history of philosophy is not whether to accept or reject Greek or Jewish wisdom. Both kinds of *sophia*—with all their subspecies—need conversion, as do all not-quite-faithful specimens of thinking that have surged *within* the history of the Christian community. Medieval theology was an attempt to transform the wisdom of centuries into an intelligent and well-practiced faith, but the inherited categories were not entirely appropriate for thinking the Word as speaking and spoken, as addressing and challenging, and as demanding a response from the hearer to its absolute radicality. This seems to be a task for today: how we, as rooted in faith and in solidarity with all, can develop conceptual structures that permit us to understand speech as speaking, events as spoken, and the figure of the crucified as the Word that God addresses to us about the mystery of God's concern for humans.

About Salvation

NINE

Philosophy and Salvation

On hearing the word "salvation," a philosopher wonders what constellation of words, images, concepts, and relations it involves and what tradition or traditions it conveys. A word sometimes presents a whole world and an entire history, and this is certainly the case with the word "salvation." In order to reconstruct its historical context, one would have to be familiar with the history of theology and participate in its current debates. A Western philosopher who wishes to proffer something meaningful about such debates must, at least to some extent, be acquainted with the Christian constellation in which "salvation" functions, but as a philosopher he will have to concentrate on those aspects that may be clarified in a language general enough to be understood by both Christians and non-Christians. However, by identifying phenomena and employing concepts that are available to believers and nonbelievers alike, he puts many aspects of the issue at stake between brackets. From the perspective of philosophy, all unproved convictions become hypothetical, but this does not necessarily require a separation between philosophy and theology.

Salvation is not given as an immediate phenomenon, although the prophets and evangelists, the poets and the mystics provide us with many texts and images in which salvation is evoked. If human life is essentially oriented toward salvation, we may expect that the longing for it should be reflected in a great deal of Eastern and Western literature. But would not then also a phenomenology be possible in which, on the basis of spiritual, theological, and literary texts and contexts, a universally valid concept of salvation could be constructed by analyzing the "universally human" elements of experience? However, such an undertaking involves great difficulties.

A first difficulty lies in the question of whether an *isolation* of "universally human" elements from their Christian context is at all possible. Will they not retain a host of connections with Christian elements? Can they be separated from their affinity with the milieu to which they belonged? How is it possible for elements that have been separated from a historically grown constellation to retain an existence and meaning of their own? Abstracted elements immediately form a new context with each other and such a context inevitably develops into a world of its own. We have seen how, during the last centuries, several elements that were separated from the Christian universe have formed an un- and anti-Christian world, but this new world is not wholly separated from Christianity; it is either obsessed by it or one of its no longer Christian heirs.

A second difficulty that emerges is the following: how are we able to *distinguish* universally human aspects of salvation from Christian salvation? Do we have a criterion that enables us to recognize what, being not typically Christian, is universally human (and then, of course, also nontypically Jewish, Buddhist, Muslim, primitive, or modern)?

We have grown accustomed to the concept of a nonspecific humanity, a human nature that can be determined without reference to particular religions or cultures. For a long time philosophy has been regarded as the territory in which the basic patterns of such a generic, prespecific, or metaspecific humanity had to be located. The result was an abstract picture of the typically Western, modern, scientific, utilitarian, and rights-oriented human being; not a universally human structure, but the outline of a concrete ideal in which modern Western culture is manifest. The fact that this culture contains the possibility of a global culture is something for which one can be grateful, but it neither justifies the thesis that "man," as exemplified in Western philosophy, coincides with the essence of all human beings, nor that his idea of "salvation" (*sōtēria, salus*) exactly coincides with the ideal longed for by all people in the East and the West.

While the question about salvation resembles the questions about *eudaimonia, beatitudo,* happiness, *Glückseligkeit,* which have been answered in various ways by Aristotle, the Stoics, Plotinus, the English empiricists, Kant, and many others, these questions do not exactly target the same reality. Not only does the desired goal acquire a name of its own in various philosophies and theologies, its meaning depends upon their overall portrayal of man and the world. Yet we recognize those thematizations as cognate and interpret them as various quests for something unifying and ultimate. If we are right in doing so, we still must answer the question of whether Christianity should be understood as a synthesis of all other pursuits for happiness and salvation, or, rather, as one among many variants of a single quest?

While "salvation" itself is not a given fact that can be immediately perceived, nearly all philosophies and theologies, and large portions of world literature, express people's longing for salvation, their fears and expectations, doubts and hopes concerning the ultimate success or failure of their existence. Longing for salvation is, indeed, a phenomenon that can be described, and it seems not too audacious to state that all sorts of people can recognize it as an authentic and profound desire. Does it occur everywhere and always, is it a universal desire that can be determined by a universally valid phenomenology?

If so, our difficulties do not yet disappear. First of all, does not the desire for the ultimate, as a radical longing, dominate us so intensely that it escapes descriptive and analytic observation? The necessary distance seems to be lacking here. Longing is behind and beyond all efforts to grasp it; we are at its mercy; it precedes all forms of self-consciousness; it refutes all attempts to capture it by means of a definition. A description of it must always make a detour through its expressions, such as exclamations, evocations, narratives, expectations, disappointments, delights, feelings of gratitude or remorse and so on, all of which show an intensity that cannot be mastered conceptually. Yet we are guided by a strictly immediate awareness of longing, which is neither objective nor thematic. Even before we are capable of wanting or knowing something, we are animated and ruled by the radical dynamism of a drive that is not within our power, though it inspires all our striving and speaking. This drive announces itself in all desires, needs, moods, and emotions. Poetry, art, and especially religion, represent and express the energy of this shapeless ec-stasy that cannot be fixed in any particular form.

A second difficulty with which we must cope, is that we lack a generally accepted idea of the ultimate *desideratum.* In using such words as "salvation," "bliss," or "happiness," we are not even sure that our interlocutors mean the same realities as we. There is a multitude of conceptions about desire and happiness. Many people deny that there is such a "thing" as one ultimate desire with one target, while those who accept its concept greatly differ in conceiving its content. Not only do the expressions of longing, evoked above, have a history, but so do their nature, scope, and quality. For example, the idea that human salvation is realized by participation in God's own life would have been considered sheer folly and arrogance by Plato and Aristotle, who nevertheless strongly emphasized that *erōs* rules the universe. Should we then suppose that they—though unconsciously— were driven by the same desire as the Christian mystics who could not stop at anything less than Godself? Or should we rather believe that their most profound desire differed from the 'mystic' longing that characterizes not only Christianity but other religions as well? Does *erōs* itself have a history?

It sounds rather haughty when Christians declare that all people, including heathens and atheists, are *actually* driven by the same longing as an ideal Christian. Unless they can offer strong arguments for this hypothesis, for example, by showing that it is the only possible explanation for such phenomena as the unity of humankind and the radical nature of human desire. Aristotle dared claim that things are in motion because of their desire for the one who has infinite self-knowledge; Plato had Socrates say that everything receives its being and its truth from the Good, which itself is neither an idea nor a totality but something infinitely different and greater; the classics of Christianity maintained unanimously that a human heart can only find rest in God. Such answers are not popular at present. Perhaps they never were, but in today's mindset they seem to have lost even their respectability. Justice, peace, social, and ecological care are highly esteemed, but few people accept "God" as a meaningful answer to the search for meaning. Yet life with God seems to be the essence of salvation as hoped for by Christians.

Why has the desire for God become devalued? Has it been overrun by moralism, dogmatic theology, and ecclesiastic politics? Those who, in former times, said that they experienced what John and Paul wrote about participation in God's life, were regularly treated with suspicion, particularly in their own church. Many of their writings indicate with sufficient clarity which affective and practical conditions are necessary for a lucid understanding of salvation, union with God, and "human longing." Thus they exemplified a fundamental rule of phenomenology that is too often neglected: in order to see what there is to be seen, one has to have good eyes; in order to find out that beautiful things are beautiful, one must have good taste; in order to discover what is really important, one should be interested in the right manner; in order to discover what I myself "basically" and "essentially" long for most of all, my affectivity must already be purified. The application of this rule not only requires a great deal of *askēsis,* but also illumination, weeding out, and suffering—and thus much struggle and tolerance. Only purification can liberate what is most radical in us, so that the rest of our life can adjust to it. To answer the question about the scope of our longing, certain historical and personal conditions must be fulfilled. The mere asking of that question already requires a vivid awareness of its depth and the emotional thicket in which it entangles us. A proper phenomenology of longing presupposes a purified sensibility.[1]

However, by indicating a few problems with tentative answers concerning salvation, I do not wish to suggest that it is now up to theologians to employ the Christian doctrine of salvation in order to determine the nature of human longing. The following considerations, indeed, speak against such an approach.

In the first place, there is no uniform "Christian doctrine of salvation." The various interpretations of "God," "incarnation," "liberation," "union with God," and so on, differ so considerably that even some Christian interpretations of salvation show more affinity with certain Jewish or Muslim theologies—perhaps even with certain forms of atheism—than with other Christian theologies. Fundamentalism, for example, creates a kind of community among fundamentalist adherents of different religions. The same might be surmised of the affinity experienced by a liberal Christian in conversation with a liberal Hindu or Jew. [2]

Furthermore, it is not a priori evident to a philosopher—nor, presumably, to a theologian—that "the" Christian interpretation of human longing, even if it is true, is complete. Christianity as a whole, including its theologies, is a geographical and historical phenomenon with its own languages, literature, and morality, as well as its own emotional, legal, aesthetic, and religious features, all of which are interwoven with the eternal realities of its faith.

"The essence of Christianity"—and therewith the essence of Christian salvation—is not an idea transcending time; it is both a given fact and an answer to the eternal question of meaning, which transcends the contingencies of history. It is a fact that is already given and yet must be discovered continually. As the ultimate truth about desire itself, salvation requires both revelation and discovery.

───────────

The historicity of the Christian and non-Christian attitudes toward salvation has produced a multitude of theoretical, practical, and affective interpretations. Due to the peculiarities of persons, times, and languages, salvation assumes different shapes, while at the same time remaining unique in its own diversity. A simultaneous and successive pluralism is required in order to experience its generosity. Ever since the discovery of the world and universal history, the idea that one particular mode of philosophy or theology could be perennial has become unbelievable. Relativism is the general mood pervading contemporary intellectuality. Yet it is impossible to consider either philosophy or theology as nothing more than symptoms of particular languages, periods, cultures, or personalities. Each epoch can be characterized in broad terms, though one must remain aware of the violence that is involved in such generalizations. The same is true of a language or a style and, in general, all characterizations. They always leave open the ultimate meaning of that which transpires in a specific (and therefore relative) language, time, personality, or economy. Just as temperament, nationality, or a person's character do not determine one's ultimate destiny, neither can the ultimate meaning of a collective history be fixed by its contextual aspects. "Salvation," destiny, and meaning are not reducible to their functioning within texts and contexts. This already follows from the fact that one and the same time produces saints and monsters and that one and the same personality structure admits of both good behavior and delinquency. No period whatsoever in world history is simply a time of salvation or a time of doom; every time is ambiguous; it is both good enough for salvation and bad enough for corruption. Salvation requires time, but it demands more than history can give.

Longing

With the preceding reservations in mind, I now will offer some brief phenomenological remarks about longing.

Being human can be characterized as a particular way of "ek-sisting," standing out, and longing for salvation. In reflecting about one's life, a human being experiences itself as having-always-longed-for, even before the awakening of one's self-consciousness. Once it becomes a conscious desire, longing is accompanied by the question "What do I really long for?" Initially, my longing is so indefinite that I cannot answer this question. Where will my longing carry me? How far does it reach? It keeps me moving, not toward some precise goal or the achievement of a clearly definable task, but rather to discover what it is that drives and obsesses me. Every satisfaction I encounter in my attempts to bring my longing to rest is in the end disappointing. Desire reaches further than all the ends we try out by possession, enjoyment, power, or achievement. Longing without end instructs me by means of the negations that fail all modes of enjoyment. Enjoyment is always a mixture of satisfaction and disappointment; it thus urges me not only to repeat my attempts but to reach further. Every experience of beauty or goodness is wistful; besides delight, it also causes melancholy. I want "more." More, or rather something very, radically, different? In any case, more of the same will not do, for that would only lead to boredom; and boredom causes disgust or doom.

Our desires have been shaped by familial, economic, political, cultural, and religious traditions. The longing that animates them is a relentless urge, which guides, but also complicates and often pains our life. We normally follow the customs and codes of the surrounding culture, but no established order can seduce us completely, even if we could adjust it to its ideal form. Longing does not find rest in any home. To be at home in the world seems impossible. Romantic escapes in the form of amorous, literary, or philosophical intimacy are tempting; but even these fail to respond to the depth and breadth of our longing, the more so because they exacerbate our loneliness.

Repeated experiences of the distance between our being at home in the world and our reaching out to something else may convince us that the "thing" we are longing for cannot be accomplished or conquered, but only met or received. Even if the difference between transcendence and the world can be clarified by revealing words or holy lives, even then their testimony must be recognized through some sort of experience; at least it must resonate within the subjectivity of the person who is reaching out. Recognition can lead to conversion, but all of these turns are impossible without receptivity, which demands humility. Striving then becomes a form of looking forward and hoping while enduring, a kind of waiting that orients and supports the searcher's activity. However, longing is very different from demanding.

Although I cannot become happy without that which I long for most, I would certainly forfeit the possibility of receiving it if I claimed it as a right. It differs too much from the rights and rewards that are considered normal within the framework of an economic style of morality. Claiming, being entitled to, deserving, or defending as a right are enemies of the most desirable. Longing points to an order of freely giving, an order of grace.

Although desire makes us uneconomic and in that sense unworldly, its authenticity and correct attunement depend on the earthly loyalty it summons. It is only by developing my bodily and mental possibilities that we begin to discover what drives us. That which occupies one's heart is shown by the works of one's mouth and hands. A philosophy of human self-realization is therefore an integral part of an erotic phenomenology. Though the economy of our being-with-others-in-a-world-that-is-happening can neither fathom nor replace the transcendence of longing, it cannot be despised or skipped. From the perspective of longing, any worldly economy both evokes and hides the ultimate. The earth does not allow itself to be betrayed; what we must learn is therefore an erotically appropriate—i.e., a salutary—engagement in words and works that do justice to both the world's own demands and its suggestions about its lovely beyond. Salvation realizes itself for those who are well-attuned to the *cantus firmus* that sustains all things. The glory of God demands loyal eyes, hands, and hearts; it shines when the earth begins to sing.[3]

Debates

Every description of longing and salvation is only *one* attempt to speak about something that is beyond our grasp. Hence it also has to make room for other attempts to point out the one thing that ultimately matters. Such openness responds to the all-encompassing radicality of the most important questions. A *certain* relativity is therefore inherent to the question of salvation. At the same time, however, a profound confidence seems legitimate, if salvation is a universal destination. For this conviction would justify the belief that all serious attempts at preparing oneself for salvation will converge somehow somewhere. Differences of opinion within the horizon of such an ecumenical belief are inevitable. When the discussions that emerge from those differences satisfy certain conditions, they are salutary. One of these conditions is that the participants are neither aiming at a triumphant dogmatism, because this would prevent the salvation of a *free* humanity, nor indulging in the indifference of a relativism that shows how little they are concerned about anyone's salvation.

As long as modern faith in reason prevailed, the participants in the discussion staked their hopes on the eventual victory of logical analysis and arguments in support of their one true point of view, thereby defending a modern version of the ancient Greek idea that the Logos gathers all minds by surpassing paradoxes and contradictions. Hegel saw that differences of opinion can be fruitful, but he maintained that the truth lies in the concept that reconciles all differences. The tradition of the gathering Logos continues whenever one tries to understand present-day pluralism from a higher or metaviewpoint, for example, by regarding all convictions as variations on a general, but very formal scheme or structure. The content of all beliefs is then committed to relativism, but unity is sought in the formal elements that underlie those contents.

Many attempts at consensus about truth and salvation are looking for generalities that all people can endorse irrespective of their particular traditions. They operate within the dimension of universal, supraparticular, and supraindividual intelligibility. Does such an intelligibility reach the root(s) of our questioning? Is it, in other words, sufficiently radical to serve as a standard for the truth of longing and salvation? Or is salvation always a question of unique individuals, none of whom coincides with any instance of a universal concept?

Philosophical criticism of abstract universality and logical rationality is not an invention of our time; but what is the source from which it derives its inspiration today? Salvation is no more to be found in universal essences than in arbitrary choices or conventions. But should we not begin with a certain confidence in the unicity of exemplary lives and the particular, but time-tested traditions with which they feel familiar? Is not a valuable part of the truth lost by separating what is special and unique about individuals and traditions from the universal concepts that capture their common essence? Should we not rather consider each person's life experiment a unique story that continues to develop in critical dependence on traditions that relate to the worldwide history of revelation?

Truth and salvation realize themselves in unrepeatable, though intertwined, lives of unique human beings in particular connections. Even if general characteristics of successful human existence are useful for our orientation, we would still impoverish the history of salvation if we isolated them from their entanglements with the concrete experiments and adventures of unique persons.

When words and works are genuine, they are also unique. The irreducible unicity of irreplaceable people is what essentially and ultimately matters, especially in debates about salvation. Ownness and singularity are not the dividing elements that universalist logics have taken them to be. Difference and unicity are conditions, not impediments, for love. As constitutive for friendship, they are also necessary for a discussion, especially when something as comprehensive and inexhaustible as salvation is at stake. Reflection on each others' life stories and acquaintance with the past and present experiences of singular existences contribute more to the debate than a metatheory that neglects the differences.

The concrete universality of a well-differentiated manifold in earnest dialogue brings a hidden convergence to light along apparently conflicting paths. We need not know the all-encompassing formula that reduces all paths to one, but we cannot believe in our own path toward salvation if we do not assume that, in one way or another, it leads in the end to salvation for *all*. This belief does not deny that many traditions and adventures—in a way that escapes us—are held together by One that is the Same for all who are driven by the most profound desire. It does, however, deny that thetical exclusions and general overviews are the best ways to truth and salvation. If caring for our own unicity is at once caring for everyone else's unicity, we are on the way to a concrete form of universality that creates cohesion, even if we do not have a neat concept of its truth. Under certain conditions the conversation between irreplaceable individuals is a better form of communication than general theories. However, all communication demands purification. Acquaintance and affinity go deeper than conceptual agreement. If salvation lies in union with God, and thus with one another, it cannot come to life through a universally valid theory. At best, it will remain hidden underneath the surface of argumentative discussions because its gathering force is more radical than shared theory. A pluralism of views does not contradict the radical unity of an attunement that precedes all speaking. Religion is not a theological institute but, "from Abel onwards,"[4] the communion of convergent divergences. As a community of hopeful gratitude and memorable expectation, it participates in a multilingual revelation that uses the whole of space and time in order to develop its many possibilities to the end. In all languages and cultures, and in all the histories of unique human existences, we hear a multitude of witnesses proclaiming the same message: what matters is the Spirit.

God across Being and the Good

The following sketch of an approach to God through being rests on several presuppositions of which I can here only give an extremely brief summary.[1]

1. My fundamental presupposition is the thought that ontology and ethics cannot be separated because the essence (or being) of being and the essence (or being) of goodness cannot be adequately distinguished.[2] In defending this thought I take the liberty of giving the largest possible meaning to the word "ethics," so that it encompasses everything that one ought to do, say, feel, or want concerning all that presents itself and thus affects the human impulse to deal with the given universe. In this large sense, ethics embraces the whole of human praxis, including all that is good, appropriate, proper, decent, beautiful, recommendable, admirable, and appreciatable in daily life, art, philosophy, scientific practices, moral customs, legal demands, codes of politeness, hospitality, and good taste in all sorts of pursuits. I hope that the rest of my remarks will show what advantages one can gain from using the word "ethics" in this expanded sense. Of course, this position does not deny that a complete ethics must also delineate and justify the more restricted senses of the word "ethics," particularly in the context of interpersonal and social relationships.[3]

If one opposes being and good or the study of both in ontology and ethics, one has already restricted being to a domain that, as such, is neither good nor bad, while goodness is then declared not to be.[4] However, every manner of being is a mode of addressing certain demands to the subject confronted by it, an invitation to recognize that which offers itself here and now in all its splendor or horror. Every phenomenon requires that I greet, accept, and respect its mode of being and that I *respond* to it in an *appropriate* manner.[5] The proper, inviting, and provocative being of a being cannot be recognized in the purely descriptive, normatively neutral language of a nonethical ontology; every description that is fair to the phenomena by taking it as it gives itself, every concrete phenomenology, is *ipso facto* ethical inasmuch as it attempts to respond adequately to the interesting, touching, demanding, amusing, or repulsive essence of all that presents itself. The most fundamental goodness is as constitutive of all beings as their "essence" (or being or "beingness") that must be pointed out by any ontology, even the one that tries to ignore its own implicit ethics.

In other words: to the extent that the consideration of a phenomenon's being expresses or awakens our interest, it has the character of something interesting. This character is specified in a variety of the good, the beautiful, the pleasant, the admirable, the monstrous, the detestable, but it can neither be abolished, nor separated from the being of phenomena that have attracted the phenomenologist's attention. Attention is always a mode of being affected, pleased or pained, attracted, fascinated, anguished or astonished. Affective neutrality is impossible if one pays enough attention to discover how a given shows itself to be. No theory is disinterested and no being exists for affective indifference.

2. My second assumption belongs to a phenomenology of human desire and correspondence.[6] Desire motivates human beings to engage in a praxis that is at the same time an investigation of all beings and their being, and a search for the incomparable good that surpasses the universe of all that is desirable. The mode of being of the ultimately Desirable cannot be known in advance; it is precisely what the search must discover. Is it the possession of some thing or of all things? Is it peace with oneself and the entire universe? A certain form of life? In any case the search passes through many attempts to deal with the ensemble of beings and events.

In its search for the Desirable, our deepest desire is a question to which the given beings respond with offers that are also demands. In perceiving what happens around, within and to us, we ought to respond in a correct manner: we must "correspond" to it. Successful correspondence presupposes that Desire allows beings to unfold in their own and proper manner. This however is possible only if we are pure enough to honor what and how they are when freed from all distortions or "in themselves." The path of desire therefore implies purification, but this takes time. As soon as this necessity has dawned on us—which implies a conversion—we find ourselves on a journey toward the purified modes of being that open themselves for clearer eyes.

3. Recognizing the various modes of being and disentangling their constitutive elements constitutes a complex operation. Each culture is a specific arrangement of the beings and events it deals with according to a characteristic combination of their dynamic phenomenality and its own modes of receptivity, practice, and production. Individuals who approach the phenomena that are displayed, have adopted the tastes and prejudices of their culture, although they can still vary them in more or less original ways; but the desire that animates them (as it animates all history and culture) provides them with a critical distance to the prejudices they share with their culture. In order to realize their liberation—condition of their purification on the way to correspondence—Desire demands that they pay attention to the hints through which the essence of the given guides their wish to honor the constellation of the beings that greet them.

4. At each stage of its purification, Desire is characterized by an (implicit or explicit) specific ontology: the universe of beings is lived, sensed, and spoken of in a typical manner of typifying them. Every ontology is an ethics insofar as it shows that the beings that manifest themselves demand the thinker to welcome them in a manner that corresponds to their self-affirmation. The more or less successful correspondence expressed in such an ontology finds itself challenged to pursue a still more adequate discovery of the given by the relentless desire that precedes, accompanies, and follows every responsive attempt.

5. At each stage of the erotic movement, it is necessary to unfold the ontology of which a wayfarer is capable. One cannot wait until one has acquired the perfectly pure openness that allows for a perfect correspondence. Only such a correspondence can procure the epistemological condition for an ontology without defect. I will therefore attempt to sketch some lines of an ontology to which I am drawn at the stage of thought that here and now seems to be mine.

The Analogy of Being Good

I would first like to insist on the analogy of being, which is also an analogy of good. When modern philosophy, seduced by the sciences, reduced being to objectivity, it exacerbated a tendency of its Western tradition that is perhaps its original sin. Since the allegorization of Greek mythology and the abolition of the dialogical dimension by a more cosmological ontology, *ta onta* (beings) have been treated as more or less homogeneous things (*res*). Despite the warnings of Aristotle, the majority of philosophers have spoken of plants, animals, events, men, women, and infants as if they were things that could be differentiated by the addition of specific differences to their generic being or by accidental transformations that leave their substantial and homogeneous character intact. Phenomenology has renewed the foundations of metaphysics by reformulating the question of the original differences between the various modes of being (or "essence"). Heidegger's analyses above all have reopened this path through his descriptions of things, objects, instruments, words, temporality, worldliness, and so on, but are we sufficiently convinced that a decisive meditation on the ontological difference between the essence of beings and the essence of being itself is impossible unless we first characterize *all* the main types of being and the differences that keep them distinct, while at the same time uniting them thanks to "being itself"? At least, the various modes in which affectivity, speaking, intersubjectivity, the religious, and the divine *are,* must be thought before we can concentrate on the essence of being as such.

As far as personality and interpersonality are concerned, Emmanuel Levinas has focused on the exceptional mode of the other human's presence. A face that speaks to me questions me. Neither your nor my way of being fits into the world, although we find it obvious that we are "in" it. When you look at me or speak to me, you awaken me to a very different kind of reception than that which is appropriate to things. A human face demands a different response from the one suggested by a tree or a work of art.[7] However, artworks, animals, trees, and *all* phenomena present us with some form of alterity, albeit an analogous and differently surprising one.[8]

Once the other human's presence has awakened us to an alterity that forbids any final generalization, we might discover that all beings display their own alterity with suggestions and demands of their own. If this insight imposes itself on our attempt to write an ontology, a radical conversion takes place. While recognizing that the encounter with the alterities of all beings' being presents itself as the privileged place where the truth of being might show its multifarious irreducibility, one feels inclined to understand "the end of philosophy" as a slogan that prevents philosophy from finally commencing or recommencing its most basic task. For where, in the tradition of modern philosophy, do we find nonreductive elaborations of the modes of being that are proper to looking, speaking, addressing, promising, dedication, devotion, displaying, offering, showing off, proposing, begging, caressing, compassion, and so on? But if we do not even know how the personal, the human, the animal, and the divine *are*, what can we say about the *being* that makes them be such as they are? The question of the difference between an ontic study of the modes in which various beings are and an ontology of being itself cannot even be posed correctly if the analogy of the actual and possible modes of being has not been studied sufficiently. Those who resist this laborious task should at least justify the hypothesis of being's univocity that seems to command their quick transition from "metaphysics" to the thought of being itself.

For an ontology that begins with human intersubjectivity, all beings begin to speak in a manner of their own. Their suggestions invite some sort of dialogue. Of course, it is neither necessary nor desirable to reduce every manner of being to the manner that characterizes the provocative existence of another person, for human existence is not a résumé or *Aufhebung* of the entire terrestrial hierarchy. But the light that surges in the relation between you and me makes it possible that we recognize in nonhuman beings as well a life of their own that lets them speak about themselves to us.

Things, too, present a face to me; they invite me to a recognition of their own "right" to be and shine. They require an appropriate respect of their qualities. The emergence of beings is offered as a response to the human desire of the ultimate desirable, but this response demands that I correspond to it by honoring the specificity of its peculiar manner of appearing. Addressing, speaking, offering, giving, demanding, and responding thus become basic categories that serve to describe the different modes of being of the various beings. These modes cannot be reduced to a concept of being that is so general that it becomes purely formal and completely void. The law of being, at this level of phenomenality, is corresponsive; the Desirable is sought as an agreement that does not abolish but confirms the difference between our central desire and all beings encountered during its lifelong exploration. Perfect correspondence between a subject's opening up and the given that surprises us constitutes a form of mutual justice, more or less comparable to the caresses through which a musician converses with his instrument. From this perspective it is no longer entirely unbelievable that the essence of being expresses a profound benevolence. If love is the promotion of another being's essence according to the possibilities of its own nobility, it generates as well the self-giving of all appearances as the blessing with which it is welcomed. Since I am not the master of the world, this blessing is a prayer. To greet a being would then always be an act of gratitude and hope; the secret of epistemology—successful correspondence—would be a religious approach.[9]

If the eye that listens becomes a caress, it will be touched by the sincerity of things. Plants, animals, stars, rocks, homes, landscapes, texts, and works of art form a choir, whose singing affects the subject with a corresponsive tonality. There are many different ways of dealing with the ensemble of existence, but it is perhaps possible to formulate some general conditions upon which such agreement depends. For example, in order to obtain the desired peace that makes us feel at home in the world, Desire must be attuned to the ensemble of beings, while preventing or surpassing the always imminent war between beings. Since one cannot simply count on a spontaneous accord of all beings, the peace of correspondence demands manners of enjoyment and suffering that surpass the injustice of discordance through agreement with the positive essence of the very beings that make one suffer. Such a suffering takes part in the benevolence with which the being of beings touches us. A fundamental ethics would thus not only imply a phenomenology of the subject's goodness in response to the goodness of being's essence, but also an analysis of the treasons that pervert this double goodness into anxiety or hatred. The search for a pacific correspondence between sincere manifestations and appropriate responses is the key to an ethical ontology that, motivated by the desire for peace, includes patience and tolerance.

By his untiring analyses, Emmanuel Levinas has shown how the narcissism that distorts Desire is refuted by the discovery that mineness consists in responsiblity for the life of others and that the suffering implied in this responsibility confirms me in a manner of being more my own than the search for happiness. The longing that motivates human beings is not egotistical, though its concretization might always be more or less perverted. If it is true that Desire has dedicated me before I had any chance to accept or reject this dedication, it has also ordered me to take care of the life that is entrusted to me as mine, without leaving me a single instant at my disposal to choose or refuse this task. The consent necessary to embrace and accomplish this task comes later and the quality of this consent characterizes my response to the existence of the "I" that I sense in myself "as an other."[10] The devotion to this "I" in myself can and ought to be as "disinterested" and as interesting as the devotion that makes me responsible for the other. By insisting too exclusively on the opposition between my being-for-the-other and the pitiless advance of my spontaneous inclinations, I would forget that my most fundamental and pure spontaneity lies in the longing of the unchosen Desire that constitutes the human essence. If my selfhood excluded the heteronomy of my being-for-the-other, I could never fully rejoice in others' being-good and being-well.

Whatever the exact relation between my benevolence toward others and my concern about my own well-being may be, it is important that the erotic striving toward a summit of fulfillment be transformed by the discovery that it is better to give than to receive. Along the way it becomes clear that longing orients me towards a generosity that, like Desire itself, is granted, rather than chosen or invented. The gift of self implicit in the devotion that precedes my choices is given—at least virtually and as a vocation—before self-consciousness begins. From its start every human movement attempts to be a praxis of autodonation. It realizes such a praxis by concretizing its desire in more or less adequate responses such as gestures of respect, acts of justice, signs of friendship, services of compassion and acts of love, thus producing more or less good constellations of being. Does the success of such concretization compose overall well-being? Giving oneself is central in the being-good that corresponds to the proper essence of humanity, but if this giving is given to me neither by the other nor by myself, the appropriate response to it cannot be limited to the perfection of interhuman relations.

God

If God loves the universe of beings to the point that He/She/It grants them not only shining and splendor but existence itself, God is the originary and exemplary giving. He must then be the desirable and lovable by excellence and transcendence. However, God is neither a being nor an event, nor the totality of all beings, for all of that (*ta onta, ta panta,* or *to pan* of the philosophical tradition) is too finite to be absolutely desirable. The model of an ascension by degrees, as well as that of the step-by-step voyage towards an ultimate figure of human praxis carries with it a danger: God is not a summit, nor the end of a pilgrimage, nor the highest being, nor the final accomplishment of a promise that holds human life in suspense. If some great metaphysicians have sometimes used the names *ens supremum, causa prima,* or even *causa sui* to speak about God, these names cannot be understood to suggest a reality above, below, or outside the framework of a universal hierarchy.[11] If it is difficult to understand the language of philosophical, poetic, or scriptural theology as a language that is neither ontic nor ontological, the reason resides in our inability to approach God through a direct access. Only a broken and doubled language, in which each phrase is partially refuted, then reaffirmed in order to be negated again, can refer to that which our deepest desire surmises, without possessing any concept or representation that could alleviate the extreme urgency of attaining at least a glimpse of it.

God is neither the summit nor the basis of a hierarchy. "The Most High" is not a superlative, but the *Incomparable.* In their encounter with Desire, all beings refer us to God by giving themselves as given in their giving of themselves, but there is an infinite abyss between their self-giving and the giving that conditions this gift. Nevertheless, we cannot separate the absolutely Desirable from the desirability of the beings we encounter in our exploration of the universe.

Every being speaks a language of its own, which signifies its givenness as given by a more original giving. Everything that happens suggests a giving that constitutes its very existence; it is given as a giving of itself. To signify what one is as a self-given gift testifies to a grace spread throughout the universe of being. If all is grace, the being of beings is sacramental.

The human response to the appearance of beings lends them a voice. It attempts to say what this voice signifies to the Desire that listens to it and to respond as well as it can through an appropriate comportment. But how should we translate the testimony of beings about their being given into language? How can we unfold the sacramental signification of all that exists? How can we verify the feeling that the absolutely Desirable can be found neither outside, above, at the end, or at the beginning of the history of beings, nor in the totality or in a part of this ensemble? How can we understand the "in" of the presence in such phrases as "God is *present in* the world, history, the soul, life and death?"

If God reveals Godself, this is done only by providing the appearance of beings with a theomorphic signification and by giving human beings a sense for deciphering this signification. This sense must accompany the Desire that prepares and surpasses our discoveries. If God creates the universe because he loves it before it even exists, all is grace. Thus, the essence of all beings must be marked by a gracious manner of appearing. Our welcoming of the phenomena presupposes then that we acquire a sensibility, a taste, an ear, eyes, and a mouth that are sufficiently purified to testify to this grace. An appropriate response to the different varieties of being thus recognizes the gracious character of their self-giving as gifts of grace.

But how can a "self" be given? How can one think of a substance that is autonomous enough to give *itself* and yet, at the same time, signifies and materializes an Other's love? This would be impossible if this Other were a being or the being of beings (which, as such, would necessarily be finite and thus opposed to another self). It seems possible, however, if the Other is nothing other than a Giving that gives everything it has or is without diminishing either its own grandeur and glory, or the glory and grandeur of the beings to which it gives itself. Such a donation of oneself posits, strengthens, and enhances the existence and the value of its other in letting this other be itself, without reducing its alterity. The original self-giving generates or creates other self-givings that are either equal or similar to itself and thus reveals itself as that which conceals and reveals itself in the givenness of its others.

In his treatise *On the Trinity,* Richard of Saint Victor explicates how such a generosity constitutes the life of God himself. Starting with the Anselmian axiom that God is greater or better than which nothing can be thought, Richard appeals to an experience that everybody can have and according to which "nothing is better or more perfect than charity."

> Let everyone interrogate his or her own experience; without any doubt or contradiction one will discover that, just as there is nothing better, so there is also nothing more delightful than charity.[12]

This axiom permits the transition from an ontology to a theology of the Good by identifying the perfection of being with the Good beyond the being of all beings. The infinite essence of charity is that which does not allow the thought of anything that is greater or better. It is tempting to think that this charity is exhausted in creating the universe by love and saving humanity by compassion. Such condescension reveals indeed why we love charity beyond everything else that is desirable. However, the charity of God cannot stop at loving the created universe, for this cannot be loved with the unsurpassable manner "greater or better than which" one cannot think of anything more charitable. Creation is an infinitely dissymmetric relation between two incomparables. In it everything that comes to existence is given, but God cannot love this gift with an infinitely infinite love, because it is, as finite, not infinitely lovable. Unsurpassable charity can only be realized perfectly in the self-giving by which God gives Godself totally and divinely. As *being the Good* whose *essence* is the infinite *goodness* of divine self-giving, God gives everything that God is, even divinity itself. It is given to an Other who, in virtue of this giving, always already has received divine existence as his own. The original Gift is the gift of the divine essence itself, while the Other to whom this gift is given, is the same self-giving, but now as given to him. The primary self-giving generates the hypostasis of a God-Self who gives itself insofar as it is given. This Gift is also the first Speech that resounds in all the speeches and languages of the universe. The Word that is generated in God is understood diversely in what the phenomena tell us: human others, the trees, the stars, the animals, the rocks, and our own selves address themselves to us in their own idioms and accents. Appropriate responses to this speaking constitute Correspondence, when Desire in us responds to the Word that translates the self-giving life of God into the limited idiom of beings' voices. Where in the universe does the Speaking of that Word become so audible that one cannot doubt it? There where created beings, even at the risk of losing their pleasures and life, give themselves to others by giving testimony to the Origin. In other words, there where Desire drives people to share their goods and to accept the pains that accompany all serious love.

The monument of this suffering love and the model of all serious giving is found in the Passion of Jesus Christ. Here the initial giving attains a *kenosis* that makes it almost unrecognizable. The perfect gift of self in compassionate solidarity with finite beings—the emptying of the infinite—renders God so humble that he strangely seems to disappear. God reveals God's strange grandeur by being scattered among finite beings in a terrifying universe that seems abandoned, cold and graceless, without charity. The positivism of finite beingness is the great temptation of every philosophy that narrows the scope of Desire to the totality of beings. The truth depends on the perspicacity with which we distinguish the desperate nothing that permeates the universe from the "None of all that" which is the incognito of grace.

The Passion in which God reveals the secret of giving is repeated everywhere in more or less convincing ways. As a sacrament of self-giving, the Cross resounds in the suffering of all the mothers and fathers and friends who accept to live and die for those whom they love. Among animals we find echoes of this charity and some poets have thanked flowers, fruits, and trees for their generosity.[13] Even the inexorable law of universal generation and corruption might be interpreted as a trace of the "diffusive" generosity of the Good that accepts death so that others might live.[14]

Faith and Thought

Is this interpretation of the universal being-given not simply pure speculation rather than justified by a phenomenological analysis of lived experiences? Without discussing here what we could learn from three thousand years of experience, revelation, and rigorous thought, I would simply like to state that all of my remarks presuppose the impossibility of separating the elements that modernity calls "philosophical" from the great spirituality in which Jewish and Christian faith has unfolded over time.[15] Educated in this heritage, one cannot be a *tabula rasa,* and this is a great fortune for those who refuse to replace this faith with the faith in autonomy that characterizes modern philosophy. If this chapter has proposed an *argumentum convenientiae* that resembles certain arguments of the past in an attempt to actualize them in contemporary language, it was motivated by the hope that its "convenience" is recognizable as a phenomenological expression of authentic experience. In this hope I would like to end this chapter with the following conclusion.

The encounter of Desire with the universe of finite beings includes the humble experience of a grace spread throughout and a kind of suffering that paralyzes every attempt to justify this suffering. Peace is not possible unless we learn how to reconcile the enjoyment of the world's splendor with the acceptance of its horrors in the hope that together, in some hidden way, they make sense. If, thanks to the sufferings and joys of purification, we discover that, in the final account, the Desirable coincides with the practice of self-giving and that this practice historically is accompanied by suffering, this passion for the Other is not merely a beautiful speculative idea, but a purified life. If, with Richard of Saint Victor, we think that such a passion, as inherent to the Good, is the essence of God, this thought can resound as the response that is desired from time immemorial. If compassion, as actuality of that passion, is the life of God on earth, Desire implicates us in "l'amor che move il sole e l'altre stelle."[16]

Freedom and Grace:
Some Reflections on Gratitude

Some popular interpretations of the Christian religion have integrated, and thereby consecrated, a pre-Nietzschean but modern conception of freedom. Should we see this absorption as an authentic translation of faith, or rather as a distortion that is all the more seductive insofar as it appears to allow Christian theology to catch up with the modern world? A response to this question requires a critical examination of the modern idea of freedom. One may think that the central criterion for such a critique is to be found in the experience of Christian life as lived in exemplary fashion independently of any scientific, philosophical, or theological reflection. However, as I will try to show, experience itself demands a critical purification from all of its anti-Christian ingredients.

To compare the spirit of modern philosophy to the spirit of the Christian religion is obviously a vast task. I will restrict myself here to some reflections on one element of Christian life that seems fundamental: *gratitude,* while focusing on the contrast between Christian gratitude and a particular conception of freedom. More specifically, I will defend the thesis that one typically modern conception of freedom and liberation is too narrow to do justice to the Christian experience of gratefulness. However, we must also submit this experience to a critique of its authenticity and in so doing learn from modern and postmodern criticisms of religion.

Freedom and Rights

Modern philosophy defines freedom as autonomy of the thinking Ego. "I" project and determine my actions by my own choices, which are or should be led by my insights. The law that rules my actions is not foreign to me. Instead of being imposed by other persons, the state, or the church, the fundamental moral, political, and religious law is what is most proper to me. My reason itself is my law. To act well is to obey reason, that which is most essential in myself. I obey "my innermost self," "myself." To live humanly means to develop my ownmost possibilities as expressions of my autonomy, to make my empirical existence rational, or to incorporate and materialize my freedom. I show my liberty, the "I can" of my freedom, by enacting my self-actualization in obedience to human reason in me.

Since all humans are in need of corporeal and thus worldly self-realization, competition and conflict are inevitable. How can the multiplicity of autonomous egos be prevented from degenerating into war? As soon as we become aware that there are many "egos," we discover that freedom implies rights, for right is nothing other than the demanding aspect of an ego's autonomy insofar as this faces other egos. A theory of autonomy thus necessarily develops into a philosophy of human rights. The only ethics possible on this basis is a philosophy of justice in the strict sense of the word: render to each what belongs exclusively to him or her! From the perspective of a thinking ego who surveys individual humans (i.e., egos that are demanding and therefore in competition with each other), such a philosophy develops institutions that must guarantee their equality. It unfolds a systematic theory of the universe, according to which the meaning of the world depends on the unfolding of human freedom. It demands a practice that, through planning and technique, creates a more just world in which each individual has a place and a chance to acquire status, space, and property. A universal overview guides the hands and mouths that transform the world into a "second," more human and just, "nature" through diplomacy, peace treaties, revolutions, and reforms. Everyone is required to participate through democratic mechanisms in the domination of nature and the utilization of the material and human resources that are needed for this grandiose project.

What could be more admirable than the desire for a world shared fraternally by all adults and children, a world in which everybody renders unto others what is their due? However, this world is animated by *demand*. Nothing is gratuitous. What gives itself gratuitously is called, sometimes contemptuously, "charity." Anyone who fails to contribute to the construction of a free and just world through work or political engagement is not worthy of respect, but we will tolerate such persons on the fringes of society as long as they do not disturb our great project. Good human beings, however, are workers who transform the world into useful property.[1]

Disappointments

Existence under the aegis of rights and freedom is in the end disappointing. The ideal of equal opportunity has not been realized, and it will never be realized as long as egoism has not disappeared—except perhaps for a short time within small groups of real friends. The widespread desire to unleash one's powers and enrich oneself necessarily leads to domination by those who enjoy a greater opportunity than others through their natural constitution or legacy, or through their own efforts. In order to abolish all inequalities, it would be necessary to prevent or repress not only all differences in nature and fortune, but also the possibility that individuals make themselves unequal in power, influence, ability, or property. Such a repression would suppress individual choice in the name of universal freedom. Even if the desire for such equality is not a form of jealousy (and thus itself an expression of egoism), its effect is murderous. Moreover, many bad things, such as jealousy, hatred, loneliness, and contempt cannot be repressed by external means.

The many disappointments that, in the meantime, have disturbed the enlightened prospects of modernity have caused a widespread pessimism. If we fight this pessimism in the name of altruism or the common good, we have already broken the circle of modern autonomy because we then advance a principle that differs from the ego's demands: other persons should be considered to be at least as important as I, and there is no longer any reason to call the subject whose self must be respected above all, "I" or "ego," and not you, she, we, or they. Likewise, the zeal to overcome the solitude and suffering of those who arouse compassion presupposes a principle other than that of a multiple "I." You and he and she are as important, as absolute, and as much a starting point, as I.

The "free world" has kindled considerable resentment, not only amidst the great mass of those who have limited opportunities, but even amongst the elite itself. The loudly proclaimed ideal of fraternal freedom has not been capable of realizing itself. Those who proclaim it do not practice what they preach; even if their intentions are sincere, they have not fundamentally changed the discriminating institutions. Most of them live on the prosperous side of the world; while proffering ideas about equality and universal development, they enjoy the agreement of their happy club. Words like "fraternity" or "family of man" have become diplomatic slogans that protect their power and wealth against those who live in the margins until the moment when they might become in turn masters and possessors of the world.

The "free world" is at a loss concerning the justification of the massive suffering it continues to inflict on its slave nations, colonies, and international underclasses. Social and political suffering has often been interpreted as an inevitable phase in the ongoing liberation of peoples from fatalism and poverty, while whatever fails to fit our utilitarian conceptions is viewed as devoid of meaning. Those who do not share in that liberation are deemed to suffer uselessly. They have no consolation apart from the hope of another world, identical to this one in all respects except that those who are unhappy here will finally receive their share of liberty and happiness there. What one cannot attain by the work of one's own hands, however, must be hoped for as a gift of charity.

The disgust spawned by such a hypocritical world easily develops into a form of hatred. If hedonism is no more than an illusory evasion, and if heroism is too superhuman, rejection of this world is almost inevitable, and this can degenerate into a boycott of existence: systematic carnage, self-destruction, and warring against procreation.

A critique of modern freedom is not complete unless it evaluates the goals that the project of autonomy wants to realize. Two distinct tacks deserve attention here: (1) that of well-being, which the modern epoch has primarily developed in its practical and theoretical varieties of utilitarianism, and (2) that of a moralism that considers all forms of utilitarianism to be expressions of self-centered hedonism. Kant tried to formulate a synthesis of these two finalities, when, like Job's friends, he founded the demand for ultimate happiness on the exigency that good intentions, though willed for their own sake, should be rewarded, whereas evil, the result of seduction by sensibility, ought to be punished. Because Kant could not conceive of happiness in any other way than as a deserved or undeserved happiness, he represented God as the ultimate judge who dominates the world in order to separate the sheep from the goats. Is Kant's conception paradigmatic for modern ethics? Does the modern idea of freedom necessarily submit philosophy to a combination of moralistic exigencies and hedonistic utilities?

Hope and Gratitude

A reflection on the relation between the Christian religion and freedom must define to what extent the modern ideal of freedom is in accordance with or contradicts the liberation heralded by the prophets and Jesus Christ. Does the Resurrection correspond to a refurbishing of human society? Is the Revelation a move toward greater justice and universal happiness? Can we interpret the Promise through the preferred concepts of modern history?

The Promise, realized obscurely as a principle of Resurrection and Transfiguration, proclaims a Life beyond life, and a Kingdom beyond the kingdom of "this world." Is it possible to understand all these expressions without falling back into another "world" that would simply be the prolongation or double of "this world here"? The promised Life bursts and breaks all the images and concepts of life that we are able to construct through our idealization. However, that Life must be discovered here and now, through a transformation of the world by other ways of living and celebrating it. True Life is neither a posthumous reward à la Kant nor a spiritualist heroism that scorns the satisfactions of corporeal existence. If it involves human liberation, it must emancipate our body and our history through a kind of inspiration that no worldly impossibility can destroy.

Here and now, the promised life comes about in the mode of *hope* and *gratitude*. Without being a fulfilled presence, it is really present despite its "not yet" and thanks to its "already past." It touches and summons from out of a past that always holds and a future that already rouses those who believe. Gratitude and hope are characterized by a certain art of receiving whatever gratifies us, who cannot make it happen ourselves. Neither fully productive nor purely passive, they reach out toward the completion of a reality whose essence has already been given. Neither what I hope for nor that for which I am grateful can be demanded as a right, however. Summoning someone to be generous destroys the other's generosity and my own gratitude by transforming them into aspects of right. Generosity, giving, grace, gratitude, and hope introduce a dimension that is "more" or better than right. If the secret of life were found in the demands of modern freedom, donation and gratitude would be marginal or superfluous.

If I hope to succeed in accomplishing a task, or if I feel gratitude after its completion, my feelings testify to the fact that I am not the absolute master of what I am joyous about; even the result of what I choose to do is a kind of fate that happens to me. Also in relation to myself, gratitude and hope thus exceed the demands of free and righteous activity.

Hope and gratitude are more radical experiences than autonomy. All that I have and all that I am, I owe to an Other whom I will never be able to replace. Let us look at this more closely with regard to gratitude.

Three elements here seem essential. (1) There is in gratitude a certain joy or contentment due to the existence of a situation, an action, an event, a thing of beauty. (2) This existence and the joy it brings me here and now are not or not entirely produced by my own efforts, but, at least to a certain extent, are also "given." (3) What happens to me is not a result of chance, occurring "just like that"; the occurrence of this constellation, the fact that the "given" comes about here and now and in this unique way, has a meaning, a meaning that is favorable to me. Through my enjoyment I admit that there is someone or something that "wishes me well."

I can delight in a situation, a gift, a success, but also in my own activities or talents. In both cases, I experience them as received from and "given" by some other reality. I then affirm that someone or something other than me "wishes" me well and "wants" me to have what I delight in. I am happy about what happens to me or because of me, thanks to a "benevolence" that is not my own.

In a religious context, gratitude professes that all things are given. "*Tout est grâce*."[2] Not only do I find myself "involved in" and formed by the history and culture from which my life borrows most of its content, but on a more radical level, I am also aware that we are carried by something or someone that encompasses the ensemble of our histories, both great and small. Through this experience, an experience that surpasses any simple emotion, I recognize that an "Other" arranges a certain whole to which the singular here and now is related. It awakens in me an almost imperceptible peace quite different from the climate that surrounds the righteous sovereignty of a universal Judge. "To hold the world in one's hand" can have two meanings that are utterly opposed: it can indicate the technological project of submitting nature to the demands of an emancipated utilitarianism, but it can also refer to the concern of a benevolent providence that surpasses usefulness by wisdom and intimacy. The enjoyment felt in gratitude for the latter's "murmuring breeze"[3] is very different from that experienced in the boisterous domination of a universe. These two interpretations of our being in the world do not necessarily exclude one another, but they compete for supremacy.

Critique

The experience of gratitude as it has just been described invites a critique, not only because of modern philosophy's suspicion about all affective experiences but primarily because the very desire that drives us to seek God is the potential critic *par excellence*.[4] Because it is discontent with all the satisfactions that claim to be definitive, Desire judges them too shallow and impure to terminate the quest.[5] It breaks out of the circle that encloses Ego's autarky by prompting us to less possessive discoveries. What does this entail for gratitude?

Before critiquing the phenomenon of gratefulness as such, we must question the language in which it has been described above. In applying the metaphor of *gift* to the constellation God-World-Subject, do we not run the risk of falling into a cheap kind of pious imagery? Believers are fond of grateful expressions, but how can we translate their sentiment and the grace to which it responds into a reflexive language?

God is not outside, above, or behind the world. He is not a subject that I can meet and see before me as I can others. When I confess that the universe originates in God, I know that I cannot speak to him in the way that I speak to human interlocutors; God is not an alter Ego with whom I can associate in a friendship similar to human intimacy.

I am not absolutely separated from the world either; my sensations and my life story witness to my entanglement. If everything I possess and do, even my very existence, is given to me, how can I conceive of the necessary distance between my received existence and my ego that receives it? I cannot take a distance from myself so as to accept my being-there from the hands of God, for this would presuppose that I exist before actually existing. And yet my experience of my existence contains a qualified kind of acceptance. I can open myself to the whole of my always-already-being-in-existence and embrace it in grateful confirmation of my ability to give thanks, but I can also respond to it with grumbling bitterness. My openness and my always already given existence encompass one other: through an act of total reflection I realize that my existence (including all reflection) is not justified by any necessity, though I am invited to approve of it in gratitude. One can bless both the totality of one's own being and that of the whole universe while joyfully acknowledging the contingency of their existence.

Gratitude and Modernity

If we try to clarify the phenomenon of gratitude by using the ontological language of our culture, this does not mean that we impose the constraints of the latter's patterns on the former. These constraints themselves and the entire conceptuality tied to modern experiences and projects deserve to be critiqued by showing their possibilities and impossibilities. However, once we have examined the constraints of modern language, should we not retrieve and correct that language from the perspective of a more authentic religion than the one that modern thought has been able to thematize? If so, the project of emancipation and the construction of a universally just world could, perhaps after purification, be transformed into elements of contemporary religion. Once again, we would be instrumental in the theological baptism of an originally non-Christian philosophy. Once again, a "profane" philosophy would have contributed to the renewal of revealed religion.

Such a hermeneutics presupposes that the mainspring and the essence of modern philosophy is not completely alien to the religious experience we want to express with its help. If they were contradictory, the dimension of religion could only be recovered through a rigorous mortification of secular thought. Then we should be much less friendly to modern philosophy than we would like to be. If modern conceptuality is rooted in an existential ground that is incompatible with gratitude and adoration, it cannot serve to translate the essence of religion unless it is *radically* converted and transformed. This would explain why, with few exceptions, modern philosophies of religion have taken the form of reductions or attacks. At the same time, it would explain why much religious thought has taken refuge in the literary genre of spiritual or mystical writings, whereas its theology has clung to paraphrases of classical texts, weakening their force by mixing in some modern elements without sufficiently transforming them.

Wonder

An attempt to speak of gratitude in a philosophically respectable language can begin from a fourth element of grateful "feeling," one we have not yet named, but which bridges the elements described above. Between joy and the affirmation of the meaningful "givenness" of all that exists, there is a kind of *wonder-and-admiration*.[6]

The existence of the beings for which we are grateful cannot be understood as self-evident. The amazement they cause cannot be abolished by understanding their structure and content, not even by a complete reconstruction or recreation in thought, if such were possible. The project of theoretical mastery collapses here. The fact that "things," we, the universe, happen to exist, does not correspond to any necessity or right. No one can claim existence; neither can anyone demand to be such and such. The very fact of our existing eludes all calculation and surpasses any reason that attempts to deduce the possibilities and demands of freedom. Yet the existence of those beings is reasonable and understandable, though not fully comprehensible, if generosity is the principle of all principles.

For one who sees everything in the light of the Good, nothing is a matter of course, but all that happens suggests a reason for approval. The truth of existence is then not to be reinvented via deduction, but, more than being an invitation to thorough reflection (which should not be neglected) it prompts us to admiration and delight. Certainly, the occurrence of evil in its many forms cannot be admired as the incarnation or shining of the Good, but, as the partial destruction of a more primordial order, it can be recognized as derivative. The horror inspired by it can tempt us to a certain dualism, but it cannot eliminate our admiration for the splendor that is contaminated or spoiled by it.

Wonder and admiration are not primarily caused by extraordinary or unheard-of things, but rather by the most simple and daily things and events that unexpectedly appear in a new light. Volcanic eruptions or tornadoes are too theatrical to open up the "dimension" of truth. All too easily, they fix our attention on themselves, or they make us believe in gods who enjoy melodrama. The truth that beings, through their being, reveal to us depends on the quality of the eyes that see them and the light that makes them perceptible.

Neither does wonder resemble the kind of curiosity aroused by inexplicable things. For it knows from the outset that even if we find an explanation, this would not in any way eliminate the amazing aspects of their existence: the fact that such a thing, such a history, such a being comes to exist here and now in its own surprising way remains wonderful. Thus, there cannot be an end to wonder. Therefore, it is not true that the task of philosophy commands us to transform an initial *thaumazein* into the lucid coherence of a self-evident system.[7] Admiration of being as such encompasses all other experiences and thought itself. In some sense, it is "without end."

Freedom itself, long imprisoned by the Kantian dilemma that opposes the *necessary* law of practical reason to the *arbitrariness* of a will assailed by sensible tendencies, receives a new meaning when being as such is disclosed as "given." Admiration refers to a higher and deeper reason or meaning than that which controls, calculates, demands, comprehends, and, in all cases, possesses and rules itself. This new meaning is called *goodness*. It cannot be captured through conceptual integration, which would progressively remove the surprising character from all that is or happens. On the contrary, the more the experience of splendor is internalized with the help of reflection, the greater grows one's awareness of a profound deficiency in comprehension. This should not be a cause for distress, however, because the inadequacy of integration only proves that the overwhelming "part" of being far outstrips our capacity for mastering. The only way to assume the new meaning announced in wonder is to enter into the movement of goodness that is disclosed by it and to participate in its generosity by becoming not only grateful but also generous oneself.

Gratitude, like affirmation, admiration, contemplation, and joy, expresses itself either by a silence that "caresses" the contours and qualities of all that shines, or else in a language that, far from looking down on daily reality, may emphasize its meaning through poetic or religious exaggeration.

Two opposing temptations that spring from the same source threaten us here: (1) the temptation of doubling the historical world, by imagining an eminent, perfectly simple, beautiful, reasonable, absolutely nonviolent and happy superworld, the order of which we try to glimpse in this, the only real, world; and (2) the temptation of bracketing or repressing the question of God. The latter, provisionally or decidedly atheist, option cannot be accompanied by admiration unless it divinizes the world. The being of the world is then celebrated as an autarkic substantiality and wonderment discovers itself surrounded by gods and demons. In the first option we should ask ourselves whether the critique of religion from Feuerbach to Nietzsche and beyond have not shown that such a superworld robs human existence of its own grandeur.

To escape pantheism or polytheism, the biblical tradition has rejected all hypostases outside God and criticized all the images that claim to capture the divine. At the same time, it cherishes a host of metaphors to name the unique God, while denying that they really describe the One who shatters idols.

Metaphors

Perhaps religious symbols are first and foremost attempts to articulate the admirability of natural and historical beings. In pointing to the "Origin" or "Source," metaphors emphasize and intensify the impressive appearance of the given. Analogical imagination is a marveling way of interpretation.

To know what a rock is, one must realize that it is "given" by One who is "like" a rock, but at the same time "gives" and, in some obscure sense, "is" mountains, trees, flowers, bees, men, women, children, oceans, storms, silence, and a realm of peace. But in playing on the "like" that separates and binds the worldly phenomena to their "Origin," how can we avoid making God a double of the world, a sublime Reality behind this one, a Totality gathering all the archetypes of the copies found here below, and a complete Satisfaction that overwhelms all our unsatisfied needs and desires and disappointments?

What exists is not only semblance. It seems to occur "just like that," but symbolic celebration confesses that its concrete existence contains a secret. It reveals something that through and in and as all beings approaches us without ever becoming an object: a source of light that is neither light nor source, although all beings owe their own being and shining and truth to it. Without making those beings themselves divine, symbolism lets them express what permits them to exist; it lets them "speak." By highlighting their perfection, the metaphoric evocations do not split the universe into different parts, one worldly and the other divine, but they shed a light that emphasizes the finitude of all beings and their pointing beyond.

The illumination of the world through religious metaphors points toward a light that we can neither see nor imagine, an invisible light, a nonlight that grants meaning, and thus illuminates: an illuminating obscurity.

Symbolic constellations that are limited to the stage of aesthetic interpretations culminate in the free contemplation of a self-centered regard. One must transcend this level to be open to God's own clear-obscure. By using symbols that are mutually or intrinsically contradictory, we may overcome imagination and comprehension, but not through the integration of their contradictions into a higher totality, nor by an absolute destruction. While adjusting and purifying our most promising analogies, we simultaneously keep and degrade them. The nothing to which the mortification of metaphors refers the searcher has the structure of a "Yes-and-No-and-Yes" that, as a doubly negative kind of Amen, can neither be replaced by a conclusive

Aufhebung, nor by a purely destructive No. A quest that follows metaphoric references may develop into an adoration that no longer knows how to name its orient.

The danger of all religious symbolism is that, behind or above this world, it can create a realm more ideal than, but still very similar to, the only reality in which we live. Symbolism must free the phenomena of this world to make them speak of that which, without constituting a superworld, escapes the intentionality of dominating egos. Through mutual annihilation, metaphors can prevent us from representing God. If, in this context, we must speak of dialectic, we should remember the dialectic of Plato's *Parmenides:* the attention of the soul is freed up, not to perceive or comprehend, but to affirm the One that cannot be represented or conceived. The war of metaphors can be seen as imaginary counterpart to the systematic destruction of the conceptual categories we are tempted to apply in our thinking about the Unique. However, the opposing images and concepts of this sort of dialectic do not have equal power, for even if an assertion is endlessly challenged and dismantled by its imaginary or conceptual negation, in the end it returns— enhanced by its negations—and prevails. The dialectical "No" is no more an annulment of the "Yes" it purifies than the devil is the murderer of God.

The following question then arises: how can we devote ourselves to this mortifying work? It presupposes a decentering of our attempts to grasp the beyond, but which force can bring about such a decentering? Our most profound desire. But even if this desire is our greatest critical force, the question remains: how do we awaken to its urgency? As Emmanuel Levinas has shown, it is the human other who awakens me: the search for God passes through ethics. Transcendent metaphors presuppose the other's transcendence.

Affective Elements

A critique of gratitude cannot be restricted to the concepts and images that express this experience more than anything else, it must examine its affective side. If happiness, joy, or peace are essential elements of gratitude, do they not make us fall prey to some sort of subjectivism, be it sublime or not?

As a first response to this objection, we can underscore the gulf that separates the pleasure of self-sufficient use and contemplation from the grateful pleasure of singing the glory of God. The peace that goes with gratitude is neither demanded nor accepted as a right; it is received as a surprise

("I didn't count on it and I didn't deserve it") or as an *excess* (the gift given to me surpasses everything I thought I needed). The gratuitous character of existence as gift, the excess of its grace, is experienced in a special type of indifference: if my acceptance welcomes shocking and painful surprises with the same eagerness as enjoyable ones, it shows that the very gesture of giving is more important than the gifts it gives.

Fidelity is tested by suffering. Are there other methods to conquer the ambiguity of pleasure? Would a pleasurable existence without interruption be able to be authentically grateful or would it inevitably drown in hedonism? One can attempt to violently mortify oneself in order to overcome narcissism, but the meaning of such an endeavor remains ambiguous. The satisfaction hidden within the disdain for easy satisfactions accompanies our asceticism right to the summit of the slope. Very often it contains a sufficiency that does not open me to the Gift. Too much self-will hides in spiritualizing attempts to overpower our addictions through moralism, even if it is a moralism of the sublime.

A more authentic negation, and a suffering better protected against hypocrisy, is imposed by the existence of others. What is the religious significance of the ethical responsibility to which I am obliged by other humans? I owe myself to them. By revealing to me that my center is relational, the other breaks the hedonistic cycle that endlessly refers me only to myself alone. But in replacing the satisfactions of my exclusive self-possession, the other offers me a new meaning in which I can rejoice. Because the other exists, I can be devoted. Thus I discover a meaning beyond egoism. Although this meaning defines me, it also exceeds me: I will never be able to fully achieve what I—as devoted to others—already am. Thanks to the other, I am no longer "good for nothing."[8] The other grants me the possibility of giving thanks for my being here.

God and History

The ontology of a masterly ego is refuted by the other. But the meaning to which an other introduces me does not depend on the other's will; it is inherent in the other's and my being-there. The basic obligation imposed on me is not an effect of the other's power; the other's will itself is exceeded by it. The moral meaning of my life as revealed in the other's existence comes from a beyond that exceeds both of us. Being-for-the-other directs the history in which I participate and provides it with a human meaning. The other demands and is more than she is. Not, however, as if she represented a means for me to serve an Other who is greater than both of us. The human other can only be an "end," but my dedication to her coincides with my devotion to God. I have not chosen this double-sided dedication; it was born with me. Neither does it depend on the other's choice, nor is it the other's gift. By their very existence, my neighbor presents me with the other Other, who, without appearing, speaks to me through the words of human mouths.

The history of this one unique real world is the only domain in which we can prove our attachment to God. Once the purification of religious experience has reached the height of total dedication, we no longer desire a lonely tête-à-tête with God's transcendent Thou; to desire God's presence includes then the historical task of charity and justice without end. By participating in this history, one can become a gift—part of the movement by which the Good creatively overflows. Love of God is then experienced as coincident with love of all. Even the duality of an ascent that is followed by a return to the cave, though valid on a psychological plane (where times for prayer and times for action alternate), is then no longer an adequate image for the most radical "level" of our attachment to God and the neighbor. For to seek God *is* to devote oneself to others and vice versa. Here we concur with the humanistic projects that modern ethics has tried to legitimate. True believers cannot remain on the fringes of contemporary society, but the spirit that guides their participation is neither aggressive nor possessive.

Passion

The suffering that best delivers us from hypocrisy seems to be neither ascetic nor altruistic. When we must suffer without seeing how it could benefit either others or ourselves, our suffering seems to be meaningless. This compels us, then, to make an ultimate choice: do I bet on an ultimate meaning of existence or is the whole "business" in the end absurd?

Both despite and because of his misfortunes, Job learned to be amazed about the beauties and the horrors that fill the universe. Together they compose a gesture that invites us to a "Yes" without "but." To accept pain as much as joy, without posing conditions, to bless without controlling, is saying: "Amen." Despite everything, all is good. Gratitude does not abolish suffering, nor does it scorn pleasure. The happy indifference at the bottom of alternating emotions does not cling to any image or emotion that claims to capture God. Driven toward ever greater purity, Desire comes to recognize that even the most sublime experiences still involve too much self-will. All self-generated experiences must be overcome; for if we cultivate them for themselves, they form a shield. As finite modes of relation, experiences are only pointers. If we become too attached to them, they prevent us from concentrating on the real issue: the Uniquely Necessary that for and in itself is worthy of adoration. The indifference (or poverty) caused by the loss of all conceptual and imaginary certainty transcends all modes because (without ever seeing or touching) it is already touched, or even wounded by the completely "modeless."[9] As modeless and beyond all essence, God can neither be "had" nor "found," or rather God can be found only as remaining forever the one who is being sought (*ho zetoumenos,* to use Gregory of Nyssa's phrase).[10] To desire God without indulging in phantasmagoric romanticism implies that all the feelings, metaphors, names, concepts, philosophies, and theologies that have served us to approach him, are progressively consumed, so that we become very poor and eager to enjoy whatever the One who surpasses all, loves to share. Thus the extremism of Desire verifies that the search has no end, even though it thrives on constant communication with the Sought.

In renouncing fulfillment, I want myself to be as I have in fact become. Through poverty, I find myself in harmony with the hand that holds and directs history. Beyond the difference of joy and pain, the One's gesture dispenses both according to a plan that remains both generous and obscure. Some saints have convinced us that we can love this gesture more than the gifts it gives. They have discovered that "all is grace." The excess of peace they were allowed to experience crowned their insouciance even concerning their own salvation. True liberation seems to consist in overcoming all desires except the ultimate one: the desire to love God unconditionally.

Affective Theology/ Theological Affectivity

Complaints about "the God of the philosophers" have become commonplace. But who cares? Are we not agreed that philosophy is secular through and through? What about theology, however? Is its God better? More desirable, admirable, lovable, adorable? In order to be true, the God of theology should be as inspiring as the God of meditation, prayer, and devotion. Do we experience such an inspiring God while reading theological studies? If so, they are written in a spirit akin to the classics of contemplation; if not, what causes their deficiency?

Theological classics—and all theologians that continue the premodern tradition of Christian *theologia*—express a double responsibility: while instructing other members of the community to which they belong, they meditate about the God who brought them together. Theology is a kerygmatic charisma within their Church and, as apostolate and apologetics, a public enterprise in the surrounding culture. Within the community of faith theologians speak to the assembly, but as a response to God's revealing deeds and words, their speech is addressed to God. Responsivity with regard to God and responsibility for the faithful community together mark their language. Both orientations have a dialogical structure; but is this structure not often overwhelmed by a speaking *about* without end?

Theology

Following the development of Western epistemology, theology has become scientific, instead of remaining contemplative, anagogic, and mystical. Many Christians regret this development; but can we return to the contemplative forms of teaching and writing practiced in premodern times? Can we overcome the objectifying character of theology without losing the benefits of universally valid (and thus antisubjectivistic) thought? The following reflections focus on the responsive and dialogical character of contemplation. In particular, they emphasize some affective moments of any attempt to honor God as the *living* God.

Speaking

Science, literature, philosophy, and theology are modes of speaking (or writing) about things, persons, events, or other issues. Speaking can be done in many ways: by allusion or suggestion, narratively or evocatively, in a meditative or instructive manner, in letters, treatises, or prayers. Science and modern philosophy have insisted on the objectivity of their observations and thoughts. They study objects and try to capture data in the empirical and conceptual nets of their objectifying approach. A specific attitude is required for this approach: instead of being biased by "subjective" preferences or presuppositions, one should adopt a neutral stance toward objects in order to generate only those theses that others can recognize as universally valid. The overall perspective is panoramic: the universe lies open for an Archimedean point of view; to be discovered, it demands a freestanding location from which everything is observable. If subjective involvement is unavoidable—for example, when the issue is mortality, the meaning of life, or love—one should, as much as possible, bracket one's own interests to concentrate on the "objective" reality alone. Epistemologists still debate the meaning of the term "objective" in this context, but for the purpose of this chapter it can be characterized as either uninteresting or universally—i.e., not merely individually or particularly—interesting.

However, "objectivity" itself is the product of a *particular*—and thus unilateral—attitude. Therefore, to proclaim that the "objective" attitude is the only truthworthy one expresses a fundamental bias. Once caught in the objectifying attitude, one no longer sees or hears or tastes or smells or feels any other aspects than those that distinguish ob-jects from phenomena that show up in other, non-objective, ways. Indeed, things can be posited, dis-played, collected, numbered, dis-assembled, reconstructed, but many "data" do not fit into the framework of such objectivity, for example, smiling, speaking, thinking, feeling, moods, trust, love, confidence, friendship, engagement, concentration, action, motivation, person, and least of all, God.

Amazingly, the specialists of objectivity seldom notice that their own speech and writing show a structure that differs from the subject-object model, which many believe to be the supreme and universal one. In talking *about* the phenomena, they adjust them to the parameters of their objectifying game, but they cannot prevent themselves from *speaking to* others. Their interest in objects is overarched by another kind of interest: what they have discovered *about* their topic must be told, offered, handed over, *communicated to* and *shared with* other people.

There is no way to reduce speaking—or, in general, communication—to some form of the relation between a subject and an object. As *addressed to* another person, speaking is similar to giving, facing, greeting, turning toward, devotion, service, and other manners of addressing, all of which approach someone not as a "direct object" or "accusative," but instead as a "dative." *An addressee is not an object.* The addressee, the act of addressing, and the "addressor" disappear from our awareness as soon as we exclusively concentrate on the objective features of a person in front of us. We then no longer *face* this person; if our speaking treats her as an object, we speak *about* her, but this is possible only if we speak (about her) *to* her, *to* a third person, or *to* ourselves. By objectifying her, we are no longer involved in a personal relationship with her, although we might know many truths about her body and mind.[1]

Modern phenomenology has made us aware of several other intentionalities than the objectifying ones; but I do not know of any exhaustive description of *all* modes of phenomenality. Especially, the characterization of facing and being faced, greeting, addressing, giving, honoring, thanking, forgiving, and so on, is still quite underdeveloped, although worthwhile beginnings have been made. And yet, are not such phenomena more revealing about human existence, including religion, devotion, and faith, than all the objective, useful, and aesthetic phenomena that have been described and analyzed at length? Philosophy will hardly have begun, as long as we do not know what and how, e.g., greeting, praising, or thanking are. Does theology know these things already?

Speaking can be understood as a metaphor for all kinds of addressing, even those that originate in nonhuman phenomena. Dogs and birds, flowers and trees, even things and machines can speak to us, as many fables and myths have demonstrated. *All* the phenomena of the universe can be perceived as addressing us, each in its own characteristic way. The analysis of speaking might thus offer us a universal paradigm for clarifying the essence of phenomenality as such. If everything "speaks" to us, we are always invited to "respond" to such "speech." Which kind of openness and perception, which attitudes and reactions are suggested by the various instances and dimensions of this amazing universe?[2]

When I hear someone speak to me, I am forced to react: even silence is an answer, though it might express my contempt or anger or indifference. Speaking thus necessarily generates a response. If the response is spoken, the roles are reversed, which is the beginning of a dialogue. To speak is to be engaged in an exchange of questioning and responding. Appropriate responses do justice to a preceding address, and each response is a new provocation to new responses.

Some remarkable features of speaking are often neglected in philosophical studies of language. First, exclusive concentration on its systematic, structural, or textual character forgets the motivation and mobilization that language owes to its user's speaking. No text says anything unless an author brings it to life by addressing it to someone. Second, no one speaks unless he or she has been spoken to by other speakers. How, otherwise, would we have learned to speak? The history of speaking does not seem to have a beginning; when speaking, we compose variations on an ongoing tradition that enables us to communicate with interlocutors who belong to the same or another tradition.

An ethics of speaking could begin by reflecting about the exchanges demanded by any address. How do I respond appropriately when you turn to me in saying "Hello"? Appropriateness is honoring or being fair to the address that provokes us. My response must be right, fitting, befitting, adequate, decent, honest. The address itself suggests the contours of a befitting response, even if it leaves much to the addressee's trial and error. It excludes certain attitudes (for example, the objectification of both the speaker and the addressee) and it indicates some properties of a respectful answer, but it leaves several variations open. "Correspondence" could be a name for the perfect relationship between a phenomenon and the way it is accepted, perceived, allowed to exist and manifest itself.

The preceding remarks are much too sketchy for a phenomenology and ethics of speaking, but I hope that they are sufficient as introduction to an analysis of the communicative structure that characterizes not only speaking proper, but also human affectivity.

Affective Correspondence

To be exhaustive, phenomenology should pay attention to all the phenomena that compose the universe. But do all phenomena deserve attention? If a phenomenon draws our attention, it must be interesting, at least to some extent. A complete description of its being would therefore include a characterization of the mode in which it awakens our interest. What we deem interesting suggests that it has some (real or putative) worth or value. "Value" is therefore an aspect of all phenomena that succeed in drawing our attention.

Every phenomenon has its characteristic appearance and worth. It is the task of phenomenology to accurately distinguish and describe the entire variety of modes in which all kinds of things and persons, situations and occurrences draw our attention by being worthwhile. If such a reconnaissance of the universe succeeds, we will have acquired an overview of "the many ways in which being is."[3]

The most immediate dimension of our contact with the phenomena is found in affectivity. Phenomena affect us: in confronting them or being involved in phenomenal constellations, we are "touched." To be touched or impressed or affected is not a mere sensation, however; it is also a challenge— e.g., in the form of a shock or a temptation. A phenomenon that impresses me not only invites me to welcome its appearance through an appropriate mode of perception; it also guides my attempt to react in an appropriate way. To perceive what and how something *is,* I must be open to it: it wants to be taken for what it shows itself to be. It depends on my attitude whether a thing or person will be allowed to display its own being or rather is distorted or mistaken for something else. Not all phenomena are beautiful or welcome, but even the monstrous ones invite an appropriate response. *Affection is our basic form of responsivity.* The mixture of splendor and horror that fills the universe provokes the mixtures of our affectivity: admiration and horror, enthusiasm and anxiety, sympathy and avoidance, hope and fear, desire and hatred in many shades and degrees correspond to the phenomena's many modes of impressing us.

When myth and fables evoke the "speaking" of birds and trees or the ocean and the sky, they emphasize the "dialogic" structure of our dealing with the cosmos. Even on the level of our most immediate moods we are summoned to responsivity with regard to the being of all beings that emerge. Correspondence seems to be the law for all the levels of our dealing with the universe.[4]

The appropriateness of our responses to the phenomena that "speak" to us includes not only openness and sensitivity, but also attunement. Some appearances suggest joy, others call for anger or fear; still others make us fall in love. Emotional perfection presupposes accuracy and proportion; it heeds and respects, without understatement or exaggeration, all that comes to the fore. It is fair in evaluating each being's manifestation. It admires or abhors the *aisthetically* revealed *ousia* (essence) or *idea* of all occurrences.[5] Each thing or person or event demands an emotional response that fits and befits its challenge.

That each phenomenon contains a demand becomes clear when we realize that our affections are accompanied by a self-critical feeling that tests their degree of authenticity. On all the levels of our awareness, *experience evaluates itself* as soon as it takes shape. Emotions are a good example: while being angry or enthusiastic about something, I am already beginning to feel whether my reaction is genuine or fake, justified, proportionate or exaggerated, or otherwise failing in "justice."

With regard to our surroundings, our home and workplace, and the universe insofar as it concerns us, our affective response, rather than being a constellation of particular emotions, consists in a general and diffuse attunement that is so deep and permeating that often we are not even aware of it: a mood. We are in touch with the world by feeling ourselves involved in it, more or less at home or exiled, more or less at peace or struggling, and in any case, profoundly tuned by its rhythms and dispositions. In its difference from particular emotions, a basic mood is the way in which we let the universe attune us.

If perfect appropriation respects the phenomena, whereas many emotions in fact miss, mute, or exaggerate their appeal, an ethics of emotions and moods is necessary. How do we learn to be affectively accurate and just? What is a well-attuned mood if we have to live in this world, which is neither hell nor paradise?

Appropriation is not a one-sided task, as if either the human subject or the phenomena would sovereignly determine mutual agreement. Phenomena too can be primitive, underdeveloped, deficient, or cruel. What affects us, moves us, often urging us to change the affecting entity. For example, a block of marble may suggest its reshaping into a more harmonious form. Or the sight of a limping dog might move me to care for it. Or the atmosphere of a house might be so depressing that we have to change its windows and furniture. Or someone who shows a mixture of talent and lack of skill might make us wish to educate this person.

When some thing or situation suggests that I change it, my action and motivation should follow the orientation they seem to indicate. My intervention is normal and "natural" if it allows the challenging phenomenon to unfold in a "natural," "normal," and—if it is very promising—an ideal way. Such a response would at the same time make my dealing with the world proportionate. Correspondence can thus lead to peace and harmony. However, some horrible events or actions cannot lead to peace and harmony unless I oppose them through an appropriate degree of hostility and counter-violence. An ethics of our dealing with evil would prescribe appropriate expressions of indignation and hatred. Justice includes the courage of an honest fight.

Desire

Nothing could move me if I were not sensitive to its motivating force. What makes me respond to its challenge? All phenomena that interest us motivate us to active involvement, at least to some extent. But how could we be motivated toward such activity without moving ourselves, and how could we move ourselves without desire? Of each and every phenomenon that touches us, it can be said that it "moves by being desired" (*kinei hōs erōmenon*).[6]

Desire (*erōs*) is the innermost motor of all we do, but it would not move us, were it not awakened by a call from elsewhere. Of many desires we are not even aware until some phenomenon reveals to us that we "always already" have wanted it. Do we know—can we ever know—what we ultimately and originarily desire? That the ultimate desideratum differs from all the desiderata of our competing desires, needs, wants, and inclinations, becomes obvious through the endless repetition of disappointments that accompany our most satisfactory experiences. Though we find pleasure, joy, delight, and even bliss in the happy moments of our lives, all these moments also testify that we have not yet found the ultimately desirable. That does not show up among the phenomena of the universe, and the universe itself is not desirable enough for the insatiable passion that devours us. What we "in the end" and originally desire reveals its desirability via and through the many ends and "objects" that seem to promise it, but then again, in full experience, it disappoints our greatest passion. The Desirable is what we continually seek, although we never seem to find it. That it continually hides and withdraws, while motivating all we do, does not disprove its reality—on the contrary, it shows how infinitely open and erotic we are—but it teaches us that seeking itself, if done correctly, is the way of keeping in touch with the Sought.[7]

What then is the correct method of this approach? Since we focus here on human affectivity, our first question regards the role of moods, affections, and emotions in the ultimate quest.

If all the phenomena of the universe show themselves to be desirable or undesirable, what then makes them so? A tree, a girl, the sun, the light, a friend, the beloved, beauty, justice, love itself impress us as admirable and attractive, tempting, worthy of love—enjoyable. On the contrary, war, violence, greed, and arrogance confront us with the destructive presence of evil, awakening our scorn and wrath. Why do we enjoy or abhor certain facts?

Let's concentrate on the enjoyable ones first. If we welcome them in the right way, they make us feel content, at home, capable, growing in knowledge or strength, confident, reconciled, at peace. There are so many levels and forms of enjoyability in the universe! The Greek word *hēdonē*, covers many— not only quantitative, but primarily—*qualitative* differences in desirability and enjoyment. To be affected (i.e., touched and moved) differentiates into attraction, inspiration, enlightenment, shelter, warmth, appreciation, love, and so on. Each kind of phenomenality has its characteristic appeal; all kinds together reveal the manifold powers of *being* to captivate and "please" us. The worthwhile features of the universe respond to the multiplicity of our desires. Do they also respond to that Desire that seems to be disappointed each time it attempts to grasp the Desirable *par excellence:* the Orient that has no precise name, because it seems to be always "more" and "better" and different than anything that can be had?

Analogy and Denial

Being impressed by a particular phenomenon, I experience that it does fulfill some desire, but not completely. Its desirability is not a final answer to my erotic questioning: while offering itself, it stresses its limitation to "only this," "no more than this." Repeated enjoyment does not solve the question, but rather intensifies our nostalgia for a better answer. The enjoyable phenomenon "tries what it can," if I try to be as welcoming as possible, but it never wholly succeeds. It thus refers to another fulfillment that is really full: fully desirable without any disappointment. However, such a referral does not yet reveal the essence of the Desired itself.

The reference signified by the sun, the heavens, the ocean, the mountains, the landscape, the flowers, the friends, the upright, the truth itself, goodness, and all beauty not only refers, but also expresses. According to Bonaventure and others, the phenomenal universe is a mirror (*speculum*) through which we catch glimpses of the utterly Beloved.[8] God is radiant, friendly, lovable, great, just, benevolent, powerful; nothing greater and better than God can be thought; God is the greatest, the best, the highest . . . But God is also—and more so—different.

The similarity between the Good itself and all other goods, as suggested by the phenomenal references of Desire, is so dissimilar—their similarity is crossed out by an abyss so "great" and deep that no analogy survives unless it is *also*—and intensely—*denied*. While embracing some being as an image or trace of the Beloved, we must also experience the infinite difference that separates the Incomparable from all ("other") beings, including ourselves. This experience is the pain of never being able to grasp, see, touch, embrace, or feel the Sought itself. Such an experience is the highest or deepest form of suffering. What apophatic theology points to in words, affectivity experiences as an overwhelming emptiness. Any enjoyment of heaven and earth is then destroyed by the general disgust that hollows all phenomena. Though these continue to satisfy our needs and desires, they reveal a void—even a horror—more profound than all splendor, a nothingness that terrifies us as long as we have not learned to tolerate the loss of all satisfaction. The test of Desire lies in living without or despite, or even against, all desires, i.e., in the tolerance of not being *fully* and *radically* touched and moved by anything else than the One who makes the ultimate and original Difference. An element of agony and ongoing death (which cannot be chosen, but only consented to) belongs to the emotional verification of the ultimate quest. Without any shade of it, negative theology is a vain-glorious theory: a lie.[9]

That the apophatic confrontation with emptiness does not paralyze a "man or woman of desires,"[10] is due to their loyalty in embracing the dynamism that determines the human mode of being. A human being is an erotic animal and only idols can stop us from searching further. Further than the limits of the phenomenal universe. Or deeper. Or differently. In any case, *beyond*.

Since *beyond* is neither a spatial or temporal, nor an imaginative or conceptual determination, the dynamics of Desire keep us oriented despite our inability to represent the principle that moves us. Blindly we follow the orientation of a most original Affection. *Kineitai hōs erōmenos.*[11]

"Beyond" does not entail separation. God cannot be set off against the universe, as if God were only greater, better, "more beingly" than the—necessarily futile—totality of phenomena. Hegel's argument against any conception that understands the difference between the finite and the infinite as a separation is solid: a separated infinite would be finite because it leaves something out: an other, albeit "smaller" substance, which would fall outside God's completeness.

If the infinitely Desirable is not opposed to the universe, it does not compete with any part or whole of it. Therefore the affective, imaginative, conceptual, or ideal negation of the universe (which, as universe, is necessarily composed and therefore finite) cannot by itself provide the answer to the question of how we may find God. Apophatism and affective *kenōsis* can only be half-truths, parasitic moments of a more truthful discovery. If God cannot simply coincide with the totality, while God's difference transcends all opposition, God is neither separate, elsewhere, absent, far above or before, nor a part or the whole of our universe. In an exceptional, obscure, and incomprehensible sense God is present "in" and "as" the phenomena, whose dissimilar similarity darkly signifies that "presence." The phenomena form a mirror "*in*" which we dimly descry God's hidden presence. Somehow God is not outside or absent, but rather—though in an utterly uncommon sense, wholly different from any temporal or spatial presence—inside, present, close, and extremely intimate. Neither here nor there, neither far nor close, neither separated nor identical, God determines that in us which predetermines us—our Desire—while at the same time affecting us "*through*" *and* "*in*" the universe. It is God's desire in us that moves us to God's desirability "in" and "beyond" all desirables.

"In" and "beyond" together define the finite infinity of the human universe. Analogy and negation, universal enjoyment and suffering, radiance and deepest obscurity together compose the mixture of "pleasure and pain" that marks the best kind of life. As mortals, we cannot escape this mixture. But who cares for "happiness," if such a mixture makes us good?

Appropriate Affection

A mixture is not a synthesis. If we pursued an analysis of the *conceptual* structures involved in the mixture of analogy and apophatism, we would have to discuss Hegel's dialectical synthesis of affirmations and negations as complementary moments of the one and total Idea, which originates, encompasses, and *is* the totality of the finite. As "identity of identity and non-identity,"[12] the Idea doubly unifies all differences in a contradictory attempt to think the coincidence of infinity and totality, missing thereby the incomparability of the only true Infinite.

The paradox of God's pres/absence "in" the universe does not allow for a third, higher, all-encompassing concept (a totality that would enclose God and the universe) in which the similarity and dissimilarity of the Incomparable would be fully integrated. However, if it is true that both the *via affirmativa* and the *via negativa* are held together by the reference of human Desire to God's beyond, would this not indicate an *affective* answer to the question that arises from their mixture? Is a *via eminentiae* opened by the erotic dynamism that relates the analogical totality of the comparable to the incomparable otherness of the infinite beyond which escapes all names?

A long tradition of spiritual theology has explored the experiential quest for God as a transformative dialogue between "God and the soul."[13] This dialogue has not erased the natural, social, and historical world in which *all* "souls" are involved, but strong concentration on "inner" experiences and adventures has sometimes led to an exaggerated spiritualism. Where this danger was avoided, the world was perceived as a universe of ambivalent desiderata whose God-oriented references had to be freed from their seductive potentialities by purification and mortification. Among these desiderata the most revealing was (and still is) the human person, especially in the form of the neighbor. Loyal to the most fundamental conviction of Christianity that love of God, love for God, love of Jesus Christ, and care for the neighbor imply one another, the masters of spirituality have insisted on the

coincidence of union with God and perfect charity toward all humans. However, the theological explanation of this faith and the experiences into which
it unfolds have not been as elaborate as the more spontaneous descriptions
of the moods and emotions that characterize the affective approach to God.
One of the reasons for this disproportion may lie in the underdevelopment
of a philosophy that shows how much personal relations, such as encounter,
respect, compassion, and friendship, differ from all impersonal relations. The
"objectifying" perspective of Western philosophy, mentioned above, and
the neglect of "face-to-face" relationships can be detected in many theologies, but a scholarly treatment of the diagnosis indicated here and the paradigm shift needed for a more "dative" thinking demands much time and rethinking.

A Proposal

The foregoing considerations lead into a multiplication of questions and
suppositions rather than to a conclusive theory. In order to summarize the
perspective from which they were formulated, I will indicate here some
(hypo)theses that together would constitute a sort of research program.

(1) To find the ultimately sought, God should be given, but such givenness can be granted only by God (Him-, Her-, It-)self. Godself must address,
touch, affect, impress, and thus provoke us to an appropriate response. In
order to be touched by God's address, we should allow it to impress us—in
the first place on the most immediate, affective level of our moods, passions,
emotions, likings, affections, and dispositions.

(2) God is never given in a face-to-face relationship. Divine invisibility
includes our inability to hear, smell, taste, feel, intuit, or comprehend God's
own presence. God's self-givenness is a hidden one, beyond senses, affects,
images, words, and concepts. Does this mean that this givenness always remains foreign and absent, never close or present? No: God's "presence" is
neither opposed to, nor suppressed by an immemorial past or an always-
delayed future. God's "time" is different: its presence—or rather essence[14]—
is simultaneously past and future, and thus none of them but beyond time
(and thus beyond the present).

(3) Godself is hiddenly given "in" and "as" our historically experienced
universe (which includes the secular and religious interpretations of its
meaning that constitute our heritage). Responding to God's givenness coin-

cides with our responses to the actual situation of the human universe, insofar as this profoundly hides and reveals God's creative and redeeming "presence," "past," and "future." Appropriate correspondence makes us feel, perceive, hear, welcome, and handle all phenomenal givenness in gratitude and hope—not merely as a constellation of symbols, but as the enigma of data that call us to integrate their lovability into the unchosen Desire that orients all human lives. Such an integration coincides with the overall recognition of God's always-and-never-being-past, always already having come and still coming "presence."

(4) The givenness of the phenomena and their challenge remain ambiguous so long as our affectedness hesitates at the crossroad indicated by their enigmatic character. When "the book of nature" (with an emphasis on the personal and communal adventures of humanity) is read in light of the scriptures and the hermeneutical illuminations of its mysterious side, this reading may result in valid commentaries; but all testimonies remain empty as long as they are not authenticated by an appropriation that adjusts the speaker's passions to the double-sided presence of the immediately given but enigmatic world.

(5) Among the phenomena, you and all other persons constitute the most emphatic and enigmatic presence of the hidden "Presence" that challenges me "in" and "as" the (visible and invisible) universe. Your facing me is the most impressive way in which God's blinding obscurity and thundering silence calls for an appropriate response. Amazingly, the most accurate revelation of that Presence occurs in the humiliation of innocent persons who accept their passion as the sacrament of God's compassion. The human history of this compassion is the phenomenon in which God's givenness crosses the boundary between phenomenal self-sufficiency and the dimension of a very para-doxical attunement. This attunement is a *pathos*. The Christian tradition of "spiritual" life has described it through a constellation of words like "acceptance," "confidence," "patience," "*kenōsis*," "humility," "sacrifice," and "mortification." Though overuse has worn them out, these words may still be reanimated, on the condition that we think their content as inseparably united with gratitude, loyalty toward the earth, enjoyment of life, and hopeful reaching out to the always already present and still desired proximity of the hidden Speech.

The Address of the Letter

THIRTEEN

Excessively simplifying the model according to which Western philosophy has conceived of truth, one might say that it has sought the place of truth in a coherent ensemble of theses and that it has understood a thesis as "saying something about something."[1] In this chapter, I begin with the assumption that it is indeed the main task of philosophy to demonstrate a coherent ensemble of well-founded true propositions. I will attempt to show the consequences of such a conception for the structure of our speaking, but then venture a succinct analysis of speaking and writing that suggests a different relation of philosophy to truth.

I.

If the truth can be affirmed in the form of "saying something about something," and if this saying has to be justified by reasons, the search for truth will be governed by the twofold question "What?" and "Why?" The procedure that follows leads to a conception of the universe as composed of determinate beings which, by their essences and mutual relations, constitute a totality both founded in and crowned by the supreme being, cause and end of all beings. Philosophy will thus develop into an onto-theo-logy (though not quite in Heidegger's sense, for from Plato and Plotinus to Saint Augustine and Nicholas of Cusa, "metaphysicians" have clearly recognized the difference between God and a highest being or *causa sui*). In classical ontotheology God is the supreme and fundamental "Being" that is neither a being, nor the being of beings. Rarely has this God motivated thinkers to address prayers to him. To dance and make music before this God—activities which Heidegger sees as necessary expressions of authentic religiosity—are not so difficult with respect to this God, but can we still adore this "Highest Being"?[2] As the summit of a system in which all beings find their destination, God is thought as the unique One who is absolutely universal, but insofar as God is *thought,* he cannot be *addressed.*

As long as thinkers continued to recognize extraphilosophical authorities, either mystical, religious, moral, or aesthetic, the circle of ontotheology could not be closed because the extraterritoriality of such authorities contradicted the belief that philosophy can comprehend everything that prompts human admiration. Since modern autonomy stipulated that all truth can be found by the rigorous unfolding of a transcendental Ego, the circle of the universe has been closed: being both the foundation and completion of truth, Logos was proclaimed to be the integration of the All that is One and the One that is All. In theology, and even more so in spiritual and mystical experiences, it has always been understood that God is neither a summit nor a gathering, neither a particular being nor even the "common" being of all beings. At the same time, one knew that in calling God a person or in attributing personal properties to God, this was insufficient to evoke the one who is not simply Someone or some One. But how should we think the truth that is experienced in prayer? If some philosophers have called God *causa prima et ultima,* they are hardly understood by modern and postmodern thinkers whose use of *causa* is dominated by the efficient kind of cause; but even by introducing all sorts of modifications into the concept of One who needs nothing, one does not yet change fundamentally the mode of God's presence within the limits of a thematizing ontotheology. Indeed, thematization does not permit the manipulation of a loving and beloved or adorable and adored God. Certainly, the category of personality must not be lost in the course of a theological itinerary; we must traverse it without drowning it in some natural or cultural metaphoric, but by themselves, the words "personality" or "interpersonality" are not sufficient to name the specificity of the relation that relates human individuals to their God. For this relation is experienced in gratitude and trust and hope and love, not primarily in cognitive certainty.

II.

A philosophy bound to the limits of "saying something about something" is dominated by the question "What must be said about what and why?" Would a more complete analysis of human discourse then not render the horizon broader so that it even might be possible to think the distinct reality of prayer along with faith in a truer God?

It is quite obvious that every saying is said by someone to someone else, and that "saying something about something" is the act of someone who addresses words or statements to someone who might listen and understand these words as a message from the speaker or writer. There is no saying without someone who speaks—let us call the speaker "I" or "Ego"—and I cannot speak without addressing myself to someone who, insofar as my address goes, appears to me as you. The one to whom I speak is always a singular you or a plurality of "yous" gathered together in the unity of a particular "all of you." If I say "I speak to her" or "I speak to them," the addressee of this sentence is a "you" and not the third person ("she" or "he" or "them") to whom the sentence refers. "I speak to us" is a strange expression that perhaps has no sense at all, whereas "I say or said to myself" expresses an interior distance, through which I experience myself "as an other," i.e., as someone about whom I am concerned in a serious way. The distance between I who speak and myself to whom I address myself creates a certain tension that suggests a temporal difference. Is this the reason why such phrases as "I said to myself . . ." or "I have said to myself . . ." sound more normal than the present of "I say to myself"? Whatever the case may be, the second person (you or "all of you," but particularly the singular "you") seems to be the paradigm of the one to whom all saying is directed. All speakers normally experience themselves as egos (or as members of a "we") addressing "yous" who in turn can address themselves to their interlocutors. The question "Who speaks to whom?" can thus be resolved by stating that wherever there is speech, "I address myself to you *about* something of which I say something *to* you."

How do you present yourself to me in the situation that this more complete formula of speaking describes? You, to whom I address myself, are neither an object nor an end or a means, but the *dative* to whom I present my words. This dative has an absolute character to it insofar as you, who hear me, can neither be perceived nor mastered as a subordinate moment of something else. For example, I cannot reduce you to the roles or functions that you accomplish as a member of a collective history or of a grand Spirit. And, in general, *you are never a mere moment or link or facet or component of a context or movement to which you would owe the meaning and being of your existence.* As you, you are *irreducible.*

Under the domination of the conceptual pair "end and means," Kant has failed to find a better concept for explaining this phenomenological fact than that of "end-in-itself" (*Zweck an sich selbst*), while the scholastics used the expression *finis cui* to indicate the final character of this absolute dative. Others, you, one's "dignity" (*Würde*), as Kant called it, cannot in any way be or become relative; I cannot turn you into an element of my perfection, be this my union with God. In my speaking, your irreducibility is always at stake. But if I say to you: "You are not an end, but the one to whom I address myself," this sentence, by saying something *about* you, does not avoid making you a theme or object. However it is *to you* that I address this (quasi)-objectifying statement. My action here does more than what the sentence would be able to say if it were not directed to you as addressed by me, but instead abandoned to itself. I touch you in addressing to you a saying in which you figure as a "direct object." Similarly I can speak with you about yourself when you consult me about some psychological or existential problem. If we are both concerned with your health and happiness, we can unite in focusing on you as a case of human desiring beset with difficulties. But insofar as you are a case about which you and I are concerned, you are different from the you to whom I speak and about whom, along with me, you are concerned. As soon as we perceive you as a psychological case or as a soul that has to be saved, we (you and me) view you as caught in a system of roles and functions, of bodies and qualities, of subjects and psychological, social, linguistic, or cultural relations from which no one can escape. Such a system is not powerful enough to suppress completely (except by murder) the unique you with whom I converse about yourself. You, the unique one to whom I speak, are not to be found in the cases of a system of which you are *also* a mode just like all the other things and persons that compose it. Within the horizons of systematic discourse you cannot come to the fore as the you to whom I speak, not even if such a discourse thematizes intersubjectivity, "youness," or the unicity of a you in general. This is probably the reason why "youness," the essence of you as you, has hardly been noticed by the Western tradition of philosophy.

However, you were not absent from the philosophical *practice* when, as in the Middle Ages, the work of thought was carried out by way of a *disputatio* where individual thinkers confronted one another in offering arguments *pro et contra*. That their discussion turned into a spectacle for a public less interested in the truth than they does not take anything away from the dialogical thrust of their thought. The spectacular character of such tournaments paved the way for the modern conception of speculative dialectic, according to which it is the solitary hero of thought who had to master all the "yeses and nos" that emerge from the universe by an all-encompassing and profound reflection.

Must we regret that the literary genre of philosophy has become more and more identified with the monologue of a treatise, apt to solicit other monologues? Should we rather write dialogues? It is not, however, a question of *writing* dialogues, for the author of a dialogue (what a strange expression!) is never multiple enough to exactly imitate the struggle between different interlocutors that an authentic dialogue enacts. We rather should dialogue in fact, being aware that we always think in response to other thinkers whom we try to provoke to their answers, even though this fact is often forgotten or concealed. If a dialogue is written by a single author, the speakers put on stage hardly escape the role of pawns in a game that is conducted over their heads. The author, who divides himself into a plurality of people in order to create some order in his chaos, knows more than the actors of his play. From the outset he knows that he will take away the victory as the judge who pronounces the verdict, unless he truly does not know how to choose between the possibilities defended by his characters. In the latter case, a written dialogue is indeed more than a monologue in disguise; however, most so-called dialogues are more monological than a magisterial lecture in which the master does not hide his struggling without end. An authentic dialogue is practiced by several persons who have not yet come up with the last word. As such they expose the structure of an "I" who speaks to you and a "you" who responds to "me," without reducing "our" expressions to components of one final thought.

III.

When I speak to others, to my students for example, it concerns them. As Socrates shows in Plato's *Symposium*, philosophical *erōs* is not exhausted once it has risen to the ocean of Beauty itself; as a non-narcissistic dynamism, it is at the same time a generous procreation in beauty. Those to whom Socrates addresses his speech are his friends and real or potential lovers of the good. Having awakened them to the true *erōs*, he offers them a chance of becoming philosophers themselves, while remaining different from their educator. In order to seduce his students to the practice of philosophy, a master does not shower the treasures of his wisdom on them, but, from a distance, provokes them to take responsibility for the questions and responses that emerge from their own erotic quest. Far from lacking seriousness, his irony incites them to seek the real issue in their own, differently appropriate way. However, the content of the master's lessons and the efforts of the students do not fall under the same category as the dative of the address with which the latters' quest has begun. The results of their conversation can be desired as an end, but the pupil is the addressee.

The difference between an addressee to whom one speaks and an end that one wants to acquire or accomplish must be seen in order to grasp the importance of the attention by which one turns toward an interlocutor, even abstracting from every finality. This attention is not exhausted by looking at or listening to the other, with or without admiration, kindness, compassion, irritation, or hatred; it is inhabited by a characteristic intention. Speaking to someone intends some change in the other: it gives or does something to her; it engages her, for example, in a confrontation with unknown facts or persuades her to study a text. But all by itself, even abstracting from all contents and realizable ends, the intention of an address provokes in the other the virtuality of an initiative, a work, or a responsibility. If you were not invited or encouraged by signs of confidence, by a master or father, or by the expectation of those who have discovered your talents, you would not be able to begin anything at all; you would not have enough confidence in yourself, perhaps not even any strength at all. Because there are people who look at you or speak to you, you can discover how to do or say something. Certainly attention, demands, and expectations are not enough, you must also learn the necessary know-how; but all learning presupposes that a teacher cares for you.

IV.

Emmanuel Levinas has shown that the other's face and speech awaken me to a responsibility that precedes every awakening of consciousness and from which I cannot escape. When you look at me, I discover myself as destined to support you. Without wishing or willing it, I am devoted to you with a "pre-original" devotion that is older than any receptivity. This involuntary devotion addresses me to you before all speech and action for which I can take the initiative. All of my activity with regard to other persons is mobilized by a dedication that precedes my will and by a desire that addresses me to you. I discover myself dedicated to you, but by whom or what?

The devotion of my always-already-being-addressed reveals your "height" to me: not only your respectable unicity, but an absoluteness that I might not yet have discovered in myself. The excellence of your being-there is expressed in the asymmetry of a relation that is revealed between you and me: without my knowledge or even to my regret, I am truly yours. And since I am dedicated to you prior to the possibility of any initiative, my words inevitably convey this devotion. I discover myself as dedicated *to* you *for* your good.

V.

But how can I do, say, or be good for you? What can or must I offer to my interlocutor when I speak to her, for instance in philosophy? What do I have to offer you that you do not already have—especially in philosophy, where people claim that there is no authority besides reason and experience?

The study of history has shown abundantly that almost everything that can be said in philosophy has been said before in one way or another. Everything that I offer you is a variation, a paraphrase, an imitation, a parody, a caricature or—in the best of cases—a surprising transformation of some heritage. Our heritage thus seems to be a paralyzing burden rather than a source of new opportunities. The Greek, Roman, German, and Christian traditions, along with Western civilization as a whole and the national patrimonies that have formed our spiritual body, cannot be annulled, even if we have lost faith both in them and in ourselves as their heirs. The very modes in which we react to the discovery of other civilizations and to the decline of our own culture is a typical expression of Western modernity: our human sciences, museums, universities, manners of data-processing, even our versions of relativism and nihilism, are nothing but variants of our own brand of universalism.

VI.

Among the gifts and burdens of our heritage, texts occupy a special place. In order to see their importance we must consider the relation between writing and speech.[3] Plato's apology for the spoken word points out that a speaker is present to and thus can assist the words as long as they are remembered by hearers. The speaker can clarify, defend, and amend his utterances, for example to protect them against misunderstanding. Thus a speaker remains as close to her words as to the listener to whom she addresses her words. In writing, on the contrary, the words seem abandoned, left to defend themselves, condemned to an obstinate silence and delivered over to the deformations that some readers may impose on them. However, the text is still addressed to someone and its sender is still present, albeit in a distant mode whose revival depends on the reader. The reader cannot perceive the text as "to be read" if he does not recognize it as a missive, that is, as having been sent by someone to some addressee(s), even if these are unknown to the sender.

The analysis of a letter can clarify these statements. A letter contains a fragment of a conversation, but this fragment is dissociated from its production insofar as it takes some time to know whether the addressee has received, read, and understood it. It is not certain that the intended exchange is going to continue or to get off the ground, but if the text is not addressed to any reader, and if it does not refer to an author, it cannot be perceived as a letter. Both the delay that a letter imposes and the possible absence of a response can create the impression that its text can be detached from the intersubjective relation within which it originated and thus become independent. However, in conversation, likewise, a certain lapse of time separates the expression of a thought from the comprehension by a listener, and even the interior dialogue of the soul with itself shows a somewhat similar kind of temporality.

Addressing remains essential for the text of every letter, as does the intention that the other will respond. For although many epistolary or quasi-epistolary messages do not count on a written response, they nevertheless want to elicit some practical, emotional, legal, or financial response from the receiver.

The delay between the sending and the receiving of a text is, in some way, annulled by the reader. In reading your letter here and now, I render myself present to your (previously) writing to me, or—what, in a rather enigmatic way, amounts to the same thing—in reading what you have written to me, I render you present to my reading. A kind of presence, with a certain duration, unites your "before" with my "after"; but that does not make them coincide, for meanwhile many things have passed that may have changed the facts and the meanings that interest you and me.

Whatever one might say about the relative independence of the text, it is nothing more than a dead score if nobody brings it back to life by lending it the audible or silent voice of a new reading, and if the memory or imagination of the reader does not attribute an author to it. To a certain extent, therefore, the structure of any text is analogous to that of a letter: sent and addressed by someone, it looks forward to a reader in order to actualize its meaning.

Certainly, just like public announcements, a book or an essay is normally destined for an indefinite number of anonymous readers, but that does not annul the fact that addressees as well as addressors belong to the essence of textuality. Neither intimacy nor acquaintance with the concrete personality of the reader(s) are essential for the structure of a letter. Some letters are less personal than scientific treatises, which presuppose at least that the readers and the author share a common interest. The decisive point is that the anonymity of the readers imagined by the author does not suppress the fact that he *addresses* his text conditionally and hopefully to each of them, and that the figure of the author imagined by the readers, however vague, does not abolish his presumed existence. Many writers and editors, especially of ancient and sacred texts, have fallen into anonymity, but even their writings cannot be read as if they are not addressed by an author. Writing is not an end in itself; its target is a future that is not wholly in its power. There is an abandonment in writing. The hope in which it lives corresponds to the gratitude for its own possibility.

If a text is addressed to me by a friend or a teacher in order to make me understand an important truth, I cannot treat it in whatever way comes to mind. Gratitude obliges me to a kind of loyalty in my way of receiving: by being addressed to me, the text demands an appropriate interpretation that renders life to lifeless letters. Only a new animation can transform a fossil into a (re)inspired address. Thanks to our readings and re-readings there is a literary and philosophical life.

Here, however, even more than in the case of a normal letter, the delay between writing and reading renders the demand of hermeneutic fidelity problematic. On the one hand, one can see the point of those who emphasize that all the texts of our heritage fundamentally transmit the same "metaphysical," "heliocentric," and "onto-theo-logical" message; on the other hand, we must recognize that our temporal distance from ancient texts grants us a possibility of renewal and a special responsibility for avoiding lifeless repetitions that deny their promise by suffocating their inspiration.

The double structure that thus appears is prefigured in every address. In wishing to say something to you, I must offer you a coherent discourse.

According to the model of "saying something that is coherent and well-founded about something," I must perform a certain synthesis, with all the characteristics that it implies. In offering it to you, however, I make you an interpreter and judge; I take my distance and abandon my discourse to you. In speaking I invite you, I even urgently demand that you make your own what you have understood of my words in your own way and by means of different conditions and presuppositions than mine. I not only think it possible for you to transform my words into a different text, I count on it and desire it. The history of speaking and writing is a history of transformations that happen to given discourses, but in the case of classical texts, the community that possesses them wants them at the same time to be restored to their own context and reactualized in the later context of another history. The continual transformation that is part of their tradition must guarantee a nucleus of indestructible meaning, but this is at the same time hidden and revealed in a shifting history of various interpretations.

The need for interpretation that characterizes all texts is particularly obvious when the presuppositions of a certain author are no longer ours; but so long as we can hear or read a discourse as concerning us, we recognize in it certain questions and responses that are also ours. We must, so to speak, swallow the texts to discover their strength and worth. In destroying the force of philosophical or literary texts with cynicism or petty "corrections," one renders them even more dead than they already are; an inspired civilization or a living faith, on the contrary, gives them a new fecundity.

If Plato has criticized writing because of its power to render memory superfluous, he wanted above all to protest against a literalism that would condemn us to producing only dead letters. If it is necessary to "feed" on ideas and texts in order to produce a meaning that is at once faithful and new, it is thanks to a certain distance with regard to all writings—and not just by a fusion of horizons or historical contexts—that we can recognize them as particular versions of questions and responses that concern all humans.

Hermeneutics finds itself ruled by an ethics of responsibility that begins with gratitude and tries to fulfill ancient promises that until now remained unfulfilled. Hermeneutics thus presupposes a certain faith in the authority of the ancients as well as a certain form of repetition.

Am I naïve? Is it not rather "metaphysics" or the objective and absolute Spirit, Life, *Physis*, Destiny, Language, or Being itself that make us affirm what we say or write? Against the Elements and the Powers that have neither mouths nor ears, it is high time to reaffirm that Language has never spoken, that Being does not exist, that Life needs living beings in order to live and that an objective Spirit can neither speak nor write. Only individual existents can live a human life, spiritually think and speak or write thanks to predecessors from whom they have learned how to express themselves in a wide but limited variety of forms of life and language.

I speak because others have spoken to me out of a common heritage. Their versions of this heritage surround me with a number of limited possibilities of life and thought. Even if I had no choice of codetermining my proper style of life and work, my words and acts would still testify to a certain consent that implies at least some degree of gratitude to those who have spoken before me.

VII.

If the true life of philosophy consists in a multiplicity of interconnected chains of unique interlocutors who strive for truth while retrieving various traditional and hermeneutic gestures, the history of philosophy does not coincide with the history of social or cultural ensembles; the history of language, commonality, economy, politics, or intertextuality cannot replace the history of living thought. Philosophy and literature concretely exist as layers and processes of a much more modest history: the history of a community of particular individuals who discuss a small part of the literary and philosophical world literature. The purpose of this "small" history is that the participants present opportunities to one another for thinking by referring to thoughts of certain classics in the hope of thus preparing other partly new, but equally limited thoughts. The exchanges that constitute philosophical life emerge within the framework of anonymous structures and powers, but they preserve aspects of a spontaneous and enigmatic generation. In emphasizing the individual responsibility and originality of an authentic thinker, it is not necessary to deny the anonymous and collective aspects of the conceptuality and the approaches that we have in common. With certain reservations we can even agree that the philosophical community of the West should be characterized as a "metaphysical" or "ontotheological" kind of thought, but such a sweeping characteristic—like every other generalization about the "Idea" or the "Spirit"—fails to capture the essence of history because it concentrates on the question of generic elements or powers, without paying enough attention to the unique way in which each thinker metamorphosizes preceding thought into his or her characteristic, old and always new, experience. The paradoxes of metaphysics, for example, cannot disqualify the metaphysical enterprise, if we are able to reproduce them in new, self-experienced ways. Like all particular languages, metaphysics has its own limitations and impossibilities, but only a "nostalgia"[4] that despises irreducible particularity can be distressed by this. It is given to us (*"Uns ist gegeben"*[5]) to think within the limited space opened up by the history of Greek and Roman conceptuality, biblical religiosity, and Western languages. The confrontation with radically different forms of speech and writing should not seduce us to deny our particularities, but on the contrary, encourage us to become more genuinely what we are able to be: particular and unique in a way that is so profound that we somewhere converge with the most profound thought of the others. Without such an expectation—the hope that at bottom and in the end all human existence is guided by the same questions, orientations, suspicions, and truths—we might have to abandon the idea of humanity as such. All this in no way implies, however, that we are capable of formulating the unifying core of such convergence in a transcendental theory. Under certain conditions the polyglot and polydox pluralism of our "small history" is perhaps one of the best ways to be "in the truth."

Provocation:
Can God Speak within the
Limits of Philosophy? Should
Philosophers Speak to God?

"The God of the Philosophers"

To oppose the God of the philosophers to the God of Abraham, Isaac, and
Jacob (who is also the God of Moses, David, Jesus Christ, and the community of the Spirit) is not exceptional in the history of Western Christianity.
From St. Paul and Tertullian to Kierkegaard and Karl Barth this contrast has
accompanied the tradition, which, for the most part, has tried to critically
integrate the Greek heritage of philosophy into the theological elaboration
of Christian faith. However, the concept of philosophy has not always remained the same from the ancients to our time.[1] In our postmodern situation, philosophy is scattered into a number of schools that do not even agree
on its tasks and meaning, and God has been eliminated by most philosophers

from their discipline. "The God of *the* philosophers" itself seems therefore to be an anachronistic expression and its opposition to the God of a living faith risks being a topic of the past. However, if a living God continues to fascinate millions and millions of people, philosophy cannot ignore this fact without abandoning the idea that it ought to think about all relevant phenomena, and especially about the most originary and ultimate ones. If some philosophers still refer to God, is their God then necessarily different from the God revered in Christian faith? If so, what is the difference, and is it the philosophical approach that is responsible for a certain contradiction between the two?

In order to avoid a lengthy examination of the philosophical project in its relation to religion and theology, I will assume that we share a general understanding of the quoted contrast and that it can still guide us to a renewal of the old question concerning the relation of philosophy to faith and theology. If I had to summarize the accusation, I would say that the philosophical God is found too pale, too cold and boring, too abstract and unreligious to interest people who have been touched by the Biblical inspiration and who experience a living faith. The God of philosophy is said to be an impersonal, immutable, uninterested substance, insufficiently alive, too unconcerned and dead to prevent an emotional and practical, or even a theoretical atheism. Often accused of being a pagan, cosmological God, this substance has not conquered Pascalian believers by being qualified as a thinking and self-knowing spirit. Neither Anaxagoras nor Aristotle have convinced those who yearn for a caring God; they are not even impressed by Hegel's attempt to demonstrate that the subjectivity of that substance is omnipresent in the legal, moral, social, cultural, and historical universe of which we are a part.

Is the absence of a living God due to the essence of philosophy? Is philosophy essentially atheistic if it is measured by the standards of Biblical faith? Or can philosophy fight back, for instance by saying that its accusers disable their own attempts at theology by not thoroughly studying the classical texts of philosophical theology, or by preferring the naïveté of imaginary languages over the rigor of conceptual and universally valid thought? In this paper I do not intend to answer the question of whether the contradiction between the two "Gods"—if it exists—stems from misunderstandings or caricatures of the metaphysical tradition, but rather argue that God, within the limits of a reborn philosophy, is much more interesting and alive than many contemporary authors seem to think. Or, to put it otherwise, I will defend the thesis that the great tradition of philosophical theology from Plato to Hegel can be retrieved on the condition that philosophy takes a new turn.

What philosophy in any case cannot allow itself to exclude, ignore, or neglect, is the religious beliefs experienced and described as all-important by innumerable people in all cultures. A little more receptivity—perhaps even more humility—than is customary among autonomous philosophers will be required. At the very least, philosophy must show that and why religion is meaningful, or else explain why, if this is not true, it is such a widespread phenomenon. However, a credible and livable religion presupposes an interesting, desirable, trustworthy, and adorable God. Can philosophy guide our thought to such a God?

I would like to offer a modest contribution to such a philosophy by reflecting on God's speaking, as documented in a host of biblical narratives, prophecies, hymns, and meditations, and continued by a constant stream of testimonies about the mystical experiences of Christian, Jewish, Muslim, Hindu, and other believers. God created the universe by speaking: "He spoke . . . , and it was." God saved humanity be speaking to Moses and confiding the sacred words of the Torah to his people. God revealed God by speaking through the prophets and Jesus Christ, who is the Word of God. God continues to reveal and to guide by speaking not only to saints and mystics, but to all who have received the gift of listening. Is philosophy able to say anything meaningful about those testimonies and experiences? Does philosophy, within its own limits, allow God to speak? If so, what would be the appropriate reaction to such speaking?

Speaking

Before we can speak about God's word, we need a phenomenology of speaking as it is practiced among us. I give here only some sketchy indications.

My starting point is Levinas's distinction between the Saying (*le Dire*) and the Said (*le Dit*). Most of the philosophical literature on speaking and writing concentrates on "the said": constellations of words and sentences, ruled by various linguistic structures and modes of expression; thematic contents as caught in syntactic and semantic patterns. Among philosophers, the saying itself (in speaking or writing) is seldom treated; most often it is altogether forgotten, while the meaning and truth of "what is said about something" (*legetai ti kata tinos*) receives the most attention. As we will see, there are reasons for this neglect, although a phenomenology of speech is obviously impossible without focusing on the fact that all that is said or written *is addressed by someone to someone.*[2]

Modern philosophers were quick to identify a speaker (or writer) as the subject of utterances, while postmodern thinkers have explored many modes of presubjective and preauthorial causalities and structures, thereby showing that authorship is always conditioned and (at least partially) determined by social, cultural, textual, emotional, unconscious, and other factors and processes. The modern and postmodern philosopher adopt a monological stance according to which the subject, as a more or less autonomous ego, sees itself confronted with a universe that is there to be conceptually conquered. Modern philosophy has analyzed and overanalyzed the central role of an ego in the manifestation of all that is, including the meaning of one's coexistence with others in one world and the complications caused by this fact. But seldom has it challenged the traditional standpoint of a lonely thinker who, in the name of all humans, tries to comprehend the universe by a universally valid theory. If the other to whom a speaker speaks appears at all in the analysis, most often he or she is seen as another instance of subjectivity, or as someone who shares the speaker's world and linguistic experience.

The most neglected element in the phenomenology of speech seems to be the addressee: the person or persons to whom a speech or text is addressed. One or more addressees are constitutive for all speech and writing, although their number and identity may vary. You can speak to one or more persons, to an anonymous audience, or even to people who are not yet born, but no speaking is possible without some intended addressee, whether real or possible. In this sense both a dative and a vocative are implied in every speech.

What happens when you speak to me? In order to focus on speaking as distinct from any spoken message, examples of speech in which very little is said are helpful. The message (and the code) is minimal in utterances such as "Hello!" or "Hi!" Words can even be replaced with sounds like "hm" or "uh huh." Even then, however, their being addressed to someone remains not only intentional but phenomenal. When you speak to me, you put me in the dative, whether or not you have a worthwhile message to deliver. This dative is preceded and supported by a vocative, through which you awaken my awareness and try to draw my attention. Your appeal to me suggests or even demands that I listen to you. The transition between my hearing your speech, as one of the many sounds and words that surround me, and my paying attention to your appeal presupposes a turn: I must turn my ear, my mind, myself to you in order to hear your call. I can ignore or refuse to receive your vocative, for example by concentrating on other events, but as soon as your words have bridged the separation between you and me by becoming a phenomenon that interests me, I am no longer completely free: your vocative (co)determines the parameters of my choice. Whatever I do, it will be a response to your demand. I am forced to choose between a refusal to listen and acceptance. As both listening and turning a deaf ear express a situated liberty, an ethics of language as communication begins here. To welcome or reject the speaking that is implied in any spoken or written word engages me in a story; because someone speaks to me, my freedom is burdened with a task that I cannot avoid.

To accept your addressing me does not entail that I agree with the message you are communicating. It is not even necessary that I understand what you tell me (e.g., because I do not know your language). It is sufficient that I recognize your sounds as some sort of language, i.e., as signifying something to me, even if your utterance seems to be no more than a beastly scream. When first listening to you, I hold your message at a critical distance, but by accepting that I am spoken to, I am drawn into a communicative intrigue for which I am as (co)responsible as you. You and I cannot be reduced to components of a linguistic process, because we not only submit to, but also rule the systemic connections and mechanisms, the codes, paradigms, and structures that constitute our language. Without us, language would be impersonal, dead, a mere *possibility* of speech and writing. It comes to life only when you or I transform its possibility into an animated dialogue. Language must be mobilized by a voice. The principle of its movement lies in our freedom, but this is situated, and thus codetermined, by an address that demands our attention.

Listening achieves the basic turn that replaces the dream of an isolated egocentrism with the towardness of intersubjectivity. If I ever was totally involved in myself alone, the first speech that draws my attention would invite me to a fundamental conversion. Once I have turned to you, my position in the world can no longer be described as the stance of an ego in the midst of a universe. Your speaking manifests my dependence on a welcoming address. I need to be provoked in order to become, by way of response, a speaker myself. The other's address invites me to become receptive and responsive. But let us first complete the description of your addressing words to me.

In your speaking to me, you reveal your unique and irreplaceable individuality. I, your listener, can be replaced by other addressees; you can even speak to an indeterminate or merely possible audience; but in addressing yourself to one or more persons, or even to other beings, you necessarily affirm and manifest your singularity. However, this affirmation cannot be perceived without a real, possible, or imaginary addressee who is aware of your words as *spoken to her or him*. Your singularity is perceptible only to someone who is turned to you, who are likewise turned to the listener. While the phenomenon of your addressing me is obvious from the perspective of a listening attitude, it disappears as soon as it is reported in stories or considerations in which you figure as a he or she who said this or that, who addressed an audience and showed your eloquence, your insights, or your feelings. Once I change your speaking *to* me into a report *about* you, I have lost sight of your singularity. You have been transformed into one of the many subjects about which I and others can tell stories or engage in studies. When you no longer regard me directly, we have replaced you with a person whose distinction from other persons must be described by an accumulation of characteristics. Talking to me is not sufficient to manifest your many properties—in order to discover them, the content of your messages might be more revealing—but it displays your "naked" or "abstract," most essential, fundamental, and unique originality: precisely that which distinguishes you from all that can be said about you. The difference between your unique self and your predicable particularities is a unique phenomenon, but it can neither be perceived, nor described from the position of a noninvolved ego or an ego that sees you as part of his or her universe. Merely studying the universe does not offer a space for the unicity that appears when you address, "face," or "touch" me. If I want to contact your ownmost self, your many properties are neither irrelevant, nor essential; I must approach you in the attitude of towardness to perceive your originariness. That you are unique and irreplaceable remains hidden so long as I am not before you as a listener who hears or regards you in your "youness."

Being confronted with a speaker is a challenge. By accepting that you disrupt the possibility that I isolate myself in a self-secured seclusion, I am confronted and provoked. Even if you do not say more than "Hello!" or "Pronto," you urge me to answer you. My answer, likewise, can be minimal as far as the message is concerned. I can, for example, say "Yes (I listen)," "It's me," or "Here I am." But in any case, your turning to me, followed by my turning to you, is not devoid of a normative aspect, a claim, a demand, an obligation. Minimally, it demands that I acknowledge your speaking by some silent or verbal gesture. Having the character of an allocution and interpellation, it urges me to respond. Your speaking awakens me to my responsivity, which is as much a natural reaction as an obligation. A phenomenology of speaking can be achieved as part of a universal phenomenology that is at the same time ontological and ethical.[3] All beings have their own modes of appearance, but each appearance implies a specific kind of claim; by surprising or "touching" or "speaking" to me, each phenomenon confronts me with a task.

Platonic *ideas* are *ideals;* all beings bathe in the splendor of the Good; every phenomenon has its own dignity, which should be respected.[4] I will not pursue this line of thought here, but it must be kept in mind when considering the metaphorical power of speaking: is speaking paradigmatic for all phenomena insofar as they, in "speaking" to me, confront me with some sort of claim and task? Can all phenomena involve me in a dialogue with normative aspects?

Pursuing the analysis of the provocation contained in your speech to me, we must state that its specific character (its "nature" or "essence") implies a characteristic claim. The ethics of intersubjectivity must manifest which particular demands are contained in your speaking and how I ought to respond to them. Your speaking invites, suggests, or demands a specific, *appropriate* response.[5]

In this context, "appropriation" stands for the right mode of accepting and answering the provocation. My reaction must be well-adjusted, befitting, attuned. This includes my allowing you to manifest and unfold your unique singularity, while I myself take responsibility for my own role in the ensuing dialogue. Retrieving the analyses of Kant and Levinas, we can describe the attitude of an ideal respondent as absolute respect for your unconditional dignity. More concrete descriptions, in which your thought, love, writing, or rhetorical skills and my more specific reactions come to the fore, depend on the particularities of your person, some of which are also revealed in messages from and about you. In addition to the esteem that I owe you for the bare fact of your emerging before me, I should also respect your "said." Though such respect does not entail approval, it excludes distortion.

Your speech has situated me as a respondent who must attempt to answer you in words that fit your appearance. You have forced me to enter into a process of *correspondence.*

Correspondence is an individual affair: no one but I can answer your addressing me. By not fencing off the engagement to which you have seduced me, I am likewise forced to display myself as this singular speaker here and now. If I succeed in responding to your speech in a more or less appropriate way, a dialogue begins. You and I are then, by our own doing, constituted as interlocutors who share a story that is ruled by free but situated users of shared necessities.

Correspondence is a question of trial and error: appropriate responses to the surprising claims of various phenomena most often require experimentation. Herein we are guided by the culture, education, examples, traditions, and customs in which former generations have expressed their attempts at wisdom. Since the wisdom of the ancients deserves critical testing, however, we are never quite sure whether the ongoing discovery of perfect correspondence has reached its goal or not.

Experimenting, critique, and testing are not possible unless we are interested in appropriateness. We would not even listen to a speech were we not driven by some sort of curiosity. The wonderful phenomenon of someone who speaks to me awakens my interest by provoking my desire to get acquainted with all that is desirable. I am driven by Desire, but this would be powerless if it were not attracted by the provocation of tempting phenomena. Speaking is one of such phenomena. It is certainly a very important one; for without being spoken to, we would not be speakers ourselves. All speaking begins by responding; and the question of how language began must remain unanswered.

Dialogue and Reflection

By provoking the listener to respond, speaking opens the dimension of intersubjective ethics. You confront me with my responsibility for an appropriate adjustment to the facts, including the situation created by your addressing me. Both you and I are now urged to pursue a meaningful dialogue as part of your and my unique adventures and our shared history. The main issue in the entire phenomenology of correspondence is the mutual turn of the one to the other, which constitutes the dialogical structure of correspondence.

The provocation that triggers the dialogue is not perceivable and does not occur unless the one is turned to the other. I must be before you, facing your facing me. Only in the position of the allocuted (the *Angeredete* or *Angesprochene*[6]) can the phenomenon of speaking—and addressing in general—be perceived. The phenomenology of speech demands a particular perspective; without a specific turn or conversion toward the speaker (or, in general, toward beings that are telling) it cannot even start.

One of the most effective ways of fencing off the challenge that provokes me to a dialogical involvement consists in deciding to concentrate on your *message* only, or in considering the exchange between you and me as a topic or *theme* for my solitary reflection. Even if I intend to draw universally valid conclusions from such a consideration, which can be shared with you and everyone else, your speaking and my responding are then neutralized, made impersonal, emptied of their vocative and provocative power. When I reflect on someone's talking to someone, without myself being involved in it, I am a third party who analyzes an event that occurs around or in front of me. It is then an instance of social interaction that I can describe without taking part in it. As a nonparticipating observer,[7] I do not experience the provocative and demanding character of your call, because I have settled into the role of a stage director. Uninvolved thematization allows me to be a mastermind; from a distance, I assign specific functions to you and your interlocutor in a linguistic universe that is ruled by systematic possibilities and historical conventions.

Reflection prevents or eliminates the stance that is indispensable for experiencing the provocative singularity of the speaker and the normative force of her address. If philosophy is essentially thematic and reflective, it remains deaf to all vocatives and singularities and the claims they imply. It is then confined to the consideration of speakers, respondents, and interlocutors in general. This is what has happened to social philosophy and ethics: the double asymmetry of provocation and response has been replaced with an overview of coexisting instances of a generic human being, insofar as these are able and required to fulfill various tasks in the community to which they belong. Instances, functions, roles, patterns, and places occupy the foreground, while people lose their own face, voice, individuality, heart, and intimacy. Instead of participating in the *dialegesthai* of concerned interlocutors, the uninvolved philosopher assigns himself the task of a dramatist. If he does not enclose himself in monologues, he writes and rules the dialogues in which other persons remain pawns in a game of which he is the master. Instead of being involved in a contemplative life, he writes texts. However, textuality cannot replace the dialogue of real life. It reduces the philosophical discussion to remembrance, imaginary *re*-enactment, *mimēsis*, but does not render what really happens in it.

Philosophy is indeed more than systematic reflection and thematization: even in its most monological form, it cannot avoid addressing itself to readers, students, or colleagues. By addressing an audience, a philosopher repeats all the gestures described above, even if she does not explicitly reflect on this nonthematized condition of all thematization. Thinking is always a combination of gratitude and renewal in response to preceding thoughts and a presentation to others of suggestions for the future. It is not imprisoned in texts, for texts and textuality are fossils if they are not resurrected from the dust of their letters by living interlocutors who care for them. Monologues that play no part in a dialogical tradition kill the most uplifting parts of life, such as encounters, awakenings, confrontations, provocations, presentations, teachings, challenges, responses, discussions, originality, and tradition.

The only way to respect and preserve the connection between the message of a "said" and its speaker is to maintain a twofold concentration: while talking to you, I can at the same time focus on your message without forgetting that you present it to me. For example, I can remind you in a letter of what your wrote to me, or I can say to you, "What you tell me now, reveals something important about you; we should speak about it." While maintaining our face-to-face relationship, we can combine the vocative and responsive position with the thematization of your and my "said." But even within such a simultaneity the emphasis of our awareness shifts from one position to the other. Perhaps we may state that the towardness of the face-to-face can heed the "aboutness," whereas the "about," left to itself, cannot save the "to." In any case, the concentration on your unicity, as manifest in your speaking, and the awareness of our being involved in a discussion force our reflection to bend back upon an event that cannot be caught in any text, even though all texts depend on it.

A complete phenomenology of speaking must do much more than I have indicated here. (1) It must also consider the various contents that are communicated, in order to discover how these elicit acceptance, adjustment, and response; (2) it must show the innovative, transformative, and (re)creative powers of speaking. Speech civilizes nature; poetry poetizes; novels stylize history; a word of hope can save or renew a life. However, the powers of renewal are not confined to the message that is delivered; the greatest surprise and the most forceful incentive lie in the very addressing itself. This can be illustrated with trivial phrases that can be used to communicate very personal and intimate messages. As the *bourgeois gentilhomme* learned to his amazement, "je vous aime" is still the best way to declare one's love, but how trite it sounds if it is not directed to the unique beloved![8]

Experience of the creative and recreative power of speaking is required to understand why it could become a central metaphor for God's saving and creative work: God spoke, and . . . it happened; God said, and . . . it was.[9]

Does God Speak?

The classical project of philosophical theology can be retrieved if we can liberate it from the many misunderstandings and caricatures that have obscured its truth. One of the conditions for its renewal is that we distinguish the question of naming God from the question of the so-called proofs for the existence of God. The impossibility of demonstrating that God's existence is entailed in the essence and existence of finite beings does not necessarily destroy the possibility of naming the God who is sought by most (or perhaps by all) human beings. Another condition for renewal is that God, if God exists, should be sought as absolutely interesting, desirable, and decisive for any human life and its struggle for meaning. This condition follows from the insight that philosophical reflection is a subordinate element within the adventure of a risky, but thoughtful life.

The warp and woof of classical ontotheology are the analogy of being and apophatic theology.[10] They are inseparable because all signs and similarities by which the phenomena refer to God's essence must be affirmed as well as denied, even though we are not able to replace them with satisfactory names. We cannot mention God without comparing the incomparable, but the enterprise itself involves us in an *aporia* that cannot be abolished, overcome, or sublated by any simple or synthetic concept.

How, for example, can we say that God is *as* a father or a mother, while at the same time affirming that He/She/It is neither a father, a mother, a he, a she, or an it? How can we call God "the maker of heaven and earth," while denying both that he is similar to an artisan and that *poiēsis* is an adequate model for creation? How can God be called Life or the source of all life, if our idea of life is borrowed from the life of plants, animals, humans, cultures, or some other instance or totality of finite beings? All that we say God is, He/She/It is not. That our language about God does not collapse altogether, however, is *due to the fact that all our denials are inhabited by a movement that points beyond the affirmations we simultaneously use and negate.* Driven by this movement—*a movement caused by Desire*—our naming God refers to the unknown Sought that is neither comparable to any phenomenon, nor indeterminate in the way *chaos, mē on, apeiron, chōra, hylē prōtē,* or *il y a* "are."[11]

If the word "being" (*ousia, to on*), may be used to indicate the totality of all that is, we must state that God is neither a being (and thus also not the highest being), nor the totality of all beings, nor the being of any being or universe of beings, even if such a beingness could be described as life or love or spirit. God is other than, beyond all being. And yet, all beings signifyingly refer to that beyond. Plato set the stage when he, in one and the same passage, called the Good an idea and insisted that it transcends all ideas.[12] The beyond cannot be respected in its transcendence unless we have recourse to the essence of all the amazing but finite phenomena that attract our desire, while pointing beyond the horizon of their universe. All analogies are false if they do not insist on the negations implied in the "as" by which they link God with light, life, truth, knowledge, justice, goodness, compassion, delight, pleasure, and so on. But all apophatism remains parasitic on the affirmations it must deny.[13] This parasitism is manifest in the works of the Neoplatonists: in order to avoid the confusion of those who put God on the same level as the utterly indeterminate (such as the *apeiron* and prime matter), they are forced to replace the negations implied in the *epekeina tēs ousias* with predicates that suggest the upward movement of an infinite desire, calling God *hyperousios, hyperagathos, hypertheos,* and the like.[14] The inseparability of analogy and denial create an almost unbearable tension, which cannot be overcome by any representation or concept or word (except, perhaps, by the word God, if this is said in a specific way). Hegel is the prime example of a *gnōsis* that claims to overcome the *aporias* in which that tension involves us. Driven by his desire to overcome all contradictions, he comprehended God as the unique and all-encompassing Spirit that is and comprehends itself as the *archē* and *telos* of the universe. The result was a God as wide as the universe, but not wider, and thus not more amazing or desirable.[15] Other methods of escaping the *aporia* can be developed by seeing it as a sufficient proof for atheism or as a justification for fideism. Still another way of coping with the unresolvable tension is to insist on one side of the contradiction by calling God *summum ens* (supreme being) or *esse subsistens* (autarkic, self-sufficient being), while immediately thereafter emphasizing that we do not know what these words properly mean.

If the aporetic structure is essential for our reflection about God, we must endure the tension and make peace with it in other ways.[16] We cannot follow Hegel's dialectical unification of positive and negative theology. Instead of construing an encompassing concept of God, we must go another way in order to respect the unity that is broken by the dim light of our reflexivity.

That we ourselves are not scattered by our hybrid language about God, we owe to the Desire that possesses us and points, beyond all ideas, notions, and knowledge, toward the most Desirable we try to name. This Desire, whose orientation makes us seekers, runs ahead of our reflections; it has its own certainty and preconscious or subconscious conscience and growing wisdom. However, before we pursue this line of thought, let us ask whether the God of philosophy can be thought of as speaking to me (which then also would open the door for God's listening, caring, protecting, guiding, and loving us).

God Speaks

That the word "speaking" can be used as a metaphor for nonhuman beings is obvious from fables, fairy tales, poems, myths, and many expressions of everyday language. Not only dogs, but also trees and flowers, events and other phenomena tell us much. Nature can easily be personified as an eloquent lady and the lessons of history are revealing if we know how to decipher them.

Sacred books and an abundance of mystical literature testify to God's revelation through prophetic words and the silent speech of religious intimacy. Though God's word is constantly contaminated in its all too human, idolatrous versions, it must be possible to recognize its purity in the messages that affect the purest tendency of our Desire. Though philosophers may not be able to discover on their own where and when God's revelation is transmitted most authentically, they cannot doubt that the ongoing history of human speech and literature somehow renders God's speaking present to humanity. On the basis of this trust, the hermeneutic task of recognizing God's own voice must be assumed. If we can meaningfully say that God "makes" the world or "causes" events or grants protection—while being well aware that all these expressions are infinitely inadequate—by the same token we may state that God speaks to us in all the words, things, and events that are desirable and true. The traditional concepts of ground, cause, origin, substance, and end, as used to evoke God, do not necessarily impose a cosmological conception of being and its beyond; they must be heard anew in the context of human culture and the history of speaking and discussion, literature and other arts, care and concern, combats and alliances, friendship and love. Nothing of all these wonderful phenomena can be missed. Philosophers who thoroughly contemplate the spiritual wealth of human history cannot but refer to a God who is alive and well—or "more than" alive: a God who speaks, regards, and affects all who have learned to listen, to look up, and to be sensitive to God's advent in all things. If such a learning is illusory, then not even theologians can explain how the Bible can state and restate that God creates and guides the human universe by speaking: "He spoke, and . . . it was"; "he said, and . . . it happened."

The apophatic element in our speaking about God's own speaking becomes manifest as soon as we emphasize that God has neither a mouth nor breath. The silence of God is not even a proper silence, because only speakers can fall silent, but it is a "telling" that "permeates" and "supports" all speaking. Just as Plato looked up to the Good as the source of the invisible light that generates all light, so we may evoke God as the inaudible Speaking that brings all speaking to life. If such a God is not alive, then what is? A telling universe reveals a concerned God, though a philosopher cannot demonstrate which particular religion is the most faithful in receiving and heeding God's Word.

That the silence of God can be experienced as a speaking that urges us to respond might be clarified somewhat by remembering that the provocation and the responsive movement awakened in us also rule the visible dimension of the face-to-face and the affective silence of invisible intimacy. The dialogical process is not confined to words, views, or emotions. Mutual towardness, not hampered but stimulated by profound asymmetry, establishes intimacy between free allies. This agreement between God and man receives its absolute confirmation in the daring proclamation that God has become flesh, while flesh itself is divinized.

However, neither philosophy nor theology can do justice to God's provocation if it is their exclusive task to reflect on such a dyadic unity, for reflection implies the standpoint of a mastermind. As we saw, a speaker can neither display her unique singularity, nor challenge an interlocutor unless the latter turns his ear and mind toward the speaker. Reflection distracts from this condition and eliminates the provocation. But how could it then be linked to a responsive attitude?

Speaking to God

God is challenging, provocative, dangerous, and desirable when met in a responsive attitude, but as long as we concentrate on study and research, God's vocative cannot reach us. A critique of the *aboutness* and the attitude that goes with it is necessary to free the philosopher from the temptation of submitting God to comprehensive mastery. God escapes the all-encompassing totality to which modern philosophy has bound our minds. Philosophers and theologians who adhere to the ideal of an uninvolved, and in this sense impartial, reflection about *ta panta* can dominate their subjects, but their *gnōsis* excludes them from any alliance with those who speak to them. If God speaks, the natural response is prayer—with or without words. Because God's word urges the addressee to a turn or conversion in order to listen and respond, God cannot enter the discussion if this is ruled by the panoptical perspective of modern scholarship. Theologians as well as philosophical theologians miss the point unless they find ways to subordinate their reflection to their faith in God, i.e., to the trust and thrust that guide the adventures of their lives. The main condition for thinkers to be true to God is that they expose themselves to that which impresses them in all phenomena as "greater" and "better" than all desirability. Such a turn or conversion creates a bias because it refers beyond the universe of all totalities.

Thus metaphysical contemplation discovers a method that is other than the customary one. Absolute (i.e., uninvolved and autonomous) reflection gets things right by giving them a proper place and function within the constellation of its universe. But God does not have a place or function. The reflective attitude is not hospitable to God. To save its relative truth, it must bend and adjust itself to the prereflective, prelingual, previsible, and preemotional movement of a life that has always already been driven by Desire. Since Desire is not different from being attracted by God, it contains at least the beginning of a trust in the truly Desirable. If philosophical reflection discovers that it is one of the activities in which a preceding engagement—the engagement of a certain faith—expresses itself, it might find this experience humbling, but a closer intimacy with the deepest thrust of life might also make it more authentic.

In the name of its faith in autonomous reason, modern philosophy has shown little trust in faith. Along several paths of thought, the history of the last centuries has shown how disappointing the results of its trust in reason are and how ineradicable a more fundamental kind of faith is, even in philosophy. Is it not time to retrieve the ancient and premodern meaning of philosophy? As the contemplative element of a life in search of meaning, it is the corresponsive quest through which a deep engagement tries to clarify itself from the margins. Though not confined to any particular religion, such a philosophy is a form of *fides quaerens intellectum.* Its God would still be a pale shadow of the living God, but its considerations would tend to replace arrogance with adoration.

N O T E S

Works given by title only are those of the author.

CHAPTER ONE. Roots of Thought

The text of this chapter is the new version of a paper that was presented at one of
the first meetings of the Association for Continental Philosophy and Theology, which
was held during the World Congress of Philosophy held in Boston, Massachusetts,
August 1998.

1. "Metaphilosophy" is an attempt at radical reflection about the nature, the
task(s), and the method of philosophy. If philosophy can boast of possessing the highest and all-encompassing theoretical perspective, metaphilosophy is simultaneously
its initial and ultimate discipline. If the most originary and ultimate assessment of
philosophy does not fall under its own competence, there must be a higher perspective. Could this then be found in life itself or in some kind of theology—or in a combination of both?

"Postmodern" is a word with so many meanings, including several vague and
confused ones, that its utility has become minimal. If pressed to define it, I would
answer that I consider G. W. F. Hegel to be the last of the great modern philosophers,
which makes me use the adjective "postmodern" to gather all attempts at inaugurating
a post-idealist way of thinking. For the shifts in meaning of the word "philosophy"
since its ancient and medieval practices, see *Historisches Wörterbuch der Philosophie*,
vol. 7, s.v. *Philosophie*, col. 573–599, and Pierre Hadot, *Qu'est-ce que la philosophie antique?* (Paris: Gallimard, 1995).

2. The mutual dependence of metaphilosophy and philosophical anthropology
("philosophy of man and woman," *not* of "mind") and the circularity it implies constitute an as yet unresolved key question of modern and postmodern philosophy.
This essay is a modest attempt to reformulate that question, which also was at the center of the ancient and medieval theory and evaluation of *theōria* (contemplation).

3. See P. Rabbow, *Seelenführung: Methodik der Exerzitien in der Antike* (München: Kösel-Verlag, 1954); A. J. Voelke, *La philosophie comme thérapie de l'âme* (Paris-Fribourg: Du Cerf, 1993); Ilsetraud Hadot, "The Spiritual Guide," in A. H. Armstrong, ed., *Classical Mediterranean Spirituality: Egyptian, Greek, Roman,* 436–459 (New York: Crossroad, 1986); Pierre Hadot, *Exercises spirituels et philosophie antique,* 3rd ed. (Paris: Etudes augustiniennes, 1993).

4. See *Historisches Wörterbuch der Philosophie,* vol. 7, s.v. *Philosophie,* col. 616–633, and Jean Leclerq, *Études sur le vocabulaire monastique du Moyen Age* (Rome: Herder, 1961), 39–67.

5. See notes 1 and 3.

6. Perfectly and paradigmatically expressed in Hegel's inaugural addresses at the universities of Heidelberg (1817) and Berlin (1818). See G. W. F. Hegel, *Gesammelte Werke,* vol. 18 (Hamburg, Meiner, 1995), 6 and 18.

7. Cf. the famous definition of Enlightenment in the first sentence of Kant's *Beantwortung der Frage: Was ist Aufklärung?* (1783): "Enlightenment is the exodus of man from his self-inflicted minority."

8. Cf. C. Esser, ed., *Opuscula Sancti Patris Francisci Assisiensis* (Grottaferrata: Ad Claras aquas, 1978), 95 and 231.

9. *De doctrina christiana,* I, 22–36.

10. *Summa Theologica* II^a II^{ae}, qq. 23–27, especially q. 26.

CHAPTER TWO.   Christianity and Academic Life

The first version of this text, titled "Christianity and Intellectual Life," was discussed with professors of Loyola University Chicago at a Consilium retreat at Lake Geneva, Wisconsin, 6–10 July 1998.

1. See also chapter 1 on *Genealogy.*

2. Cf. Saint Francis's letter to Brother Anthony, in *Opuscula Sancti Patris Francisci Assisiensis,* C. Esser, ed. (Grottaferrata, 1978), 95.

3. The indispensable role of *katharsis* in growth toward wisdom is the subject of *Elements of Ethics* (Palo Alto: Stanford University Press, 2003), 218–232.

4. For an explanation of this sentence, see chapter 6.

5. Cf. Aquinas's wonderful explanation of *caritas* as *forma virtutum* in *Summa Theologiae* II^a II^{ae} , q. 23, especially aa. 6–8.

CHAPTER THREE.   On the Relationships between Life, Scholarship, and Faith in a Catholic University

This chapter contains the revised text of an invited address to the University of San Francisco, given in February 1999.

1. There was a time when monasteries and convents were such places of contemplation, but where is their tradition retrieved nowadays, except among sporadic groups of friends or in some private centers of reflection that attempt to reconnect knowledge with existential needs?

2. Pelikan, *Idea of the University,* 34–37.

3. *Elements of Ethics* is an attempt to clarify the meaning of "a meaningful and good life."

4. Two attempts to prove this are "Bestemming en gang van het denken" (Destination and Course of Thinking) in *Gronden en Grenzen* (Haarlem: Gottmer 1966), and "Filosofie—Geloof—Theologie," in *Tijdschrift voor Filosofie* 62 (2000): 655–680.

5. A revised version of that paper was published as "Philosophia" in *Faith and Philosophy* 14 (1997) and—after revision—in *The Quest for Meaning; Friends of Wisdom from Plato to Levinas* (New York: Fordham University Press 2003), 7–22. For the ancient and medieval meaning of *philosophia,* see the literature indicated in notes 1 and 3 to chapter 1.

CHAPTER FOUR.   The Future of Christian Philosophy

The first version of this text was an address at the Symposium on the Future of Christian Philosophy held on 2–3 April 1998 at Loyola College, Baltimore, Maryland. I have maintained the style of an address.

1. "The Church is such that it constantly needs reform."

2. As the Latin proverb says: "*Corruptio optimi pessima.*"

3. For the various meanings of "faith," as I use it in this book, see also chapters 6 and 8.

4. For a commentary on Descartes' ideal of mastery and possession, see "Life, Science, and Wisdom according to Descartes," in *The Quest for Meaning,* 123–148.

5. Cf. Plato's *Symposium* and the beginning of Augustine's *Confessions.*

6. Augustine, *Confessiones* I, 1, 1.

7. Cf. also Aristotle, *Metaphysica* XII, 1072b3–4.

8. Cf. *Historisches Wörterbuch der Philosophie,* vol. 2 (Basel, 1972), 118–130, and L. Braeckmans et al., eds., *Op het ritme van de oneindigheid, Opstellen over het natuurlijke Godsverlangen* (Leuven: Acco, 2000).

9. Cf., for instance, *Ennead* 9 [VI, 9], 9.

10. "Nothing in excess!" Cf. Plato, *Protagoras* 343b and *Charmides* 165a.

11. Cf. Martha C. Nussbaum, *The Therapy of Desire: Theory and Practice in Hellenistic Ethics* (Princeton: Princeton University Press, 1994), 484–510. Thanks to this book, we have rediscovered the central role of affectivity in Epicurean, Skeptic, and Stoic philosophy. May we hope that this example will be followed by similar studies of the Platonic, medieval, and modern history of affectivity?

12. Cf. the blessing of the Easter Candle during the Easter liturgy: "*Christus—heri et hodie, cras et in aeternum.*"

13. Cf. Claudio Ciancio et al., eds., *In lotta con l'angelo. La filosofia degli ultimi due secoli di fronte al Cristianesimo* (Torino: Società Editrice Internazionale, 1989).

14. Cf. Aquinas, *Summa Theologica* I, q. 2, a. 3, c.

CHAPTER FIVE.   Does Theology Have a Role to Play in the University?

The first version of this address was given as the Cody Lecture at Loyola University Chicago in October 1997.

1. The turn away from the contemplative tradition has not prevented but rather has stimulated a proliferation of scientific studies of the social, psychological, psychoanalytical, linguistic, historical, economic, cultural, and political aspects of religions and religious beliefs. However, "religious studies" do not always show the sensitivity required for understanding the difference between a vision based on belief and the contemplative engagement of a practiced faith.

2. The necessity of some sort of synthesis, presupposed in this chapter, seems to contradict a widespread conviction according to which all syntheses are simplistic, superficial, or impossible. Fragmentation and concentration on particular issues are said to be conditions for serious scholarship and progress, while overall views should be left to private meditation and journalism. If science and scholarship are identical, syntheses may indeed have become impossible, but then the divorce between research and the life we have to live is complete, unless another kind of serious thought exists by which we can unify the many dimensions of a human life. That all attempts at synthesis simplify and therefore must be seen as provisional and open to correction does not refute their necessity. Even the word "fragmentation" itself witnesses to the idea and the desirability of a whole that—alas!—is broken up. Is the recommendation of synthetic views a typically modern gesture, especially when it is associated with Hegelian ideas of systematicity and encyclopedic unity? Must we rather choose between unscholarly narratives about the universe, on one hand, and fragmentary but well-investigated stories about isolated subjects, on the other?—No; while pleas for fragmentary research are legitimate, the demand for synthesis cannot be given up because the final relevance of all discoveries remains undecided until we know how these fit and function within the framework in which they have been obtained. The horizon of a problem refers to the horizon of the discipline in which it emerges, while all disciplines refer to one another and to the scholarly universe whose fragments they try to map out. The totality of their explanations refers in turn to the universal horizon of human existence and its meaning. None of these horizons, all of which (at least implicitly) are present in each scholar's work, can be suppressed if we want to know what is really going on. Moreover, since every fragment is by its

very nature incomplete, it invites further attempts to show how it can become part of a bigger whole.

It may well be the case that the demand for synthesis is too burdensome for human beings. However, *tentative* and provisional syntheses are needed in order not to forget what, in the end, the "university of sciences" is all about. If even theologians embrace the trend to fragmentation, how then can they maintain their belief in universal creation and salvation? A caveat is necessary, however: although theology cannot avoid attempts at synthesis, it must also show that God is neither a part (not even the summit), nor the whole of any totality. The difference between God and "all things" (*ta panta* or "*omnia entia*") does not fit well within the framework of universal scholarship, because God cannot be reduced to any being within or coinciding with the *limits* of the universe. For further qualifications of the synthetic demand that guides this chapter, see note 6 and the subsequent arguments of the main text.

3. The failure of the Hegelian and other simplistic visions of world history does not justify the condemnation of all narratives about sacred history. If it is meaningful to search for the ultimate meaning of humanity, why should the metaphor of a story or (quasi)history not be a good genre for proposing it?

4. See especially the many publications of Henri de Lubac on the relations between "nature" and grace and the discussions that it provoked, for instance *Augustinisme et théologie naturelle* (Paris: Aubier, 1964), and *Le mystère du surnaturel* (Paris: Aubier, 1965). A succinct résumé and some important literature can be found in Jean-Yves Lacoste, dir., *Dictionnaire critique de théologie* (Paris: PUF, 2002), col. 1127–1131.

5. Some thoughts about Platonic philosophy as "prefiguring" Christian theology, can be found in *The Quest for Meaning,* 34–47 and 59–72.

6. The emphasis on synthesis displayed in this paper was prompted by the focus on the role of theology within the university and its own encompassing character. Although I relativize the value of synthetic views by underlining their simplifying, provisional, and revisable features, those who reject all syntheses in the name of the fragmented character of the world and the university (which should rather be called a multiversity) will not be satisfied. Can they themselves still uphold a convincing picture of theology? Or even of human life itself? Or are they willing to divorce the factual unity of human lives from the collection of unconnected pieces of knowledge into which these are translated? The relations between analysis and synthesis, the whole and its parts, the fragments and that from which they are the fragments, cannot be fully analyzed (nor synthesized) in a paper or note on the academic significance of theology. Moreover, the questions involved in such a discussion cannot be isolated from another complex set of questions: those that regard *the persons who propose* their (provisional and always premature) syntheses to their audience. It is easy to attack any synthesis by presenting examples or cases that do not fit within it, but such attacks can only spur us to look for a better one. The main point of not neglecting the very speakers or writers who propose their views lies in the fact that a

synthesis is always a personal one (even if it is prepared by a team or plagiarized by epigones). This implies that every synthesis represents a personal perspective on the summarized whole. Because a personal perspective is founded in and characterized by the unicity of the individual who offers it, no synthesis can completely satisfy another person. Original thinkers differ more from average people than do others. Their views influence many less original individuals, but even then the vision of an original thinker is remarkably different from its imitations. Influential views are competing with one another for many reasons, but their most fundamental difference is caused by the difference between the individuals whose unicity is expressed in each one's view of human life in the universe. If this is true, any synthesis is only one interpretation, which may be thorough, brilliant, grandiose, superficial, mediocre, average, or superfluous. In realizing this, we are aware that the ultimate synthesis we are seeking—i.e., the whole truth—cannot be found in any one of the many competing interpretations. Instead of an individual perspective, we want the true perspective in which all the truths of individual perspectives are summarized without the limitations with which they are mixed. But that truth is not anyone's property. The synthesis we are seeking is the goal of a desire that goes beyond all interpretations. It is represented, but also limited and probably contaminated, by them insofar as they only can *point to* the truth. Hopefully, they converge in proposing—rightfully so, I hope—that we try out their suggestions. The confrontation of interpretations invites us to participate in a discussion about proposals whose synthetic characters are only elaborate perspectives on the hidden truth that unites by differentiating thoughtful lives.

CHAPTER SIX. Philosophy—Religion—Theology

The first version of this chapter was published simultaneously in *International Journal for Philosophy of Religion* 50 (2001): 29–39 and in Eugene T. Long, ed., *Issues in Contemporary Philosophy of Religion* (Boston: Kluwer, 2001), 29–39.

1. See chapter 1.

2. More about this level of affectivity can be found in chapter 14 below and in *Elements of Ethics*, 56–69.

3. An analysis of desire can be found in *Elements of Ethics*, 73–97 and 254–258. In the present volume, see also chapter 7 through 12.

4. An analysis of Descartes' separation between theory and praxis, as found in the third part of his *Discours de la méthode,* can be found in "Life, Science, and Wisdom According to Descartes," chapter 8 of *The Quest for Meaning,* 123–148.

5. Cf. "Hegel and Modern Culture," chapter 11 in *The Quest for Meaning,* 206–211; "Religion et Politique dans la philosophie de Hegel," in Guy Planty-Bonjour, ed., *Hegel et la religion* (Paris: PUF, 1982), 37–76; and *Modern Freedom: Hegel's Legal, Moral, and Political Philosophy* (Boston: Kluwer, 2001), 618–642.

6. That "philosophy" in antiquity was a way of life and not an attempt to realize Descartes' program has been proved by the specialists of Greek and Hellenistic philosophy. A summary of their results can be found in Pierre Hadot's *Qu'est-ce que la philosophie antique?* (Paris: Gallimard, 1995).

7. "The Universality of Catholic Philosophy," forthcoming in *Revista Portuguesa de Filosofia* 60, no. 4 (2004).

CHAPTER SEVEN.   Retrieving Onto-Theo-Logy

This chapter is the lightly revised text of a paper that was presented under the title "Religion after onto-theology?" at a conference on "Religion after onto-theology," organized by Mark A. Wrathall and held at Sundance (Utah), 23–28 July 2001. The first version was published in Mark A. Wrathall, ed., *Religion after Metaphysics* (Cambridge: Cambridge University Press: 2003), 104–122.

1. If we read "ontotheology" as an "ontology" in which the divine (*to theion*) or God (*ho theos, Deus*) inevitably emerges, we can use this word to characterize the philosophies of Plato and Aristotle and most metaphysicians, Hegel and Heidegger included. As a *logia* that studies the relations between beings and God, it could be named "onto-theo-logy." An "onto-theology" seems to stress a theological perspective on the being (*to einai, das Sein*) of all beings (*to onta*).

2. Some of them, for instance, follow the Plato interpretations of Nietzsche and Heidegger, but do not always display familiarity with the primary texts. For an analysis of the transformation that Plato's *Politeia* undergoes in Heidegger's interpretation, for example, one could read *Platonic Transformations* (Lanham: Rowman and Littlefield, 1997), 57–112.

3. As Heidegger so often writes. Whether this expression by itself already includes the thought that the word "god" in "God" and "the gods" has the same or a radically different meaning, and whether its use excludes the possibility of an infinite God, has to be shown by further analysis.

4. *Identität und Differenz* (Pfullingen: Neske, 1957), 25–37.

5. *Identität und Differenz*, 71.

6. *Identität und Differenz*, 71.

7. *Identität und Differenz*, 70.

8. Cf. *Historisches Wörterbuch der Philosophie*, vol. 1, col. 976–977.

9. *Identität und Differenz*, 54–57.

10. Cf., however, Plato, *Lysis* 219c25–d4 and Aristotle's *anangkē stēnai* in *Metaphysica* XII, 1070a4.

11. Careful reading of, e.g., Plotinus, *Enneads* VI, 8 [39], 13, 25–58 and 8, 18, 32–53 (where *aition heautou* is used metaphorically to point at the One's originality and freedom), Aquinas, *Contra Gentiles* I, 22 (where Thomas rejects the expression), Descartes' responses to the first and fourth objections to his *Meditationes de prima*

philosophia, and Spinoza's *Ethica* (which Heidegger may have read although he never showed any acquaintance with it) suffices to justify the conclusion that Heidegger's claim rests on shaky ground.

12. *Itinerarium mentis in Deum,* cap. 5–7.

13. The gods of the later Heidegger are divine (*theioi*) in the sense of polytheic myths. The God (*ho theos*) of Plato, Aristotle, and Plotinus is not any god, although some very enlightened Greeks once in a while used "Zeus" to name the One who absolutely transcends all beings, including the most "divine" ones, such as the cosmos and the gods. God (*theos* or *ho theos*) as adored and contemplated by Jews, Christians, and Muslims, is even "more" infinitely transcendent and "more intimate" than the God of Greek philosophy. As Trinity, God is simultaneously "above," "in," "around," and "deeper than" all beings and their being and none of them. See below chapters 10, 11, and 14.

14. See *Modern Freedom: Hegel's Legal, Moral, and Political Philosophy* (Boston: Kluwer, 2001), *Hegel's praktische Philosophie* (Stuttgart-Bad Cannstatt: Frommann-Holzboog, 1991), and *Selbsterkenntnis des Absoluten* (Stuttgart-Bad Cannstatt: Frommann-Holzboog, 1987).

15. *Grundlegung zur Metaphysik der Sitten,* Akad. IV, 429–437.

16. *Sein und Zeit* §26.

17. See Adriaan Peperzak, *To the Other: An Introduction to the Philosophy of Emmanuel Levinas* (Lafayette: Purdue University Press, 1992), 202–208, and *Beyond: The Philosophy of Emmanuel Levinas* (Evanston: Northwestern University Press, 1997), 82–86. I use the word "meontological" here to indicate Levinas's struggle for forging a language that transcends the boundaries of being by saying no (*mē*) to the claim that "being" is the most encompassing, "first," radical," or "ultimate" word (and not, e.g., "the Good" or "the One" or "the Other" or "God").

18. *Grundlegung der Metaphysik der Sitten,* Akad. IV, 434–435.

19. Cf. the third part of the *Discours de la Méthode,* AT VI, 22–28. An analysis of this text can be found in *The Quest for Meaning,* 123–148.

20. *Totalité et Infini: Essai sur l'extériorité* (La Haye: Nijhoff, 1961), 4–5.

21. Ibid., 3.

22. See the last six chapters below.

23. Cf. the last pages of the *Lettre-Préface* to the French edition of Descartes' *Principia,* in Descartes, *Oeuvres philosophiques,* vol. 3, ed. F. Alquié (Paris: Garnier, 1973), 779–782. Descartes achieved only his metaphysics and a part of his physics, while he hardly touched *médecine, mécanique,* and (a scientifically demonstrated) *morale.*

24. See especially chapter 5 of *Autrement qu' être ou au-delà de l'essence* (La Haye: Nijhoff), 1974. For one of my reservations, see *Beyond,* 176–177 and 226–227.

25. The last chapters of this book allude to apophatic theology, about which some clarifications can be found in "La référence érotique des négations théocentriques," in Marco M. Olivetti, ed., *Théologie Négative* (Padova: CEDAM, 2003), 83–94.

CHAPTER EIGHT. Wonderment and Faith

The first version of this chapter was presented at the Castelli Colloquium on Philosophy of Revelation, held 4–7 January 1994 in Rome and published in Marco M. Olivetti, ed., *Filosofia della revelazione* (Padova: CEDAM, 1994), 173–186.

    1. That true faith is as old as Abel's sacrifice to God, as the letter to the Hebrews declares (Heb 11:4), has elicited many commentaries from the Church Fathers to Yves Congar. See the latter's essay "Ecclesia ab Abel," in *Christus und Kirche im Lichte ihrer Analogie zum Menschenleib* (Düsseldorf: Patmos, 1952), 79–108.

    2. This phrase can be read as a summary of Thérèse of Lisieux's understanding of faith. See Saint Thérèse de l'Enfant-Jésus et la Sainte Face, *Edition Critique de ses Oeuvres complètes,* vol. 7: *Derniers entretiens,* 2nd ed. (Paris: Du Cerf, 1971), 221 and 435.

    3. This phrase could sum up the thirteenth-century Franciscan theology of creation.

    4. Martin Heidegger, *Einführung in die Metaphysik* (Tübingen: Niemeyer, 1966), 6.

    5. Since Saint Paul proclaims that Christ is "God's power (*dynamis, fortitudo*) and wisdom (*sophia, sapientia*)" (1 Cor 1:24), and since *philosophia* means love of wisdom, Augustine concludes that the true philosophy can be found in Christ only. Cf. Augustine, *Epistula* 120 (ad Consentium), cap 1, n. 6.

    6. As an outdated theology of grace claimed: grace and faith would be "supernaturally" added on top of the given human "nature." See note 4 to chapter 5.

    7. Lk 10:42.

    8. See chapter 6 for the very broad meaning of "faith" that is used here.

    9. "*Poiēsis*" means not only making or producing poetry. I use here the adjective (*poiētikos*) to indicate the aesthetic character of the ancient Greek ideal of perfection in *theōria* and *praxis*. It is not possible to oppose the Greek ideal as primarily theoretical to Christian holiness as primarily practical, even if it is true that one can be a good Christian without theoretical skills. Good *praxis* was extremely important to all Greek philosophers; however, the perfection of *praxis* (its idea of "virtue") as seen by them, is very much dominated by their contemplative ideal. Both theory, in the form of philosophy, and practice, as beauty of stance and behavior, belong to the perfection that makes human beings similar to the shining gods. The grace of Christian faith is not poetic (although it welcomes poetry), but compassionate, patient, humble—not competing with the gods, but looking up to the one and only God in a crucified man who continues to overcome death.

    10. See chapters 13 and 14.

    11. This sentence needs to be qualified, if "theology" is taken to indicate an implicit, not yet thought through but already coherent constellation of elements in which faith diversifies its pretheoretical self-understanding.

12. As Augustine and Anselm defined what we call theology. For "Christian philosophy" as a retrieval of their *fides quaerens intellectum,* one could read chapter 9 of *Reason in Faith; On the Relevance of Christian Spirituality for Philosophy* (New York: Paulist Press, 1999).

13. See chapter 1.

14. See Chapter 14 and "La référence érotique des négations théocentriques" in Marco M. Olivetti, ed., *Théologie Négative* (Padova: CEDAM, 2003), 38–94.

CHAPTER NINE. About Salvation

A first version of this text, in Dutch ("Filosofie en Heil"), was read and discussed at a conference on soteriology at the university of Utrecht (The Netherlands) on June 8, 1993. A first translation into English, under the title "Philosophical Presuppositions of the Christian Debate on Salvation," appeared in Rienk Lanooy, ed., *For Us and For Our Salvation: Seven Perspectives on Christian Soteriology* (Utrecht-Leiden: IIMO, 1994), 133–144. Thorough reworking resulted in this chapter.

1. More on purification can be found in *Elements of Ethics,* 102–108 and 218–225.

2. I use here the words "fundamentalism" and "liberalism" in a rather loose sense to indicate "the right" and "the left" of a more culturalized than orthodox Christianity.

3. A more elaborate analysis of desire and longing can be found in *Elements of Ethics,* 73–97, and in the next three chapters of the present volume.

4. Heb 11:4.

CHAPTER TEN. God across Being and the Good

This chapter is the significantly revised English version of a paper "Dieu à travers l'être et le bien," which was presented at the Castelli Colloquium on "Philosophie de la religion entre éthique et ontologie," held in Rome, 4–7 January 1996. The original French version was published in Marco M. Olivetti, ed., *Philosophie de la religion entre éthique et ontologie* (Padova: CEDAM, 1994), 111–120.

1. For more analysis of some definitions and hypotheses that are presupposed in this and following chapters, I will refer to *Elements of Ethics.*

2. I will use the word "essence" as shorthand for "(characteristic) mode of being." About ontology (and ontotheology), see chapter 7.

3. About the concept of "ethics," some precisions can be found in *Elements of Ethics,* 22–55, 121 ff., 239–241.

4. Cf. *Elements of Ethics,* 44–47, 121–175.

5. Cf. *Elements of Ethics,* 98–120.

6. The fourth chapter of *Elements of Ethics* (73–97) offers an analysis of desire. To indicate the radical difference and connection between the deepest and longest desire and the multitude of all other desires, I often capitalize the former ("Desire"). I use the lower cased to prevent irritation. For the meaning of "correspondence," as used here, one could read *Elements of Ethics,* 98–120.

7. Cf. Levinas, *Totalité et Infini* and *Autrement qu'être,* an interpretation of which can be found in *To the Other and Beyond* (see notes 17, 20, and 24 to chapter 7).

8. The analogy of being is also an analogy of good, should, alterity, identity, movement, and rest. Cf. *Elements of Ethics,* 121–175.

9. See the next chapter.

10. Cf. Paul Ricoeur's *Moi-même comme un autre* (Paris: Du Seuil, 1990).

11. See also chapters 7 and 14.

12. *Nihil caritate melius, nihil caritate perfectius* (*De Trinitate* III, 2). *Conscientiam suam unusquisque interroget et procul dubio et absque contradictione inveniet quia, sicut nihil caritate melius, sic nihil caritate jucundius* (III, 3).

13. The great Flemish poet Guido Gezelle is the foremost example of such praise.

14. Cf. the enormous influence that the characterization of the good as "diffusivum sui" had on the theology of Dionysius, "the Areopagite," and the European theology of the thirteenth century.

15. About the inseparability of experience, faith, spirituality, philosophy, and theology, which this book wants to illustrate, one can also read *Reason in Faith* (see note 12 to chapter 8) and *The Quest for Meaning,* 1–22 and 225–228 (see note 4 to chapter 3).

16. "... the love that moves the sun and the other stars" (last line of Dante's *La Divina Commedia*).

CHAPTER ELEVEN. Freedom and Grace

The first draft out of which this chapter grew via a first translation and several reworkings, was presented under the title *Liberté et grâce: Quelques refléctions sur la gratitude* at the Castelli Colloquium on Hermeneutic of the Philosophy of Religion, held 3–8 January 1977 in Rome and published under that title in Enrico Castelli, ed., *La philosophie de la religion: L'herméneutique de la philosophie de la religion* (Paris: Montaigne, 1977), 179–192.

1. This picture of modern social philosophy owes much to Kant and Hegel. On the latter's practical philosophy, which might be considered the systematic culmination of the modern tradition, one could read *Modern Freedom* (see note 14 to chapter 7).

2. "All is grace"—as Thérèse Martin (of Lisieux) said. See note 2 to chapter 8.

3. Cf. 1 Kings 19:12.

4. For the critical aspect of affection as self-affection, see also the next chapter and *Elements of Ethics,* 102–108.

5. Cf. *Elements of Ethics,* 81–88.

6. About wonder, see chapter 8.

7. Cf. Aristotle, *Metaphysics* A1, 982b10–28, 983a10–20.

8. As the French expression "bon à rien" says.

9. "*Wiseloos*" (without particular mode) is a word that Jan van Ruusbroec often uses to indicate a "super-essential" (*overweselijcke*) union beyond all particular manners of relation, imagination, and thought. Cf., for example Jan van Ruusbroec, *Van den blinckenden steen* (Tielt: Lannoo, 1981), 33–38 and 72–74, or *The Spiritual Espousals and Other Works,* James A. Wiseman, introd. and trans. (New York: Paulist Press, 1985), 153–184, especially 171–177.

10. Cf. Gregory of Nyssa, *The Life of Moses* II, 162–165. See *La vie de Moïse ou Traité de la Perfection en matière de vertu,* 3rd ed., ed. Jean Daniélou, (Paris: Du Cerf, 1968), 210–213.

CHAPTER TWELVE.   Affective Theology/Theological Affectivity

The first version of this chapter was published in Jeffrey Bloechl, ed., *Religious Experience and the End of Metaphysics* (Bloomington: Indiana University Press, 2003), 94–105.

1. About speaking (and writing) one could read *Platonic Transformations,* 189–204.

2. Cf. chapter 11.

3. Though Aristotle, in *Metaphysica* Γ (IV, 2) 1003a33, focuses on the plurality of manners in which being appears for our *legein* (saying), the various ways in which it surprises our *seeing, feeling,* and *hearing* should not be neglected. Being is also differently felt, heard, and smelled to be.

4. On correspondence, see *Elements of Ethics,* chapter 5.

5. Cf. *Platonic Transformations,* 11–14, 88–93, 104–106, 133–145. Aisthēsis does not coincide with the modern senses. Its meaning includes the sensibility that is necessary for wisdom and prudence and aesthetic appreciation.

6. Cf. Aristotle, *Metaphysica* Λ (XII, 7) 1072b3–4.

7. Cf. Gregory of Nyssa, *Life of Moses* II, 163; see above, note 10 to chapter 11.

8. Bonaventure, *Itinerarium mentis in Deum,* I, n. 5.

9. On apophatic or negative theology, see also note 25 to chapter 7.

10. *Itinerarium mentis in Deum,* Prologus, end of n. 3.

11. Are we still allowed to understand Aristotle's idea that the Absolute attracts all beings by being loved (see note 6) as a hint in the right direction?

12. "The Absolute itself is . . . the identity of the identity and the non-identity." This often-quoted sentence is found in Hegel's first philosophical work, *The Difference Between Fichte's and Schelling's Philosophical System* (Jena, 1801); cf. G. W. F. Hegel, *Gesammelte Werke* (Hamburg: Meiner) vol. 4 (1968), 64.

13. E.g., Saint Augustine, *Soliloquia* I, n. 7.

14. "Essence" or "being" should be heard here as transitive, creative, and saving being-with and being-for.

CHAPTER THIRTEEN. The Address of the Letter

The first French version of this chapter, "L'adresse de la lettre," was discussed at the Castelli Colloquium on *Religion, Word, Writing,* held 3–7 January 1992 in Rome. It was published in Marco M. Olivetti, ed., *Religione, Parola, Scrittura* (Padova: CEDAM, 1992), 145–155.

1. Cf. E. Tugendhat, *Ti kata tinos; eine Untersuchung zu Struktur und Ursprung aristotelischer Grundbegriffe* (Freiburg: Alber, 1958).

2. M. Heidegger, "Die onto-theo-logische Verfassung der Metaphysik," in *Identität und Differenz* (Pfullingen: Neske, 1957), 35–73, especially 70–71. Compare above, chapter 7.

3. Cf. *Platonic Transformations,* 189–204. See for the following section Plato, *Phaedrus* 274c–278e.

4. Marco Olivetti, *Analogia del soggetto* (Roma: Laterza 1992), 121 ff.

5. Cf. Hölderlin, *Hyperion's Schicksalslied* in *Sämtliche Werke* (Kleine Stuttgarter Ausgabe), vol. 1 (Stuttgart: Kohlhammer & Wissenschaftliche Buchgesellschaft, 1966), 260.

CHAPTER FOURTEEN. Provocation

The first version of this chapter was presented at the Castelli Colloquium on *Intersubjectivity and Philosophical Theology,* held 5–8 January 2000 in Rome and published in a volume with the same title (ed. Marco M. Olivetti [Padova: CEDAM, 2000], 305–319).

1. Our ongoing departure from modernity includes a fundamental change in the praxis and the very concept of philosophy. Philosophical distance toward the modern, science-dominated concept of philosophy as systematic (re)construction of the universe has received historical support from recent studies about the existential character of ancient philosophy and the religious framework of its medieval praxis.

2. See the preceding chapter.

3. See above chapters 10 and 12.

4. Cf. *Platonic Transformations*, 143–145.

5. On appropriateness and correspondence, see chapters 10 through 12 above and *Elements of Ethics*, chapter 5 (98–120).

6. Cf. "Daß ein Gespräch wir sind," in Bernhard Waldenfels and Iris Därmann, eds., *Der Anspruch des Anderen: Perspektiven phänomenologischer Ethik* (München: Fink, 1998), 17–34.

7. Cf. Husserl's "unbeteiligter Zuschauer."

8. In the *Bourgeois gentilhomme* of Molière (sixth scene of Act Two), the gentleman, a *nouveau riche*, learns from the *maître de philosophie* that his spontaneous "your eyes make me die from love" is much better than all embellishments of this sentence. I have taken the liberty of updating the joke.

9. See the first chapter of Genesis.

10. See chapters 7 and 10 above.

11. These words refer, respectively, to the chaos in Hesiod's *Theogony* (v. 116), the *mē on* of Plato's *Sophist*, the *apeiron* of Anaximander and other Greeks, the *chōra* of Plato's *Timaeus*, Aristotle's "prime matter," and Levinas's "there is."

12. Compare *Politeia* 508e and 534c with 509b.

13. Without negative theology, the analogy of being would fall into idolatry, but negations without analogy are empty and lead to nihilism. More about apophatic theology can be found in "La référence érotique des négations théocentriques" (see note 25 to chapter 7 above).

14. Plato's expression *"epekeina tēs ousias"* (*Politeia* 509b 9) is not just being, good, divine, but "hyper- (or above-, over-, beyond-)" being, good, divine. For Dionysius, a Christian bishop who frequently used the last three and similar expressions to name God, see, for instance, *On the Divine Names* I, 5 (593c).

15. Hegel reduced the meta-phoric dialogue of Plato's *dialegesthai* to the univocal dialectics of a conceptual monologue, thus narrowing the width of philosophical intersubjectivity and evocative theology.

16. The tension is not merely theoretical; it is and must be lived, practiced, experienced in the simultaneity of our being involved in and delighted by finite phenomena, while also being utterly detached from them and travelling through nothingness (*nada*). Cf. St. John of the Cross, *Subida del Monte Carmelo* and *La Noche Oscura*.

acceptance, 139, 146–147, 167
addressee, 183
addressing, 157–159, 170–171, 173–176,
    182–185, 189; and thematization, 188
admiration, 148–149
adoration, 154, 194
affection, 100, 162; appropriate, 165; and
    motivation, 161; as response, 160
affectivity, 130, 159–162
alterity, 132–133
Amen, 150, 153
analogy: and apophatic theology, 165;
    and negation, 165
Anselm of Canterbury (1033–1109), 137
appropriation, 167, 186–187
Aquinas, Thomas (1225–127), 40
Aristotle (384–322 B.C.): on being, 93;
    on desire, 122; on myth, 109; on
    wonder, 108–109
ascent and descent, 53
asymmetry, 188
atheism, 89, 102, 149, 191
attunement, 60
autonomy, 141–143. See also freedom;
    philosophy

being(s), 130–134, 136, 148, 150, 190;
    analogy of, 132–133, 159, 206; of

being, 137; face of, 133; as finite, 150;
    as given, 149; and good, 129–130;
    and the Good, 137; as image, 163; as
    pleasing, 162; as referring to God,
    191; response to, 137; as sacramental,
    136; speaks, 136, 150; as trace, 163;
    voice of, 138
being-for-the-Other, 152–153
belief, 25
beyond, 151, 164–165
Bonaventure (1218–1274), 163; on God,
    89; ontotheology of, 89

causa sui, 88
cause, 88
charity, 13, 28, 137–138; and science, 27
Christian philosopher, 9–15, 43, 45–46, 55
Christianity: and culture, 41; essence
    of, 123–124; and Greece, 16; and
    philosophy, 52–55; and scholarship,
    21; and the university, 37–39
Church, 44–45; Catholic, 39
Cogito, 98–99
communication, 184
compassion, 138–139, 167
consent, 134–135
contemplation, 116–117, 195;
    metaphysical, 194; method of, 194

convenience: argument of, 139

convergence, 126, 179, 198

core curriculum, 31

correspondence, 130–131, 133–134, 159–161, 186–187; to the phenomena, 167; to the Word, 138

creation, 49, 51, 101–102, 137; and grace, 65; and Jesus Christ, 104

cross, 138

culture, 131; American, 21

dative, 157, 170–171, 183

dedication, 134, 153, 174

deism, 102

Descartes, René (1596–1650), 76, 82, 88–89, 98–99; on theory and practice, 95

desiderata, 165

Desideratum, the, 121–122, 161–162

Desirable, the, 130, 133, 136, 139, 163–164, 191

desire, 34–35, 49–50, 54, 125–126, 133; and *erōs*, 122; and grace, 104; natural, 50, 104. *See also* longing

Desire, 130–131, 134–136, 138–139, 162, 164–165, 192, 205; and agony, 163; and autarky, 146; and being, 139; as called, 161; as critique, 151; and culture, 131; and desires, 163; and God, 190–192; of God, 49–51, 194; and indifference, 154; and love, 154; and motivation, 161; and nothingness, 163; and the phenomena, 163; and provocation, 187; and reflection, 192; and trust, 194; and the universe, 139. *See also erōs*

devotion, 102, 135, 173–174; to the Other, 152

dialectic, 172

dialogue, 69, 133, 186–187; interdisciplinary, 68–69; and monologue, 189; and silence, 193; as theater, 188; writer of, 172

dignity, 171

Dionysius (c. 500), 66

discussion, 172; interdisciplinary, 68–69; and unicity, 128

divine, 87

dogmatism, 126

education, 29–30

ego, 92, 99, 146, 184; and individuals, 48

egology, 93

emancipation of thought, 76

end-in-itself, 171

enduring, 125

enjoyment, 125, 162–163

Enlightenment, 7–8, 11, 40, 46–49, 80

epistemology, 132–134

equality, 141

erōs, 107, 122; and adoration, 114. *See also* Desire

essence, 130–132, 134, 136; of being, 132, 134

ethics, 35, 129, 188; and Christian faith, 27–28; of intersubjectivity, 186–187; and ontology, 129–131

eudaimonia, 121; and *sophia*, 115; and *theōria*, 106, 108

existence: as gift, 152

experience, 48, 154; as self-evaluation, 160

face-to-face, 94–95

facing, 97, 157, 167

faith, 36–39, 64–65, 75, 117; in autonomy, 139; basic, 36–37; and belief, 25; and compassion, 41–42; corruption of, 44–45; and culture, 10, 21–22, 43–45, 51–52; and ethics, 27–28; in God, 13–14, 19–21, 91; and justice, 41–42; and knowledge, 38, 44; and mathematics, 26–27; philosophical, 79–82; and philosophy, 10–12, 44–45, 51–52, 83, 103–105, 115–116, 139; and prayer, 63; and purification, 45; and reason, 12, 25–27, 83; in reason, 11,

127; and reflection, 115; and scholarship, 25–28, 37; and science, 26–27, 51; sense of, 44; and theology, 52, 115; and theory, 63; and thought, 116, 139; and wonder, 114–116

faith, Christian, 18–21, 45–46; and philosophy, 43; and *poiēsis*, 203; and *praxis*, 203; since Abel, 203

Fichte, Johann Gottlieb (1762–1814), 99

fideism, 191

foundation, 88

fragmentation, 198

fraternity, 143

freedom, 34, 140–145; and the given, 149. *See also* autonomy

friendship, 117; and unicity, 128

genealogies, 5–11; hermeneutics of, 7

genealogy: Christian, 9–11; of the Christian tradition, 22–24; enlightened, 7–8; of Enlightenment, 22–24; of philosophy, 5–11

generosity, 149, 154

given, 145, 149

giving, 136, 138, 146, 152; of self, 137–139

God, 13–15, 19, 36, 47, 51, 54–55, 66, 81, 87, 90, 135–139, 146, 149–150, 157, 163, 193–194; of Abraham, 91, 180; absence of, 13; as addressed, 169; adoration of, 169; affective response to, 165; as "all", 101; and being, 94, 169, 190–192; and beings, 135–136, 163, 169, 190–192; as beyond being, 164, 191; beyond essence, 154; beyond totality, 194; *causa prima*, 136; and *causa sui*, 87, 89, 136; as cause, 169; and causes, 89; and charity, 166; compassion of, 137–138; conversion to, 193–194; desirability of, 164 (*see also* Desirable, the); as the Desirable, 194; desire of, 122 (*see also* Desire); and the earth, 14; essence of, 166; existence of, 35–36, 190; and

facing, 167; of faith, 66–67, 91, 180–181; as given, 166; as giving, 145; glory of, 126, 151; hiddenness of, 13; as horizon, 101; and humanity, 14; images of, 149; and incarnation, 14, 193; incomparable, 136; infinity of, 102; and interpersonality, 14, 169; of Jesus, 91; as judge, 144–145; like a person, 14, 101, 169; love of, 14–15, 135–139, 153–154, 165; as modeless, 154; names of, 190; necessity of, 154; and *Nous*, 89; as the One, 89, 151, 154; as Other, 146; and the Other, 153; and philosophy, 180–182, 193–194; of philosophy, 66–67, 87–88, 91, 155, 169–170, 180–181; of prayer, 170; presence of, 13, 101, 136, 153, 164–167; as providence, 145; and reflection, 194; responding to, 167, 194; and salvation, 122; and scholarship, 194; silence of, 193; as sought, 154; as speaking, 192–194; speaking of, 182, 190; speaking to, 193–194; and theology, 194; of theology, 155; as thought, 169; and totality, 165; and the universe, 146, 164–165, 191; Word of, 138, 182, 192; and the world, 146, 150

gods, 87, 90, 148–149

good, 130; analogy of, 132; and being, 129–130; and pleasure, 35

Good, the, 117–118, 122, 138–139, 163

goodness and reflection, 149

grace, 66, 136–139, 145, 154; and human nature, 66; and nature, 65–66, 104

gratitude, 140, 144–147, 149; and affectivity, 151; and autonomy, 145; and freedom, 144–145; and modern culture, 147; and pleasure, 153; and religion, 147; and right, 144–145; and suffering, 153; and theology, 147

grounding, 88, 102

grounds, 88

happiness, 121–122, 126, 165. *See also* eudaimonia

heart, 126

hēdonē: varieties of, 162

Hegel, Georg Wilhelm Friedrich (1770–1831), 47, 89, 98–99, 195; dialectical synthesis of, 165; on God, 191; on the Idea, 165; on the infinite, 164–165; on intersubjectivity, 92; on subjectivity, 92; on truth, 127

Heidegger, Martin (1889–1976), 87–90, 93; on atheism, 89; on being, 132; on *Dasein*, 93; on faith, 105; on God, 88–89; and the history of philosophy, 88–89; on intersubjectivity, 93; on ontology, 93; on ontotheology, 87–90; on the person, 93; on prayer, 90;

height, 174

hell, 104

heritage, 174, 178

hermeneutics, 177

hope, 144–145

humanity, 120

humility, 125

Husserl, Edmund (1859–1938), 97–99

I, 98–99, 135; and myself, 170

idols, 164

imagination: analogical, 150

indifference, 152–154

individuality, 99; and unicity, 198

infinite, 94; and the finite, 94, 137–138

intersubjectivity, 14, 54, 97, 99, 133; ethics of, 186–187

Jesus Christ, 20, 117; and God, 117; passion of, 138; and wonder, 110–114; as Word of God, 118

justice, 41–42, 133, 141

Kant, Immanuel (1724–1804), 171, 186; on happiness, 143–144; on human dignity, 92–93; on morality, 143–144; on personality, 92–93

kenōsis, 138, 164

knowledge: and faith, 38; natural versus supernatural, 104; and needs, 34; and passion, 34; and wisdom, 29–30, 32–34, 38

language: does not speak, 178; and freedom, 184; and voice, 184

Leibniz, Gottfried Wilhelm (1646–1716), 98

letter, 175; reading of, 175–176; and text, 175–176

Levinas, Emmanuel (1906–1995), 93–98, 134, 151, 173, 182, 186; on being, 94; on economy, 95; on the ego, 95, 100–101; on ethics and religion, 94, 96; on the face, 132; on the face-to-face, 95–96; on God, 94, 96; on height, 95–96; on the infinite, 95–96; on intersubjectivity, 96–98; on *Mitsein,* 95–96; and modern philosophy, 96; ontology according to, 94; and ontotheology, 100; on the Other, 95–96, 100; on persons, 100; on proximity, 94; on saying, 97; on the "third", 100; on value, 95; on the world, 95–96

liberation, 143–144, 154

listening, 184

logic, 127

longing, 121–126, 134–135; and desire, 125; phenomenology of, 123. *See also* desire

love, 14–15, 134, 153; love of God, 14–15, 135–139, 153–154, 165; and suffering, 138

master and pupil, 173

me, 100

meaning, 18, 34–36; of existence, 74–75; of life, 18, 35; and satisfaction, 34

metaphilosophy, 3–5, 49, 82, 106, 116, 195; and life, 195; and theology, 195
metaphors, 150; religious, 150–151
metaphysics, 35, 50, 67, 86–87, 132–133, 178–179
mind, 99
modern philosophy: as panoramic, 98; separation from praxis, 98; stance of, 98–99
mood, 75, 160–161
moralism, 143, 152

natura pura, 104
nature (human), 120; and grace, 51, 104, 120
needs, 35
neighbor: care for, 165; love of, 14–15, 135
Nussbaum, Martha, 33

objectivity, 156–157
ontology, 89–90, 131–134, 168; and ethics, 129–131; modern, 91–92; and ontotheology, 137; and the Other, 152–153; Western, 92
onto-theo-logy, 90
ontotheology, 66–67, 85–92, 102, 169, 178, 201; according to Heidegger, 87–90; and analogy of being, 190; and apophatic theology, 190; and prayer, 91
Other, the, 97, 100, 137, 139, 145; devotion to, 152; and God, 153; and me, 152; and ontology, 152

pantheism, 102
Pascal, Blaise (1623–1662), 66
passion, 34–36, 139, 153–154, 162, 167
pathos, 167
peace, 139, 154
Pelikan, Jaroslav, 33
person, 91–93, 101, 133, 167; and ego, 92
personality, 14
perspective: first person, 97, 100
phenomenality, 158, 162

phenomenology, 94, 132, 157, 159; in the first person, 97; of intersubjectivity, 94, 101; of personality, 101
phenomenon, 130, 132, 134, 150–151, 157–158, 161–162; as affecting, 160; as claiming, 186–187; correspondence to, 167; as demanding, 160; as desirable, 163; as enjoyable, 162–163; as expression, 163; givenness of, 167; as impressing, 160; as mirror, 164; and motivation, 161; normative aspect of, 186; as speaking, 158, 160, 186, 192; as suggestive, 159–160; value of, 159
philosopher: Christian, 9–15, 43, 45–46, 55; originality of, 178–179
philosophia, 4, 9–10, 15, 37, 39, 42, 83, 106
philosophy, 3–4, 73–74, 82–84, 107–108, 120; and agnosticism, 67, 105; autarchy of, 78–79, 105; and authority, 46–47; and autonomy, 65, 73–74; autonomy of, 46–48, 76–84, 115–116; and belief, 79; and Bible, 96; and Christ, 105; Christian, 105–106, 114–118; and Christian faith, 140; and Christian spirituality, 52–55; and the Church, 47; and contemplation, 194; context of, 5–6; dependence of, 77; and desire, 49, 194; and dialogue, 83; as dialogue, 83, 172; of ego, 92; *erōs* of, 172–173; and faith, ix–x, 12, 17, 40, 43, 45, 51–52, 73–74, 77, 79–81, 83, 103–106, 116, 181, 194; as *fides quaerens intellectum,* 194; and freedom, 46; and God, 58, 66–67, 101, 181–182, 190–194; Greek, 10–11, 180; history of, 39–41, 88, 116, 178–179; horizon of, 96; independence of, 80; and the infinite, 96; inspiration, 49; institutions of, 80; and life, 17–18, 76–78, 79–80, 99–100, 116, 194; and metaphilosophy, 82, 195;

philosophy (*cont.*)

methods of, 30; modern, 11, 46–49, 67–68, 77, 81–82, 84, 92, 195, 207; as monologue, 172, 183; and non-philosophy, 169; *pathos* of, 115; of person, 92, 100; of personal relations, 166; position of, 82; postmodern, 85–87, 99, 195; and prayer, 14, 78, 91, 170; premodern, 12; and religion, 58, 73–74, 77–84, 182; as religion, 79–82; of religion, 73–74, 82–84, 88–89; and revelation, 51, 106, 117; rituals of, 80; roots of, 80, 83, 116; of salvation, 119–123; and scholarship, 17–19; scholastic, 86; and the sciences, 46, 58; social, 92, 188; and *sophia*, 115; spirit of, 52–53; and spirituality, 139; stance of, 79, 82, 105–106; subject of, 77; as system, 70; and theology, 11–15, 40, 58, 64–65, 68, 74, 104–105, 116–118, 181; and totality, 96; as a tradition, 5–7; tradition of, 5–7, 77; as universally valid, 79–80; universe of, 99; and the university, 118; as a way of life, 4–5, 80, 116; Western, 106; and wisdom, 37, 82–83; and wonder, 106–109, 113, 116. *See also* ontology; ontotheology

Plato (428–348 B.C.): on desire, 122; on dialectic, 151; on the Good, 191, 193; on speaking, 175; on wonder, 106–108; on writing, 177

Platonism: Christian, 106–107

pleasure: and good, 35; and pain, 165. *See also* enjoyment

Plotinus (204?–270), 66

poiēsis, 203

postmodern, 8–9, 195

praxis, 203

prayer, 12–14, 63, 90–91, 94, 101, 134, 194; and contemplation, 115; and philosophy, 91; and reflection, 115, 117; and theology, 117

presence: of beings, 132–133; of God, 101; human, 132

proposition, 168

provocation, 173, 185–187

purification, 50, 123, 131, 139, 165

reading, 175

reason, 10–11, 48; autonomy of, 46–48; and faith, 12, 194; and prayer, 14; trust in, 194

receptivity, 125–126

reflection: and addressing, 188; and devotion, 102

relativism, 126–127

religion, 18, 26, 36, 74–76, 78–82, 87, 90–92, 101; Christian, 75–76; critique of, 149; natural, 76; and ontotheology, 85, 87; and philosophy, 82–102 (*see also* philosophy: and religion); philosophy of, 73–74, 82–84, 88–89; positive, 76; and prayer, 90–91; and thought, 78; and wisdom, 37

religions: convergence of, 81

responding, 97, 100, 131–133, 158, 184–185; appropriate, 160–161; to being, 137; ethics of, 186

responsivity: affective, 160

Richard of St. Victor (c. 1123–1173), 137, 139

said, 170, 174, 177

salvation, 119–127; Christian, 120–123; and convergence, 128; and *eudaimonia*, 121; and exemplary lives, 127–128; longing for, 120–123, 125; philosophy of, 120–124, 127; theology of, 123–124

saying, 168, 182; about and to, 170–171, 177; and said, 170, 182, 189

Scheler, Max (1874–1928), 99

scholarship: and being a Catholic, 39–41; of Christians, 24–27, 59; democratic, 68–69; and faith,

37–39; and fragmentation, 198–199;
     fragmentation and integration of,
     30–31; interdisciplinary, 31; and
     justice, 41; and life, 31–34, 57, 69;
     modern, 33–34; and philosophy,
     65; and synthesis, 198–199; and
     theology, 57–64; and truth, 69
scholasticism: of philosophy, 85–87;
     postmodern, 99
science, 156–157; and faith, 26–27; and
     life, 57; and meaning, 57; and
     philosophy, 58; and theology, 58
Scotus, Duns (1265/66–1308), 66
self, 135, 137
Socrates (469–399 B.C.), 107, 172–173
sophia, 115
Sought, the, 162–163, 190
speaker: singularity of, 184–185
speaking, 94–95, 98, 100, 156–159, 167–168,
     170–171, 182–187, 189; about, 100,
     157, 189; and dialogue, 158; ethics
     of, 158–159; and objectivity, 156;
     phenomenology of, 157–159, 182–187,
     189; and responding, 158, 184–187;
     thanks to others, 178; to, 100, 157, 173,
     189; and writing, 174–175
Spinoza, Baruch de (1632–1677), 47,
     88–89, 98
spiritualism, 165
spirituality, 18, 165; Christian, 12, 19–22,
     26; and culture, 21; and justice, 41;
     of today's academe, 22
stance, 75, 78, 100
subject (human), 99
suffering, 134, 139, 143, 163; ambiguity of,
     152; meaning of, 153
superworld, 149, 151
synthesis, 198–200

Tertullian (c.155–225?), 10
text, 174–176; classical, 177; and
     interpretation, 176–177; and letter,
     175–176; transformation of,177

thematization, 188
theology, 10, 24–25, 37, 57, 61–64, 68,
     76, 123, 155–156, 169; and analogy,
     190–191; apophatic or negative, 101,
     117, 150–151, 163–165, 190–191, 193;
     and autonomy, 70; and community,
     69–70; contemplative, 156; and
     culture, 69; and faith, 38–40, 59–60,
     62, 68–70; and fragmentation, 199;
     and God, 59–60, 190–194, 199; and
     human existence, 59, 63, 199; of love,
     166; metaphoric, 190–192; and
     method 30; and mystery, 69–70;
     and mystics, 60, 63; and other
     disciplines, 38, 56, 58–59, 61–64;
     and other sciences, 30–31, 58,
     68–69; philo- sophical, 190–193;
     and philosophy, 11–15, 40, 58, 64–65,
     68, 74, 104–105, 116–118, 181; and
     prayer 24–25, 60, 117; and religious
     studies, 59; and scholarship, 57–64;
     and truth, 70; unity of, 70; and the
     university, 38, 61–62, 118; and
     wisdom, 38, 62
theōria, 9–10, 106, 109; and
     contemplation, 195; and
     eudaimonia, 106–108
theory: and life, 32, 98; and meaning, 32;
     and practice, 95, 98
thinking: and addressing, 25, 169;
     dative, 166
Thomas of Aquino (1225–1274), 40
totality, 94; and the infinite, 94, 96; of all
     beings, 98
transcendence, 66, 125; and the Other, 151
Trinity, 137
trust, 19–20, 64, 75; in God, 91. *See
     also* faith
truth, 168; and prayer, 169; and
     universality, 128

unicity, 128, 198
universe: as mirror, 163

university, 199; Catholic, 29–30, 40–42;
    and Christian faith, 37–39; and
    faith, 38–40, 58; and life, 32, 33; and
    philosophy, 64; and religion, 37; and
    secularity, 39; and theology, 57–58,
    64; and wisdom, 33
utilitarianism, 142–143, 145

value, 159
via: affirmativa, negativa, eminentiae, 165
vocative, 183–184; and text, 189

well-being, 143
wisdom, 35; of God, 118; of the world, 118
wonder (*thaumazein*), 106–114, 148–149;
    in Aristotle, 106, 108–109; in the

Gospels, 106, 110–114; in
    Greek philosophy, 113–114;
    and philosophy, 106–109, 113;
    in Plato, 106–108
world: being of, 149; free, 141–143;
    just, 141–142; other, 143–144,
    149, 151; this, 144; unique, 153.
    See also superworld
writing, 156–157; a dialogue, 172; and
    reading, 175–176; and speaking,
    174–175; and the future, 176.
    See also speaking

you, 97–100, 133, 167, 171; about and to
    you, 171; and I, 142–143, 170, 186;
    and me, 183–187

ADRIAAN THEODOOR PEPERZAK

is Arthur J. Schmitt Chair of Philosophy at Loyola University, Chicago.